Design Patterns in C#

By

Danny Adams

Copyright © 2024 by Danny Adams. All rights reserved. No part of this book may be reproduced in any form or by any electronic or mechanical means, including information storage and retrieval systems, without written permission from the author. The only exception is for reviewers, who may quote short excerpts in a review.

First Edition: July 2024.

Table of Contents

Intro 5
   Who Is This Book For? 5
   What You Will Learn 5
   Why Design Patterns? 6
   Gang of Four (GoF) Design Patterns 7
   About Me 8
   My Setup 9
   Github Repo 9
   A Quick Note About Top-level Statements 10

Chapter 1: Object-oriented Programming (OOP) Principles 10
   Encapsulation 11
   Abstraction 15
   Inheritance 17
   Polymorphism 18
   Coupling 25
   Composition 28
   Composition vs Inheritance 30
   Fragile Base Class Problem 31

Chapter 2: Unified Modeling Language (UML) 32
   Representing Classes 32
   Inheritance Relationship 33
   Composition Relationship 35
   Association Relationship 37
   Dependency Relationship 38

Chapter 3: SOLID Principles 39
   Single Responsibility Principle (SRP) 40
   Open/Closed Principle (OCP) 42
   Liskov Substitution Principle (LSP) 45
   Interface Segregation Principle (ISP) 48
   Dependency Inversion Principle (DIP) 52

Chapter 4: Design Patterns 57

    Behavioral Design Patterns 58

        Memento Pattern 58

        State Pattern 66

        Strategy Pattern 75

        Iterator Pattern 85

        Command Pattern 94

        Template Method Pattern 110

        Observer Pattern 126

        Mediator Pattern 140

        Chain of Responsibility Pattern 157

        Visitor Pattern 167

        Interpreter Pattern 179

    Structural design patterns 190

        Composite Pattern 191

        Adapter Pattern 201

        Bridge Pattern 208

        Proxy Pattern 217

        Flyweight Pattern 223

        Facade Pattern 233

        Decorator Pattern 241

    Creational design patterns 253

        Prototype Pattern 254

        Singleton Pattern 263

        Factory Method Pattern 270

        Abstract Factory Pattern 277

        Builder Pattern 285

Conclusion 302

For More From Me 303

Intro

Who Is This Book For?

This book is for the developer that has at least a little knowledge of object-oriented programming (OOP), and wants to learn design patterns to become a better developer. Here are some things that you should understand in order to find this book useful:

- Classes
- Creating objects from classes
- Access modifiers (public, private, protected)
- Class properties/fields/data/state
- Class methods

So, you just need to understand the very basics of OOP to find this book valuable. Any other OOP concepts – such as abstract classes, polymorphism, encapsulation, composition – will be fully explained in this book. You will also learn the very important SOLID principles.

OOP principles and the five SOLID principles are crucial to understand before learning any design patterns – which is why I have dedicated the first few chapters of this book to those topics, before we start learning any design patterns. This means that developers of all levels can benefit from this book.

All examples are in C#, so it would help if you understood the basic syntax of C#. I don't explain basic syntax, as there are plenty of free and great videos on YouTube to get you started with C# in little time.

My aim for this book was to keep it succinct, and not for it to become some slab of a textbook – so that you can actually finish it!

What You Will Learn

- All 23 design patterns ("The Gang of Four Design Patterns") with examples of where they would be applicable.
- OOP principles: encapsulation, abstraction, inheritance, polymorphism, coupling, composition.
- The five SOLID principles.
- Unified Modeling Language (UML).

Feel free to skip chapters. E.g. If you already understand the OOP principles, skip them.

Why Design Patterns?

Design patterns are essential in software development for several reasons:

1. **Reusable Solutions**: Design patterns provide proven solutions to recurring problems in software design. Instead of reinventing the wheel, developers can leverage these patterns to solve common issues efficiently. For example, to implement an *undo* feature in an application, developers could use the Memento design pattern.
2. **Standardized Terminology**: Design patterns establish a common language for developers to communicate effectively about software designs. This common vocabulary enhances collaboration and understanding among team members.
3. **Scalability**: Design Patterns promote scalable designs by providing flexible and adaptable solutions. They allow systems to evolve over time without extensive rework or architectural overhaul.
4. **Maintainability**: Using design patterns often results in more maintainable code. Patterns encapsulate design decisions and promote modular, loosely coupled architectures, making it easier to understand, modify, and extend codebases.
5. **Performance**: Some design patterns help to improve performance by optimizing resource usage, reducing overhead, or facilitating efficient algorithms.
6. **Documentation**: Design patterns serve as a form of documentation for software designs. By employing well-known patterns, developers can convey design intent more effectively, making codebases easier to understand for both current and future contributors.
7. **Best Practices**: Design patterns embody best practices and principles of software design. They encapsulate years of collective knowledge and experience, guiding developers toward solutions that are robust, reliable, and maintainable.
8. **Cross-Domain Applicability**: Many design patterns are agnostic of programming languages or domains. They can be applied across different technologies and industries, making them valuable tools for developers working in diverse environments.

Overall, design patterns facilitate the creation of high-quality, maintainable software systems by providing reusable solutions to common design problems and promoting best practices in software development.

(By the way, don't worry if you don't quite understand all of the above points; these points will become clearer as we implement and discuss each of the design patterns, SOLID principles and OOP principles. For example, many of you right now won't understand the difference between *extending* a codebase vs *modifying* a codebase. For now, relax – all will be revealed!)

Gang of Four (GoF) Design Patterns

Consists of 23 design patterns from the book *Design Patterns: Elements of Reusable Object-Oriented Software*, written by four guys – Erich Gamma, John Vlissides, Richard Helm, Ralph Johnson – in the 1990s.

These 23 design patterns can be grouped into three categories:

- **Creational**: the different ways to create objects.
- **Structural**: the relationships between those objects.
- **Behavioral**: the interaction or communication between those objects.

Creational Patterns

1. Abstract Factory
2. Builder
3. Factory Method
4. Prototype
5. Singleton

Structural Patterns

1. Adapter
2. Bridge
3. Composite
4. Decorator
5. Facade
6. Flyweight
7. Proxy

Behavioral Patterns

1. Chain of Responsibility
2. Command
3. Interpreter
4. Iterator
5. Mediator
6. Memento
7. Observer
8. State
9. Strategy
10. Template Method
11. Visitor

On completion of this book, you will understand all of the 23 GoF design patterns, where to (and where not) apply them, all five SOLID principles, and some advanced OOP concepts. You will have all of the tools that you need to become a great object-oriented software developer.

About Me

I am currently a freelance software developer and technical writer. I build fullstack web applications, Shopify apps, mobile apps, and WordPress plugins and themes. My current techstack usually consists of React on the frontend, Laravel or .Net on the backend, and a PostgreSQL database.

I am also a technical writer and enjoy writing tech blog posts, books, videos and courses. I sporadically create content for FreeCodeCamp's blog and YouTube channel.

My YouTube channel:
https://www.youtube.com/channel/UC0URylW_U4i26wN231yRqvA

Twitter: https://x.com/DoableDanny

Gumroad: https://doabledanny.gumroad.com/

FreeCodeCamp: https://www.freecodecamp.org/news/author/danny-adams/

Dev.to blog: https://dev.to/doabledanny

My Setup

I have an M1 Macbook Pro and currently use VS Code for creating C# applications. But feel free to use whatever you're comfortable with.

If you want to set up similar to me, follow this guide: https://code.visualstudio.com/docs/csharp/get-started.

I created a simple C# console app to run the examples in this book, and see their outputs in the terminal.

All code examples in this book use VS Code's "Solarized Light" theme in size 14 font.

OK – let's get stuck in!

Github Repo

All code examples are included in this repo: https://github.com/DoableDanny/Design-Patterns-in-C-Sharp

A Quick Note About Top-level Statements

In the program.cs file, it's now possible to use top-level statements where we just have to write the body of the `Main()` method, and the compiler will convert this into the `Program` class with `Main()` method for us, making our code simpler (see https://aka.ms/new-console-template for more information):

Writing out the full thing:

```
namespace MyApp
{
  internal class Program
  {
    static void Main(string[] args)
    {
      Console.WriteLine("Hello World!");
    }
  }
}
```

Or, the same thing with top-level statements, requires no boilerplate:

```
Console.WriteLine("Hello, World!");
```

In this book, I'll be creating examples with the explicit program class and main method, as well as with top-level statements.

Chapter 1: Object-oriented Programming (OOP) Principles

Before learning any design patterns, it's important that you understand some fundamental OOP principles. Here are the concepts that you'll understand by completing this chapter:

- Encapsulation
- Abstraction
- Inheritance

- Polymorphism
- Coupling
- Composition
- Composition vs Inheritance

Encapsulation

Encapsulation is a fundamental principle of object-oriented programming that involves bundling the data ("attributes" or "fields") and methods (behaviors) that operate on the data into a single unit, called a class. Encapsulation helps in hiding the internal implementation details of a class by only exposing the necessary functionalities to the outside world.

Here's a simple example demonstrating encapsulation in C#:

First, here's a bad example, with no encapsulation:

```csharp
public class BadBankAccount
{
  public decimal balance;
}
```

Users of this class now have free reign to assign `balance` to whatever value that they want:

```csharp
class Program
{
  static void Main(string[] args)
  {
    BadBankAccount badAccount = new BadBankAccount();
    badAccount.balance = -1; // Oh dear -- balance should not be allowed to be negative
  }
}
```

A better `BankBalance` class with encapsulation of fields and internal logic:

```csharp
public class BankAccount
```

```
{
    private decimal balance;

    public BankAccount(decimal balance)
    {
        Deposit(balance);
    }

    public decimal GetBalance()
    {
        return balance;
    }

    public void Deposit(decimal amount)
    {
        if (amount <= 0)
        {
            throw new ArgumentException("Deposit amount must be positive");
        }

        this.balance += amount;
    }

    public void Withdraw(decimal amount)
    {
        if (amount <= 0)
        {
            throw new ArgumentException("Withdrawal amount must be positive");
        }

        if (amount > balance)
        {
```

```csharp
            throw new InvalidOperationException("Insufficient funds");
        }

        this.balance -= amount;
    }
}
```

Then, in our Program.cs file:

```csharp
// Program.cs

// Creating an instance of the BankAccount class
BankAccount account = new BankAccount(1000.00m);

// Accessing properties and methods of the BankAccount class
Console.WriteLine("Balance: " + account.GetBalance()); // 1000.00

account.Deposit(500.00m);
Console.WriteLine("Balance after deposit: " + account.GetBalance()); // 1500.00

account.Withdraw(200.00m);
Console.WriteLine("Balance after withdrawal: " + account.GetBalance()); // 1300.00
```

In this example:

- The `BankAccount` class encapsulates the account data (`balance`) and related methods (`Deposit()` and `Withdraw()`) into a single unit.
- The data members (`balance`) are marked as private, *encapsulating* them within the class and preventing direct access from outside the class.
- "Getter" methods (`GetBalance()`) are used to provide controlled access to the private data members.

- Methods (`Deposit()` and `Withdraw()`) are used to manipulate `balance`, ensuring that operations are performed safely and according to the business rules.
- The `Main()` method demonstrates how to create an instance of the `BankAccount` class and interact with its properties and methods, without needing to know the internal implementation details.

Above, the user of the `BankAccount` class (i.e. you, other developers, classes) can't directly access the `balance` field directly, as it is marked `private`. This data is *encapsulated* within the class. Methods dictate the rules for how this data can be accessed and modified, ensuring that our program's correct rules and logic can't be violated by users, or consumers, of the `BankAccount` class – for example, it's no longer possible to withdraw more money than is in the account.

Encapsulation of the logic inside of the methods in `BankAccount` also means that users don't need to worry about the implementation details when interacting with a `BankAccount` object. For example, the user doesn't have to worry about the logic involved in withdrawing money – they can just call `account.Withdraw(200.00m)`. The implementation details are hidden and encapsulated. And if the user tries to do something stupid, like deposit a negative amount, the program will throw an error, and the user will be notified.

Encapsulation of logic within methods in the `BankAccount` class allows users to interact with a `BankAccount` object without needing to know or understand the internal implementation details of how withdrawals, deposits, or other operations are carried out. Users of the `BankAccount` class can interact with it using simple, intuitive methods, like `Withdraw()` and `Deposit()`, without needing to understand the complex logic behind these operations.

Encapsulation abstracts away the complexity of the implementation details, allowing users to focus on the higher-level functionality provided by the `BankAccount` class. Users only need to know the public interface of the `BankAccount` class (i.e., its public methods or properties) to use it effectively, while the internal implementation details remain hidden.

In summary, encapsulation allows for a clear separation between the public interface and the internal implementation of a class, providing users with a simplified and intuitive way to interact with objects while hiding the complexity of how those interactions are handled internally.

Abstraction

Reduce complexity by hiding unnecessary details. E.g. when pressing a button on a tv remote, we don't have to worry about, or interact directly with, the internal circuit board – those details are abstracted away.

Example of abstraction:

```
class EmailService
{
 public void sendEmail()
 {
    System.Console.WriteLine("Sending email...");
 }


 // ALL THE BELOW METHODS ARE PRIVATE -- THEY ARE NOT EXPOSED TO
 OTHER CLASSES. OTHER CLASSES JUST WANT TO SEND EMAILS, NO NEED
 FOR THEM TO SEE ALL THE COMPLEX DETAILS OF CONNECTING TO MAIL
 SERVER, AUTHENTICATING, DISCONNECTING.

 private void connect()
 {
    System.Console.WriteLine("Connecting to email server...");
 }

 private void authenticate()
 {
    System.Console.WriteLine("Authenticating...");
 }

 private void disconnect()
 {
```

```
    System.Console.WriteLine("Disconnecting from email
server...");
  }
}
```

The user of the class can send emails without knowing any of the internal implementation details involved in sending an email. They have been abstracted away, and life is simple for the user:

```
EmailService email = new EmailService();
email.sendEmail();
```

Without abstraction, the user would have more decisions to make, is exposed to more information and complexity than is necessary to perform a task, and has to write more complex code. If the above private methods were changed to public:

```
EmailService email = new EmailService();
email.
        ⊗ ★ ToString
        ⊗ ★ sendEmail
        ⊗ ★ GetType
        ⊗ ★ authenticate
        ⊗   authenticate
        ⊗   connect
        ⊗   disconnect
```

The methods become available via the `EmailService` public API. The user needs to know more information and understand the internal logic involved in sending an email; their code would end up looking like this:

```
EmailService email = new EmailService();
email.connect();
email.authenticate();
email.sendEmail();
email.disconnect();
```

Importantly, by using encapsulation, if any of those private methods are changed, e.g. they take another parameter, then only the `EmailService` class has to change; classes using the `EmailService` don't have to change. We can change the implementation details of `EmailService` without it affecting other classes in our app.

Inheritance

Inheritance is a fundamental concept in object-oriented programming (OOP) that involves creating new classes (subclasses or derived classes) based on existing classes (superclasses or base classes). Subclasses inherit properties and behaviors from their superclasses and can also add new features or override existing ones. Inheritance is often described in terms of an "is-a" relationship.

A simple example, demonstrating inheritance and the "is-a" relationship: a Car *is-a* Vehicle, and a Bike *is-a* Vehicle:

```csharp
// Base class representing a vehicle
public class Vehicle
{
  public string Brand { get; set; }
  public string Model { get; set; }
  public int Year { get; set; }

  public void Start()
  {
    Console.WriteLine("Vehicle is starting.");
  }

  public void Stop()
  {
    Console.WriteLine("Vehicle is stopping.");
  }
}
```

Now, all specific vehicles – such as cars, bikes, planes – can inherit common vehicle behavior, and also include fields and methods specific to that particular type of vehicle:

```csharp
// Subclass representing a car, inheriting from Vehicle
public class Car : Vehicle
{
  public int NumberOfDoors { get; set; }
  public int NumberOfWheels { get; set; }
}

public class Bike : Vehicle
{
  int NumberOfWheels { get; set; }
}
```

We don't have to write the commonly used fields and methods for every single type of vehicle. Now, if we want to change the `Start()` method, we only have to change it in one place.

Inheritance also allows for polymorphism…

Polymorphism

The word *polymorphism* is derived from Greek, and means "having multiple forms":

Poly = many

Morph = forms

In programming, Polymorphism is the ability of an object to take many forms.

First, here's an example with no polymorphism:

```csharp
public class Car
{
  public string Brand { get; set; }
  public string Model { get; set; }
```

```csharp
    public int Year { get; set; }

    public int NumberOfDoors { get; set; }

    public virtual void Start()
    {
       Console.WriteLine("Car is starting.");
    }

    public virtual void Stop()
    {
       Console.WriteLine("Car is stopping.");
    }
}

public class Motorcycle
{
  public string Brand { get; set; }
  public string Model { get; set; }
  public int Year { get; set; }

  public virtual void Start()
  {
     Console.WriteLine("Motorcycle is starting.");
  }

  public virtual void Stop()
  {
     Console.WriteLine("Motorcycle is stopping.");
  }
}
```

Let's say that we want to create a list of vehicles, then loop through it and perform an inspection on each vehicle:

```csharp
// Create a list of objects
List<Object> vehicles = new List<Object>
    {
        new Car { Brand = "Toyota", Model = "Camry", Year = 2020, NumberOfDoors = 4 },
        new Motorcycle { Brand = "Harley-Davidson", Model = "Sportster", Year = 2021 }
    };

// Perform a general inspection on each vehicle
foreach (var vehicle in vehicles)
{
 if (vehicle is Car)
 {
    Car car = (Car)vehicle; // cast vehicle to a Car
    Console.WriteLine($"Inspecting {car.Brand} {car.Model} ({car.GetType().Name})");
    car.Start();
    car.Stop();
 }
 else if (vehicle is Motorcycle)
 {
    Motorcycle motorcycle = (Motorcycle)vehicle; // cast vehicle to a Motorcycle
    Console.WriteLine($"Inspecting {motorcycle.Brand} {motorcycle.Model} ({motorcycle.GetType().Name})");
    motorcycle.Start();
    motorcycle.Stop();
 }
 else
 {
    throw new Exception("Object is not a valid vehicle");
 }
}
```

Notice the ugly code inside the `foreach` loop! Because `vehicles` is a list of any type of object (`Object`), we have to figure out what type of object we are dealing with in each loop, then cast it to the appropriate object type before we can access any information on the object.

This code will continue to get uglier as we add more vehicle types. For example, if we *extended* our codebase to include a new `Plane` class, then we'd need to *modify* existing code – we'd have to add another conditional check in the `foreach` loop for planes.

Introducing: Polymorphism...

Cars and motorcycles are both vehicles. They both share some common properties and methods. So, let's create a parent class that contains these shared properties and methods:

```
public class Vehicle
{
  public string Brand { get; set; }
  public string Model { get; set; }
  public int Year { get; set; }

  public virtual void Start()
  {
     Console.WriteLine("Vehicle is starting.");
  }

  public virtual void Stop()
  {
     Console.WriteLine("Vehicle is stopping.");
  }
}
```

`Car` and `Motorcycle` can now *inherit* from `Vehicle`:

```
public class Car : Vehicle
```

```csharp
{
  public int NumberOfDoors { get; set; }

  public override void Start()
  {
    Console.WriteLine("Car is starting.");
  }

  public override void Stop()
  {
    Console.WriteLine("Car is stopping.");
  }
}

public class Motorcycle : Vehicle
{
  public override void Start()
  {
    Console.WriteLine("Motorcycle is starting.");
  }

  public override void Stop()
  {
    Console.WriteLine("Motorcycle is stopping.");
  }
}
```

`Car` and `Motorcycle` both extend `Vehicle`, as they are vehicles. But what's the point in `Car` and `Motorcycle` both extending `Vehicle` if they are going to implement their own versions of the `Start()` and `Stop()` methods? Look at the code below:

```csharp
// Program.cs

// Create a list of vehicles
```

```
List<Vehicle> vehicles = new List<Vehicle>
    {
        new Car { Brand = "Toyota", Model = "Camry", Year = 2020,
NumberOfDoors = 4 },
        new Motorcycle { Brand = "Harley-Davidson", Model =
"Sportster", Year = 2021 }
    };

// Perform a general inspection on each vehicle
foreach (var vehicle in vehicles)
{
 Console.WriteLine($"Inspecting {vehicle.Brand} {vehicle.Model}
({vehicle.GetType().Name})");
 vehicle.Start();
 // Additional inspection steps...
 vehicle.Stop();
 Console.WriteLine();
}
```

In this example:

- We have a list, `vehicles`, containing instances of both `Car` and `Motorcycle`.
- We iterate through each vehicle in the list and perform a general inspection on each one.
- The inspection process involves starting the vehicle, checking its brand and model, and stopping it afterwards.
- Despite the vehicles being of different types, polymorphism allows us to treat them all as instances of the base `Vehicle` class. The specific implementations of the `Start()` and `Stop()` methods for each vehicle type are invoked dynamically at runtime, based on the actual type of each vehicle.

Because the list can *only* contain objects that extend the `Vehicle` class, we know that every object will share some common fields and methods. This means that we can safely call them, without having to worry about whether each specific vehicle has these fields or methods.

This demonstrates how polymorphism enables code to be written in a more generic and flexible manner, allowing for easy extension and maintenance as new types of vehicles are added to the system.

For example, if we wanted to add another vehicle, we don't have to modify the code used to inspect vehicles ("the client code"); we can just *extend* our code base, without *modifying* existing code:

```csharp
public class Plane : Vehicle
{
  public int NumberOfDoors { get; set; }

  public override void Start()
  {
    Console.WriteLine("Plane is starting.");
  }

  public override void Stop()
  {
    Console.WriteLine("Plane is stopping.");
  }
}

// Program.cs

// Create a list of vehicles
List<Vehicle> vehicles = new List<Vehicle>
        {
            new Car { Brand = "Toyota", Model = "Camry", Year = 2020, NumberOfDoors = 4 },
            new Motorcycle { Brand = "Harley-Davidson", Model = "Sportster", Year = 2021 },
            /////////// ADD A PLANE TO THE LIST:
            new Plane { Brand = "Boeing", Model = "747", Year = 2015 }
```

```
        /////////////////////////////////////
    };
```

The code to perform the vehicle inspections doesn't have to change to account for a plane. Everything still works, without having to modify our inspection logic.

We will discuss Extension vs Modification in more detail during the SOLID principles section of the book. Hold tight for now!

Coupling

In object-oriented programming (OOP), coupling refers to the degree of dependency between different classes or modules within a system. High coupling means that classes are tightly interconnected, making it difficult to modify or maintain them independently. Low coupling, on the other hand, indicates loose connections between classes, allowing for greater flexibility and ease of modification.

If classes are tightly coupled, then modifying one class could break the other, which could break our program.

Let's consider an example of high coupling followed by an improvement to reduce coupling:

Bad Example (High Coupling):

Suppose we have two classes, `Order` and `EmailSender`, where the `Order` class is responsible for placing an order on some eCommerce store, and the `EmailSender` class is responsible for sending emails. In the bad example, the `Order` class directly creates an instance of `EmailSender` to send an email after placing the order.

```
public class EmailSender
{
    public void SendEmail(string message)
    {
        // Email sending logic
        Console.WriteLine("Sending email: " + message);
    }
}
```

```csharp
public class Order
{
 public void PlaceOrder()
 {
   // Place order logic
   // ...

   // Send email notification
   EmailSender emailSender = new EmailSender();
   emailSender.SendEmail("Order placed successfully");
 }
}

// Program.cs

var order = new Order();
order.PlaceOrder();
```

In this example, the `Order` class is tightly coupled to the `EmailSender` class because it directly creates an instance of `EmailSender`. This makes the `Order` class dependent on the implementation details of `EmailSender`, and any changes to the `EmailSender` class may require modifications to the `Order` class.

Improved Example (Low Coupling):

To reduce coupling, we can introduce an abstraction (e.g., an interface) between the `Order` class and the `EmailSender` class. This allows the `Order` class to interact with the `EmailSender` class through the abstraction, making it easier to replace or modify the implementation of `EmailSender` without affecting the `Order` class.

```csharp
public interface INotificationService
{
 void SendNotification(string message);
}
```

```csharp
public class EmailSender : INotificationService
{
    public void SendNotification(string message)
    {
        // Email sending logic
        Console.WriteLine("Sending email: " + message);
    }
}

public class Order
{
    private readonly INotificationService notificationService;

    public Order(INotificationService notificationService)
    {
        this.notificationService = notificationService;
    }

    public void PlaceOrder()
    {
        // Place order logic
        // ...

        // Send email notification
        notificationService.SendNotification("Order placed successfully");
    }
}
```

The user can now easily switch between different notification services:

```csharp
var order = new Order(new EmailSender());
order.PlaceOrder();
```

In this improved example, the `Order` class depends on the `INotificationService` interface instead of the concrete `EmailSender` class. This decouples the `Order` class from the specific implementation of the notification service, allowing different implementations (e.g., `EmailSender`, `SMSNotifier`, etc.) to be easily substituted without modifying the `Order` class. This reduces coupling and improves the flexibility and maintainability of the codebase.

Composition

Composition involves creating complex objects by combining simpler objects or components. In composition, objects are assembled together to form larger structures, with each component object maintaining its own state and behavior. Composition is often described in terms of a "has-a" relationship.

Example:

Consider a `Car` class that is composed of various components such as `Engine`, `Wheels`, `Chassis`, and `Seats`. Each component is a separate class responsible for its own functionality. The `Car` class contains instances of these component classes and *delegates* tasks to them.

```
public class Engine
{
 public void Start()
  {
    Console.WriteLine("Engine started");
  }
}

public class Wheels
{
 public void Rotate()
  {
    Console.WriteLine("Wheels rotating");
  }
}
```

```csharp
public class Chassis
{
 public void Support()
 {
    Console.WriteLine("Chassis supporting the car");
 }
}

public class Seats
{
 public void Sit()
 {
    Console.WriteLine("Sitting on seats");
 }
}
```

Car class using composition:

```csharp
public class Car
{
 private Engine engine = new Engine();
 private Wheels wheels = new Wheels();
 private Chassis chassis = new Chassis();
 private Seats seats = new Seats();

 public void StartCar()
 {
    engine.Start();
    wheels.Rotate();
    chassis.Support();
    seats.Sit();
    Console.WriteLine("Car started");
 }
}
```

```
class Program
{
  static void Main(string[] args)
  {
    Car car = new Car();
    car.StartCar();
  }
}
```

In this example, the `Car` class uses composition to assemble its components – the `Car` class is *composed* of an `Engine`, `Wheels`, a `Chassis` and `Seats`. Each component (e.g., `Engine`, `Wheels`) is a separate class responsible for its own functionality. The `Car` class contains instances of these component classes and delegates tasks to them (i.e. calls their methods within its own methods).

Composition vs Inheritance

When to Use Composition:

- When you need more flexibility in constructing objects by assembling smaller, reusable components.
- When there is no clear "is-a" relationship between classes, and a "has-a" relationship is more appropriate.
- When you want to avoid the limitations of inheritance, such as tight coupling and the fragile base class problem – which we will look into shortly.

When to Use Inheritance:

- When there is a clear "is-a" relationship between classes, and subclass objects can be treated as instances of their superclass.
- When you want to promote code reuse by inheriting properties and behaviors from existing classes.

Both composition and inheritance can be used to leverage polymorphism to allow objects to be treated uniformly via their interface or parent class.

Let's now look at the Fragile Base Class Problem to show you why you should generally use composition over inheritance…

Fragile Base Class Problem

The Fragile Base Class Problem is a software design issue that arises in object-oriented programming when changes made to a base class can break the functionality of derived classes. This problem occurs due to the tight coupling between base and derived classes in inheritance hierarchies.

Key points about the Fragile Base Class Problem:

1. **Inheritance Coupling**: Inheritance creates a strong coupling between the base class (superclass) and derived classes (subclasses). Any changes made to the base class can potentially affect the behavior of all derived classes.
2. **Ripple Effect**: Modifying the implementation details, adding new methods, or changing the behavior of a base class can have a ripple effect on all derived classes. This can lead to unintended consequences and require extensive regression testing to ensure the correctness of the entire hierarchy.
3. **Limited Extensibility**: The Fragile Base Class Problem limits the extensibility of software systems, as modifications to the base class can become increasingly risky and costly over time. Developers may avoid making necessary changes due to the fear of breaking existing functionality.
4. **Brittle Software**: The Fragile Base Class Problem contributes to the brittleness of software systems, where seemingly minor changes to one part of the codebase can cause unexpected failures in other areas.
5. **Mitigation Strategies**: To mitigate the Fragile Base Class Problem, software developers can use SOLID principles such as the Open/Closed Principle (OCP) and Dependency Inversion Principle (DIP), as well as prefer Composition over Inheritance. These approaches promote loose coupling, encapsulation, and modular design, reducing the impact of changes in base classes.

In summary, the Fragile Base Class Problem highlights the challenges associated with maintaining inheritance hierarchies in object-oriented software development. It underscores the importance of designing software systems with extensibility and maintainability in mind, while also considering alternative approaches to inheritance when appropriate.

Generally, it's often recommended to use composition over inheritance, but there are cases where inheritance makes more sense. Composition results in less coupling and more flexibility. It is also easier to build classes out of various components than it is to try to find commonality between them and build a family tree.

OK, you now know some very important OOP principles. Next, we'll look at a way to model our software systems in a graphical way…

Chapter 2: Unified Modeling Language (UML)

UML is a language used to model classes and the relationships between classes. I decided to hand-draw the UML diagrams throughout this course as it is quicker for me, and gives me more flexibility to annotate them. But if you need to be super neat and tidy, you could also use a web app, such as https://app.diagrams.net/.

Representing Classes

Dog class:

```
public class Dog
{
  private string name;

  public void bark()
  {
    System.Console.WriteLine("Woof woof");
  }
}
```

Can be represented in UML as:

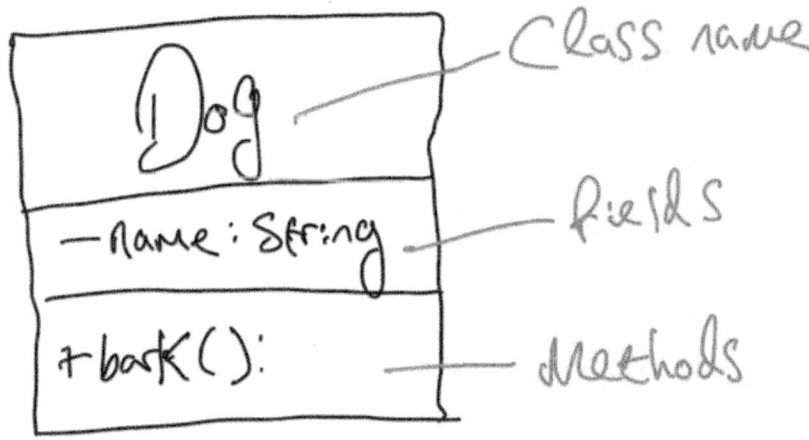

Or, if I use some using a modeling app:

Dog
- name: string
+ bark():

- "-" sign means private access modifier.
- "+" sign means public access modifier.

Value after ":" is the type. If there is no colon after the method, then `void` is the return type.

If the access modifier is omitted, in this book it should be assumed that fields are private and methods are public.

Inheritance Relationship

Represented by an arrow. The `Dog` class inherits from, or extends, the `Animal` class:

or:

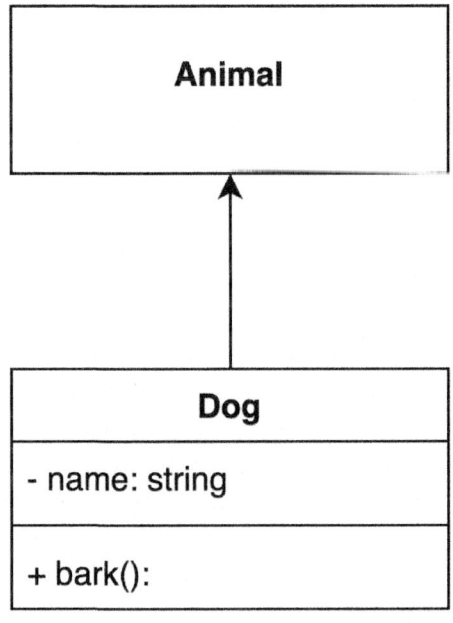

```
public class Dog : Animal
{
    // ...
}
```

Composition Relationship

Represented by an arrow with a filled diamond.

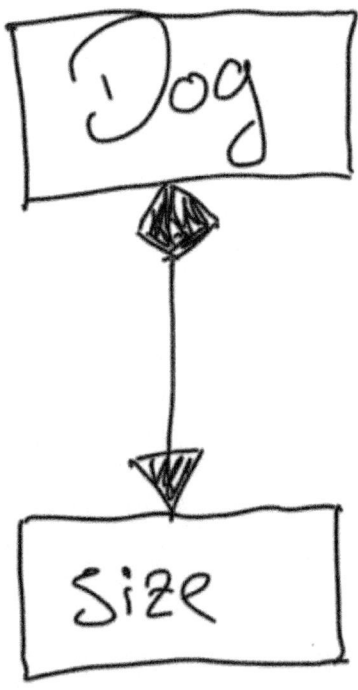

Or

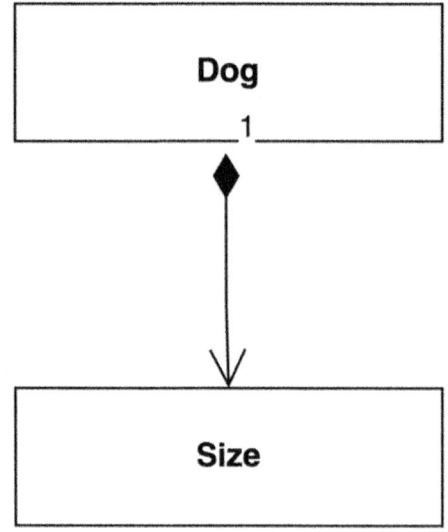

```
public class Dog
{
  private Size size;
}
```

Above, the Dog class is composed of the Size class -- i.e. in the Dog class, we have a field of type Size.

Association Relationship

Represented by an arrow:

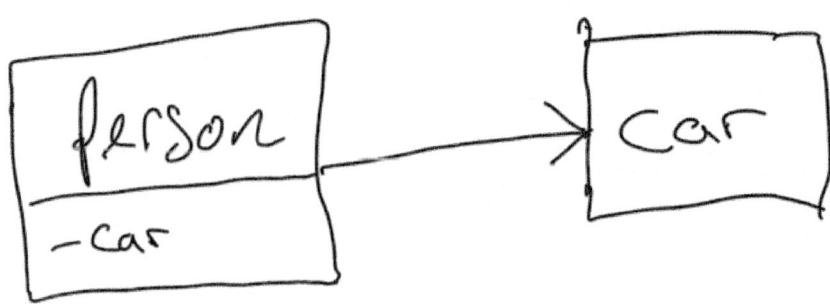

Or

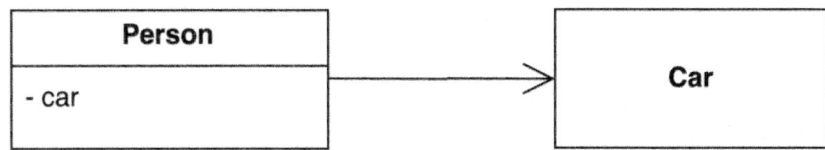

The difference between Association relationship and Composition relationship:

- Association: A Person has a Car, but is not composed of Car. A person holds a reference to Car so it can interact with it, but a Person can exist without a Car.
- Composition: when a child object wouldn't be able to exist without its parent object, e.g. a hotel is composed of its rooms, and HotelBathroom cannot exist without Hotel (destroy the hotel, you destroy the hotel bathroom – it can't exist by itself). Another example: if a Customer is destroyed, their ShoppingCart and Orders are lost too – therefore Customer is composed of ShoppingCart and Orders. And if Orders are lost,

`OrderDetails` and `ShippingInfo` are lost – so `Orders` are composed of `ShippingInfo` and `OrderDetails`.

Dependency Relationship

Represented by a dashed arrow:

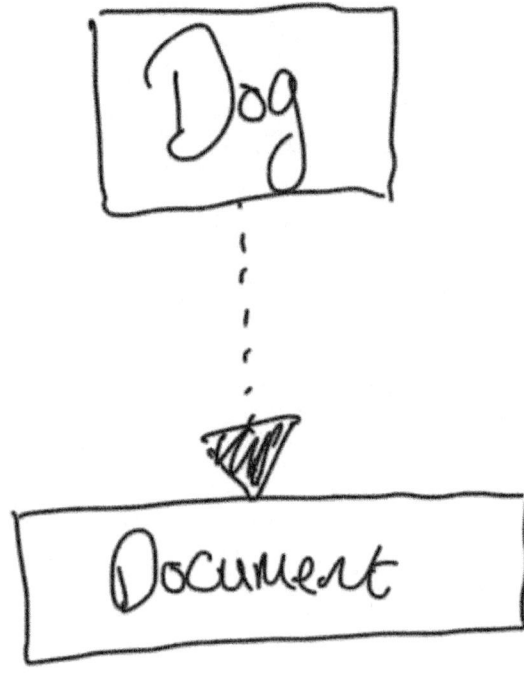

Or

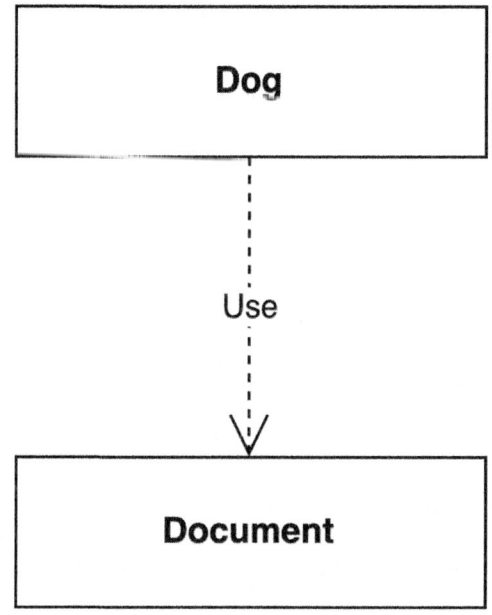

```
public class Dog
{
  public void render(Document document) { }
}
```

Above, Document is not a field in this class, but is used somewhere in the class – in this case it's a parameter, but it could also be a local variable defined in the render() method. So, somewhere in the Dog class, we have a reference, or dependency, to the Document class.

Chapter 3: SOLID Principles

One final thing that you should understand before beginning to study design patterns are the SOLID Principles:

- **S**: Single Responsibility Principle (SRP)
- **O**: Open-closed Principle (OCP)
- **L**: Liskov Substitution Principle (LSP)
- **I**: Interface Segregation Principle (ISP)
- **D**: Dependency Inversion Principle (DIP)

They were introduced by a guy called Robert C. Martin, also known as "Uncle Bob", in the early 2000s.

By following these principles, developers can create software designs that are easier to understand, maintain, and extend, leading to higher-quality software that is more robust and adaptable to change.

Single Responsibility Principle (SRP)

"A class should have only one reason to change, meaning that it should have only one responsibility or purpose."

This principle encourages you to create classes that are more focussed and perform one single well-defined task, rather than multiple tasks. Breaking up classes into smaller, more focused units makes code easier to understand, maintain, and test.

An example that violates SRP:

```csharp
public class User
{
  public string Username { get; set; }
  public string Email { get; set; }

  public void Register()
  {
    // Register user logic
    // ...

    // Send email notification
    EmailSender emailSender = new EmailSender();
    emailSender.SendEmail("Welcome to our platform!", Email);
  }
}

public class EmailSender
{
  public void SendEmail(string message, string recipient)
```

```csharp
{
    // Email sending logic
    Console.WriteLine($"Sending email to {recipient}: {message}");
  }
}
```

In this example, the User class manages user data (username, email), and contains logic for registering a user. This violates the SRP because the class has more than one reason to change. It could change due to:
- Modifications in user data management – e.g. adding more fields, such as firstName, gender, hobbies.
- Modifications to the logic of registering a user, e.g. we may choose to fetch a user from the database by their username rather than their email.

To adhere to the Single Responsibility Principle, we should separate these responsibilities into separate classes.

Refactoring the code to satisfy SRP:

```csharp
public class User
{
  public string Username { get; set; }
  public string Email { get; set; }
}

public class EmailSender
{
  public void SendEmail(string message, string recipient)
  {
    // Email sending logic
    Console.WriteLine($"Sending email to {recipient}: {message}");
  }
}

public class UserService
{
  public void RegisterUser(User user)
```

```
{
    // Register user logic
    // ...

    // Optionally, notify user via email
    EmailSender emailSender = new EmailSender();
    emailSender.SendEmail("Welcome to our platform!", user.Email);
  }
}
```

In the refactored code, the `User` class is responsible solely for representing user data. The `UserService` class now handles user registration, separating concerns related to user data management from user registration logic. The `UserService` class is responsible only for the business logic of registering a user. This separation of responsibilities adheres to the Single Responsibility Principle, making the code easier to understand, maintain, and extend.

Open/Closed Principle (OCP)

"Software entities (classes, modules, functions, etc.) should be open for extension but closed for modification."

This principle promotes the idea that existing code should be able to be extended with new functionality without modifying its source code. It encourages the use of abstraction and polymorphism to achieve this goal, allowing for code to be easily extended through inheritance or composition.

Let's consider an example of a `Shape` class hierarchy that calculates the area of different geometric shapes. Initially, this violates the Open/Closed Principle (OCP) because adding a new shape requires modifying the existing code:

```
public enum ShapeType
{
 Circle,
 Rectangle
}

public class Shape
```

```csharp
{
    public ShapeType Type { get; set; }
    public double Radius { get; set; }
    public double Length { get; set; }
    public double Width { get; set; }

    public double CalculateArea()
    {
        switch (Type)
        {
            case ShapeType.Circle:
                return Math.PI * Math.Pow(Radius, 2);
            case ShapeType.Rectangle:
                return Length * Width;
            default:
                throw new InvalidOperationException("Unsupported shape type.");
        }
    }
}
```

In this example, the Shape class has a method, CalculateArea(), that calculates the area based on the type of shape. Adding a new shape, such as a triangle, would require modifying the existing Shape class, violating the OCP.

To adhere to the Open/Closed Principle, we should design the system in a way that allows for extension without modification. Let's refactor the code using inheritance and polymorphism:

```csharp
public abstract class Shape
{
    public abstract double CalculateArea();
}

public class Circle : Shape
{
```

```csharp
    public double Radius { get; set; }

    public override double CalculateArea()
    {
        return Math.PI * Math.Pow(Radius, 2);
    }
}

public class Rectangle : Shape
{
    public double Length { get; set; }
    public double Width { get; set; }

    public override double CalculateArea()
    {
        return Length * Width;
    }
}
```

In this refactored code, we define an abstract Shape class with an abstract CalculateArea() method. Concrete shape classes (Circle and Rectangle) inherit from the Shape class and provide their own implementations of CalculateArea(). Adding a new shape, such as a triangle, would involve creating a new class – *extending* the codebase – that inherits from Shape and implements CalculateArea(), without *modifying* existing code. This adheres to the OCP by allowing for extension without modification.

Being able to add functionality without modifying existing code means that we don't have to worry as much about breaking existing working code and introducing bugs. Following the OCP encourages us to design our software so that we add new features only by adding new code. This helps us to build loosely-coupled, maintainable software.

Liskov Substitution Principle (LSP)

"Objects of a superclass should be replaceable with objects of its subclass without affecting the correctness of the program."

This principle ensures that inheritance hierarchies are well-designed and that subclasses adhere to the contracts defined by their superclasses.

Violations of the LSP can lead to unexpected behavior or errors when substituting objects, making code harder to reason about and maintain.

Let's consider an example involving a `Rectangle` class and a `Square` class, which inherit from a common `Shape` class. Initially, we'll violate the LSP by not adhering to the behavior expected from these classes. Then, we'll fix it to ensure that the principle is respected.

```csharp
public abstract class Shape
{
  public abstract double Area { get; }
}

public class Rectangle : Shape
{
  public virtual double Width { get; set; }
  public virtual double Height { get; set; }

  public override double Area => Width * Height;
}

public class Square : Rectangle
{
  public override double Width
  {
    get => base.Width;
    set => base.Width = base.Height = value;
  }
```

```csharp
  public override double Height
  {
    get => base.Height;
    set => base.Height = base.Width = value;
  }
}
```

Now, let's test out if `Rectangle` calculates its area correctly:

```csharp
// Program.cs

var rect = new Rectangle();
rect.Height = 10;
rect.Width = 5;
System.Console.WriteLine("Expected area = 10 * 5 = 50.");
System.Console.WriteLine("Calculated area = " + rect.Area);
```

Expected area = 10 * 5 = 50.

Calculated area = 50

Perfect!

Now, in our program, our `Square` class inherits from, or extends, the `Rectangle` class, because, mathematically, a square is just a special type of rectangle, where its height equals its width. Because of this, we decided that `Square` should extend `Rectangle` – it's like saying "a square *is a* (special type of) rectangle".

But look what happens if we substitute the `Rectangle` class for the `Square` class:

```csharp
var rect = new Square();
rect.Height = 10;
rect.Width = 5;
System.Console.WriteLine("Expected area = 10 * 5 = 50.");
System.Console.WriteLine("Calculated area = " + rect.Area);
```

Expected area = 10 * 5 = 50.

Calculated area = 25

Oh dear, LSP has been violated. we replaced the object of a superclass (`Rectangle`) with an object of its subclass (`Square`), and it affected the correctness of our program. By modeling `Square` as a subclass of `Rectangle`, and allowing `width` and `height` to be independently set, we violate the LSP. When setting the width and height of a `Square`, it should retain its squareness, but our implementation allows for inconsistency.

Let's fix this to satisfy LSP:

```
public abstract class Shape
{
 public abstract double Area { get; }
}

public class Rectangle : Shape
{
 public double Width { get; set; }
 public double Height { get; set; }

 public override double Area => Width * Height;
}

public class Square : Shape
{
 private double sideLength;

 public double SideLength
 {
   get => sideLength;
   set
   {
     sideLength = value;
   }
```

```csharp
    }

    public override double Area => sideLength * sideLength;
}

// Program.cs

Shape rectangle = new Rectangle { Width = 5, Height = 4 };
Console.WriteLine($"Area of the rectangle: {rectangle.Area}");

Shape square = new Square { SideLength = 5 };
Console.WriteLine($"Area of the square: {square.Area}");
```

In this corrected example, we redesign the `Square` class to directly set the side length. Now, a `Square` is correctly modeled as a subclass of `Shape`, and it adheres to the Liskov Substitution Principle.

How does this satisfy LSP? Well, we have a superclass, `Shape`, and subclasses `Rectangle` and `Square`. Both `Rectangle` and `Square` maintain the correct expected behavior of a `Shape` (in our case, providing an area), and they should both behave appropriately when interacting with other parts of the program that expect shapes.

Interface Segregation Principle (ISP)

"Clients should not be forced to depend on interfaces they do not use."

This principle encourages the creation of fine-grained interfaces that contain only the methods required by the clients that use them. It helps prevent the creation of "fat" interfaces that force clients to implement unnecessary methods, leading to cleaner and more maintainable code.

Let's consider an example involving 2D and 3D shapes, initially violating the ISP, and then we'll fix it.

Violating ISP:

```csharp
public interface IShape
{
 double Area();
 double Volume(); // problem: 2D shapes don't have volume
}

public class Circle : IShape
{
 public double Radius { get; set; }

 public double Area()
 {
    return Math.PI * Math.Pow(Radius, 2);
 }

 public double Volume()
 {
    throw new InvalidOperationException("Volume not applicable for 2D shapes.");
 }
}

public class Sphere : IShape
{
 public double Radius { get; set; }

 public double Area()
 {
    return 4 * Math.PI * Math.Pow(Radius, 2);
 }

 public double Volume()
 {
    return (4.0 / 3.0) * Math.PI * Math.Pow(Radius, 3);
```

        }
    }

In this example, we have an `IShape` interface representing both 2D and 3D shapes. However, the `Volume()` method is problematic for 2D shapes, like `Circle` and `Rectangle`, because they don't have volume. This violates the ISP because clients (classes using the `IShape` interface) may be forced to depend on methods they do not need.

```
var circle = new Circle();
circle.Radius = 10;
System.Console.WriteLine(circle.Area());
System.Console.WriteLine(circle.Volume()); // My text editor says
no problem...

var sphere = new Sphere();
sphere.Radius = 10;
System.Console.WriteLine(sphere.Area());
System.Console.WriteLine(sphere.Volume());
```

Usually, if I try to call a method on an object that doesn't exist, VS Code will tell me that I'm making a mistake. But above, when I call `circle.Volume()`, VS code is like "no problem". And VS code is correct, because the `IShape` interface forces `Circle` to implement a `Volume()` method, even though circles don't have volume. It's easy to see how violating ISP can introduce bugs into a program – above, everything looks fine, until we run the program and an exception gets thrown.

Fixing ISP
```
public interface IShape2D
{
    double Area();
}

public interface IShape3D
{
    double Area();
```

```csharp
    double Volume();
}

public class Circle : IShape2D
{
    public double Radius { get; set; }

    public double Area()
    {
        return Math.PI * Math.Pow(Radius, 2);
    }
}

public class Sphere : IShape3D
{
    public double Radius { get; set; }

    public double Area()
    {
        return 4 * Math.PI * Math.Pow(Radius, 2);
    }

    public double Volume()
    {
        return (4.0 / 3.0) * Math.PI * Math.Pow(Radius, 3);
    }
}
```

In the fixed example, we've *segregated* the IShape interface into two smaller, more focused interfaces: IShape2D and IShape3D. Each shape class now implements only the interface that is relevant to its functionality. This adheres to the Interface Segregation Principle by ensuring that clients are not forced to depend on methods they do not use. Clients can now depend only on the interfaces they need, promoting better code reuse and flexibility.

Dependency Inversion Principle (DIP)

"High-level modules should not depend on low-level modules. Both should depend on abstractions."

Dependency Inversion is the strategy of depending upon interfaces or abstract classes rather than upon concrete classes. This principle promotes decoupling between modules and promotes the use of interfaces or abstract classes to define dependencies, allowing for more flexible and testable code.

Let's start with an example violating the DIP and then correct it.

```
public class Engine
{
 public void Start()
 {
    System.Console.WriteLine("Engine started.");
 }
}

public class Car
{
 private Engine engine;

 public Car()
 {
    this.engine = new Engine(); // Direct dependency on concrete Engine class
 }

 public void StartCar()
 {
    engine.Start();
    System.Console.WriteLine("Car started.");
 }
}
```

In this example:

- The Car class directly creates an instance of the Engine class, leading to a tight coupling between Car and Engine.
- If the Engine class changes, it may affect the Car class, violating the Dependency Inversion Principle.

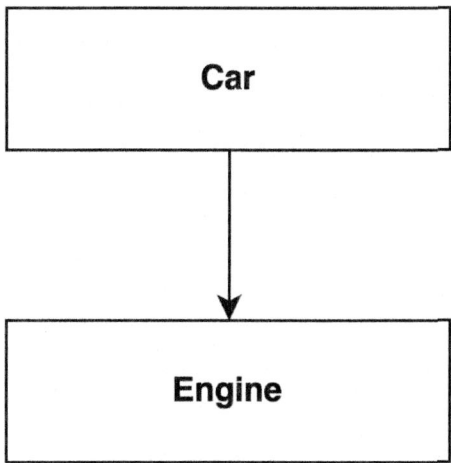

Fixing DIP:

To adhere to the Dependency Inversion Principle, we introduce an abstraction (interface) between Car and Engine, allowing Car to depend on an abstraction instead of a concrete implementation.

```
public interface IEngine
{
 void Start();
}
public class Engine : IEngine  // Engine is our "low-level" module
{
 public void Start()
 {
    System.Console.WriteLine("Engine started.");
 }
```

```
}

public class Car // Car is our "high-level" module
{
  private IEngine engine;

  public Car(IEngine engine)
  {
     this.engine = engine;
  }

  public void StartCar()
  {
     engine.Start();
     System.Console.WriteLine("Car started.");
  }
}
```

We can now *inject* any type of engine into Car implementations:

```
var engine = new Engine(); // concrete implementation to be
"injected" into the car
var car = new Car(engine);
car.StartCar();
```

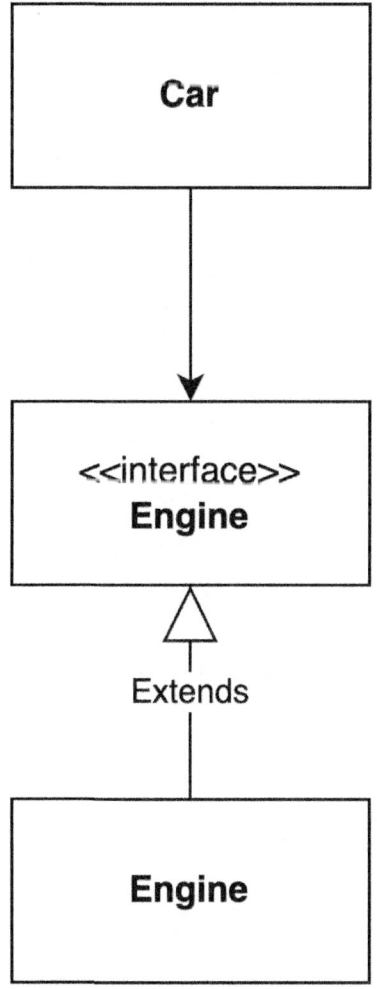

From the UML diagram above, we can see that both objects now depend on the abstraction level of the interface. Engine has inverted its dependency on Car.

In this corrected example:

1. We define an interface IEngine representing the behavior of an engine.
2. The Engine class implements the IEngine interface.
3. The Car class now depends on the IEngine interface instead of the concrete Engine class.
4. Dependency injection is used to inject the IEngine implementation into the Car class, promoting loose coupling. Now, if we want to give a car a different type of engine, e.g. a fast engine, we can inject that in instead.

5. Now, if the implementation of the engine changes, it won't affect the `Car` class as long as it adheres to the `IEngine` interface.

Dependency Injection (DI) offers several advantages in software development:

- **Decoupling**: DI promotes loose coupling between components by removing direct dependencies. Components rely on abstractions rather than concrete implementations, making them more independent and easier to maintain.
- **Testability**: Dependency injection simplifies unit testing by allowing components to be easily replaced with mock or stub implementations during testing. This enables isolated testing of individual components without relying on their dependencies.
- **Flexibility**: DI provides flexibility in configuring and swapping dependencies at runtime. It allows different implementations of dependencies to be used interchangeably without modifying the client code, facilitating runtime customization and extensibility.
- **Readability and Maintainability**: By explicitly specifying dependencies in the constructor or method parameters, DI improves code readability and makes the codebase easier to understand. It also reduces the risk of hidden dependencies, leading to more maintainable and understandable code.
- **Reusability**: DI promotes component reusability by decoupling them from their specific contexts or environments. Components can be designed to be independent of the application framework or platform, making them more portable and reusable in different projects or scenarios.
- **Scalability**: DI simplifies the management of dependencies in large-scale applications by providing a standardized approach for dependency resolution. It helps prevent dependency hell and makes it easier to manage and scale complex systems.

Overall, dependency injection enhances modularity, testability, and maintainability of software systems, contributing to improved software quality and developer productivity.

But what do you mean by "high level" and "low level" classes?

High-Level Class:
The high-level class is typically the one that represents the main functionality or business logic of the application. It orchestrates the interaction between various components and is often more abstract in nature.

In this example, the `Car` class can be considered the high-level class. It represents the main functionality related to starting the car and driving it. The `Car` class is concerned with the overall behavior of the car, such as controlling its movement.

Low-Level Class:
The low-level class is usually one that provides specific functionality or services that are used by the high-level class. It typically deals with implementation details and is more concrete in nature.

In this example, the `Engine` class can be considered the low-level class. It provides the specific functionality related to starting the engine. The `Engine` class encapsulates the details of how the engine operates, such as ignition and combustion.

In summary:
The `Car` class is the high-level class, representing the main functionality of the application related to the car's behavior.

The `Engine` class is the low-level class, providing specific functionality related to the operation of the engine, which is used by the `Car` class.

OK – you now understand the very important SOLID principles. You are now ready to learn…

Chapter 4: Design Patterns

There are three main groups of design patterns:

- **Creational**: the different ways to create objects.
- **Structural**: the relationships between those objects.
- **Behavioral**: the interaction or communication between those objects.

First, we will look at the Behavioral design patterns.

Behavioral Design Patterns

Behavioral design patterns focus on how objects interact with each other and how they communicate to accomplish specific tasks. These patterns address communication, responsibility, and algorithmic issues in object-oriented software design. They help in defining clear and efficient communication mechanisms between objects and classes.

These patterns help in making the design more flexible, extensible, and maintainable by promoting better communication and separation of concerns between objects and classes in the system. Each pattern addresses specific design issues and provides a standardized solution to common problems encountered in software development.

Memento Pattern

The Memento Pattern is used to restore an object to a previous state.

A common use case for the Memento Pattern is implementing an undo feature. For example, most text editors, such as Microsoft Word, have undo features where you can undo things by pressing Ctrl + Z on Windows, or Cmd + Z on Mac.

Here is a sequence of things that you might do in a text editor:

1. Add a title to the document: "Test Title".
2. Write some text: "Hello there, my name is Dan.".
3. Change the title of the document to "The Life of a Developer: My Memoirs".

A simple way to implement this text editor in code would be to create a single `Editor` class and have a field for `title` and `content`, and also have a field that stores each of the previous values for each field in some list:

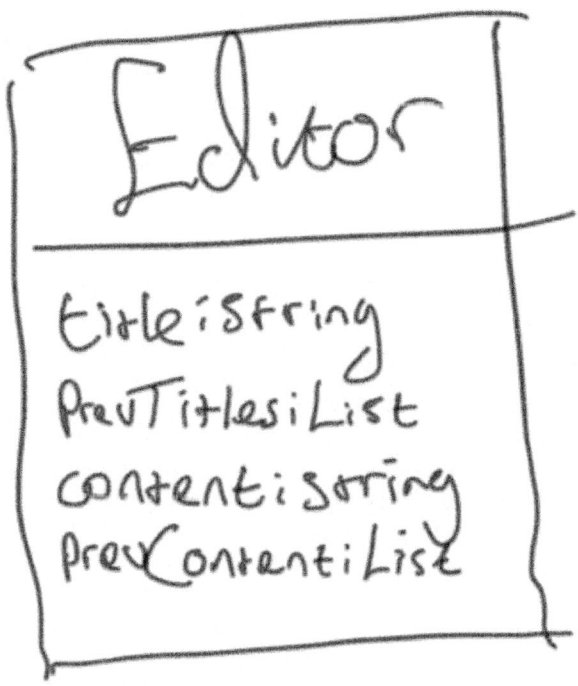

Problem: every time we add a new field, e.g. `author`, `date`, `isPublished`, we have to keep storing lists of prev states (all the changes) for each field. Also, how would we implement the undo feature? If the user changed the title, then changed the content, then pressed *undo*, the current implementation has no knowledge of what the user last did – did they change the title or the content?

How about this: instead of having multiple fields in this `Editor` class, we create a separate class to store the state of our editor at a given time:

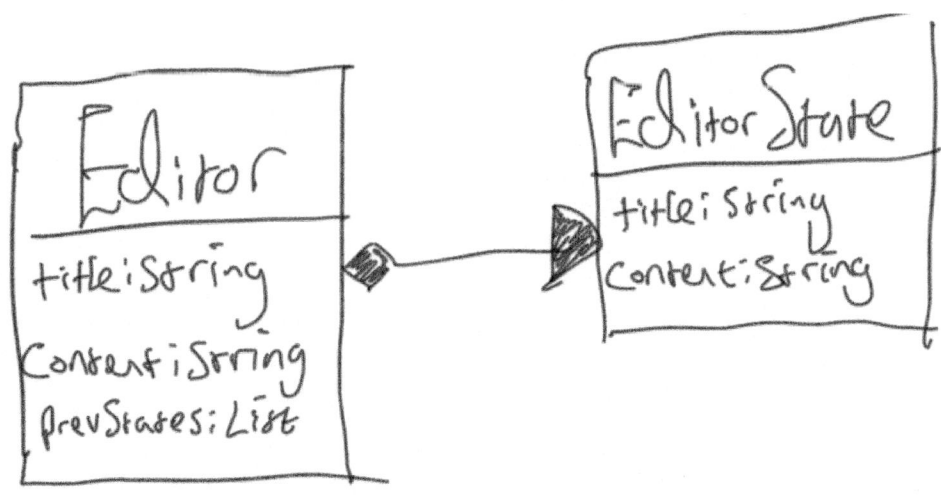

(Note the composition relationship: `Editor` is composed of, or has a field of, the `EditorState` class).

This is a good solution as we can undo multiple times and we don't pollute the `Editor` class with too many fields.

However, this solution is violating the Single Responsibility Principle, as our `Editor` class currently has multiple responsibilities:

1. State management
2. Providing the features that we need from an editor

We should take all the state management stuff out of Editor and put it somewhere else:

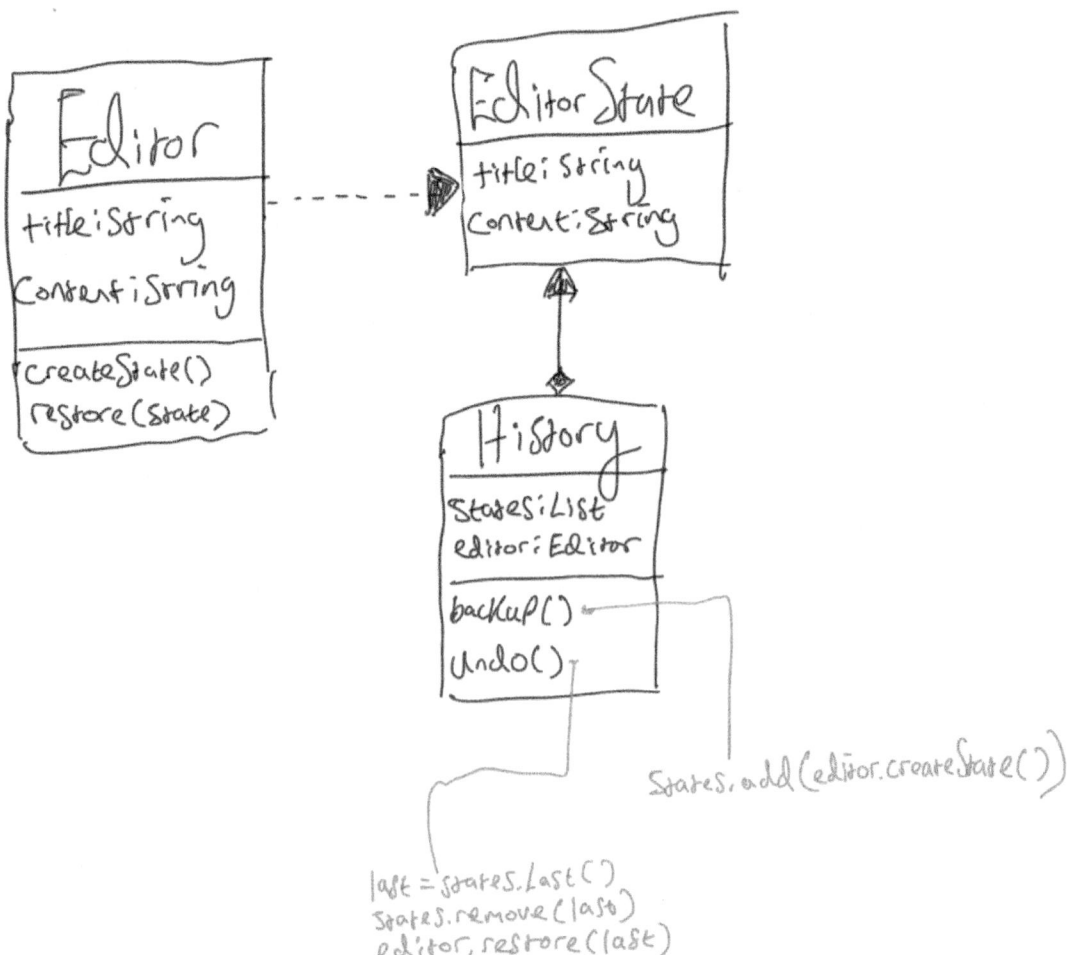

The `createState()` method returns an `EditorState` object, hence the dotted line arrow (dependency relationship). History has a field with a list of `EditorStates`, hence the diamond arrow (composition relationship).

This is the Memento pattern. Here are the abstract names that each class would be in the memento pattern:

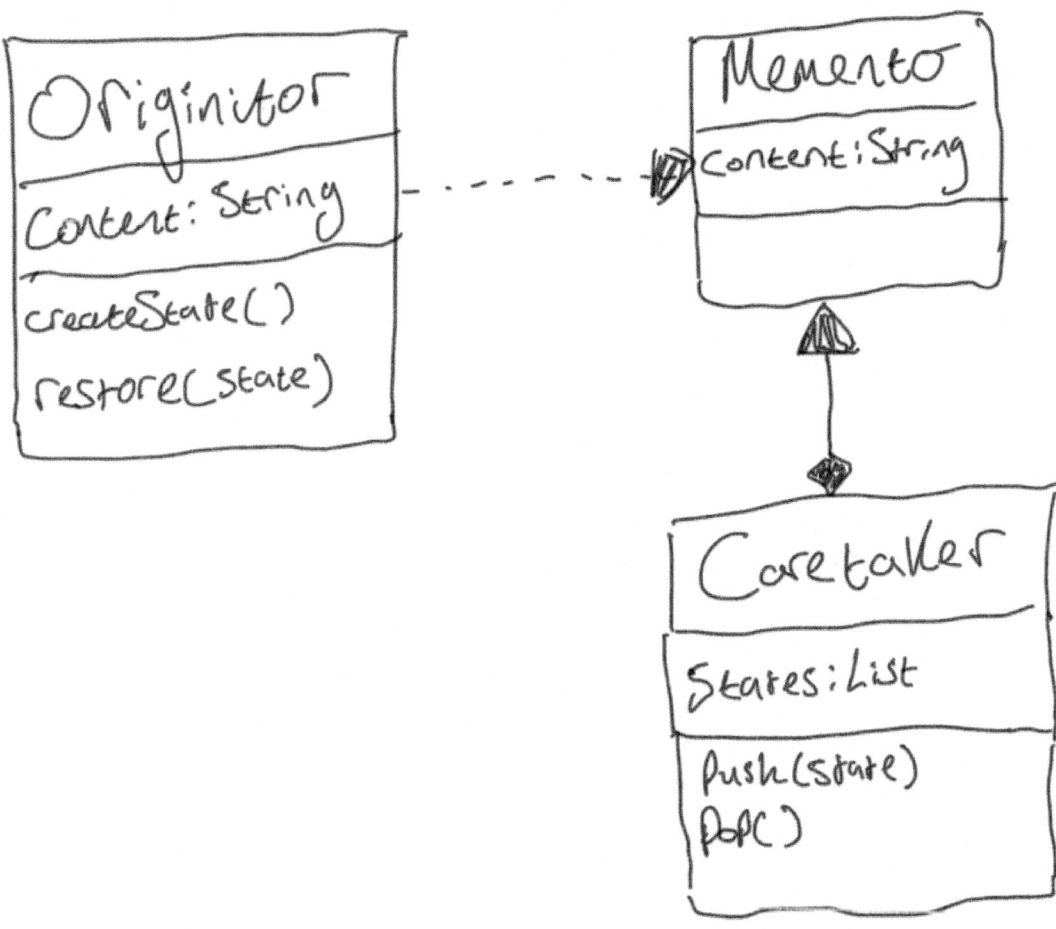

These abstract names for the classes in the Memento Pattern come from the original Gang of Four (GoF) book. Note that our solution differs slightly from the above pattern, as our Caretaker class, `History`, also has a field that stores a reference to the `Editor`, so that the `History` class can restore the Editor's state when the user clicks *undo*.

Let's now implement this in code:

```
// Originator
```

```csharp
public class Editor
{
  public string Title { get; set; }
  public string Content { get; set; }

  public EditorState CreateState()
  {
    return new EditorState(Title, Content);
  }

  public void Restore(EditorState state)
  {
    Title = state.GetTitle();
    Content = state.GetContent();
  }
}

// Memento
public class EditorState
{
  // Editor state data:
  // `readonly` so once created we cannot change it, adding robustness to our code.
  private readonly string _title;
  private readonly string _content;

  // State meta data:
  private readonly DateTime _stateCreatedAt;

  public EditorState(string title, string content)
  {
    _title = title;
    _content = content;
    _stateCreatedAt = DateTime.Now;
```

```csharp
    }

    public string GetTitle()
    {
        return _title;
    }

    public string GetContent()
    {
        return _content;
    }

    // The rest of the methods are used by the CareTaker (History) to display meta
    // data:
    public DateTime GetDate()
    {
        return _stateCreatedAt;
    }

    public string GetName()
    {
        return $"{_stateCreatedAt} / ({_title})";
    }
}

// Caretaker
public class History
{
    private List<EditorState> _states = new List<EditorState>();
    private Editor _editor;

    public History(Editor editor)
    {
```

```csharp
        _editor = editor;
    }

    public void Backup()
    {
        _states.Add(_editor.CreateState());
    }

    public void Undo()
    {
        if (_states.Count == 0)
        {
            return;
        }

        EditorState prevState = _states.Last();
        _states.Remove(prevState);

        _editor.Restore(prevState);
    }

    public void ShowHistory()
    {
        Console.WriteLine("\nHistory: Here's the list of mementos:");

        foreach (var state in _states)
        {
            Console.WriteLine(state.GetName());
        }
    }
}
```

Here's how a client could use this implementation:

```csharp
class Program
```

```csharp
{
  static void Main(string[] args)
  {
    Editor editor = new Editor();
    History history = new History(editor);
    history.Backup();
    editor.Title = "Test";
    history.Backup();
    editor.Content = "Hello there, my name is Dan.";
    history.Backup();
    editor.Title = "The Life of a Developer: My Memoirs";

    Console.WriteLine("Title: " + editor.Title); // Title: The Life of a Developer: My Memoirs
    Console.WriteLine("Content: " + editor.Content); // Content: Hello there, my name is Dan.

    history.Undo();
    Console.WriteLine("Title: " + editor.Title); // Title: Test
    Console.WriteLine("Content: " + editor.Content); // Content: Hello there, my name is Dan.

    history.ShowHistory();
    // History: Here's the list of mementos:
    // 11/04/2024 12:11:18 / ()
    // 11/04/2024 12:11:18 / (Test)

    history.Undo();
    Console.WriteLine("Title: " + editor.Title); // Title: Test
    Console.WriteLine("Content: " + editor.Content); // Content:

    history.Undo();
    Console.WriteLine("Title: " + editor.Title); // Title:
    Console.WriteLine("Content: " + editor.Content); // Content:
```

        }
    }

When to use the Memento Pattern:

So, the Memento Pattern can be used when you want to produce snapshots of an object's state to be able to restore the object to a previous state. It's a commonly used pattern for implementing the undo feature, and so provides a common solution that a team of developers can quickly understand and get on the same page with.

Pros and cons of the Memento Pattern:

- + You can simplify the originator's code by letting the caretaker maintain the history of the originator's state, satisfying the Single Responsibility Principle.

- - The app might consume a lot of RAM if lots of mementos are created. E.g., if we have a class that is heavy on memory, such as a Video class, then creating lots of snapshots of videos will consume lots of memory.

State Pattern

The state pattern allows an object to behave differently depending on the state that it is in.

Say that you're writing a blog post using the popular content management system, WordPress. The document, or post, can be in one of three states:

1. Draft
2. Moderation (under review by an admin)
3. Published

There are three types of user roles:

1. Reader
2. Editor
3. Admin

Only admins can publish posts.

First, let's create a simple solution that uses if/else statements to check the current state of the document to see whether the state of the document should be upgraded. We'll also create a couple of enums to store the possible document states and user roles:

```
public enum DocumentStates
{
  DRAFT,
  MODERATION,
  PUBLISHED
}

public enum UserRoles
{
  READER,
  EDITOR,
  ADMIN
}

public class Document
{
  public DocumentStates State { get; set; }
  public UserRoles CurrentUserRole { get; set; }

  public void Publish()
  {
    if (State == DocumentStates.DRAFT)
    {
      State = DocumentStates.MODERATION;
    }
    else if (State == DocumentStates.MODERATION)
    {
      if (CurrentUserRole == UserRoles.ADMIN)
      {
        State = DocumentStates.PUBLISHED;
```

```
      }
    }
    else if (State == DocumentStates.PUBLISHED)
    {
      // do nothing
    }
  }
}
```

We can then use this document like so:

```
class Program
{
  static void Main(string[] args)
  {
    Document doc = new Document();
    doc.State = DocumentStates.MODERATION;
    doc.CurrentUserRole = UserRoles.ADMIN;

    System.Console.WriteLine(doc.State); // MODERATION

    doc.Publish();

    System.Console.WriteLine(doc.State); // PUBLISHED
  }
}
```

As you can see, the behavior of the Document class changes depending on the state.

Can you spot the problem(s) with the current Document class?:

We are violating the Open/Closed Principle: if we add other states or user roles, many of the Document classes methods would have to be modified. With more states, this class will quickly become bloated, unwieldy and difficult to understand.

Code is very difficult to maintain because any changes in logic may require changing state conditionals in every method.

Solution with State Pattern

The State Pattern suggests that we should create state classes for each possible state of the Document object, and extract all state-specific logic into these classes.

The Document class will store a reference to one of the state classes to represent the current state that it is in. Then, instead of Document implementing state-specific behavior by itself, it *delegates* all the state-related work to the state object that it has a reference to:

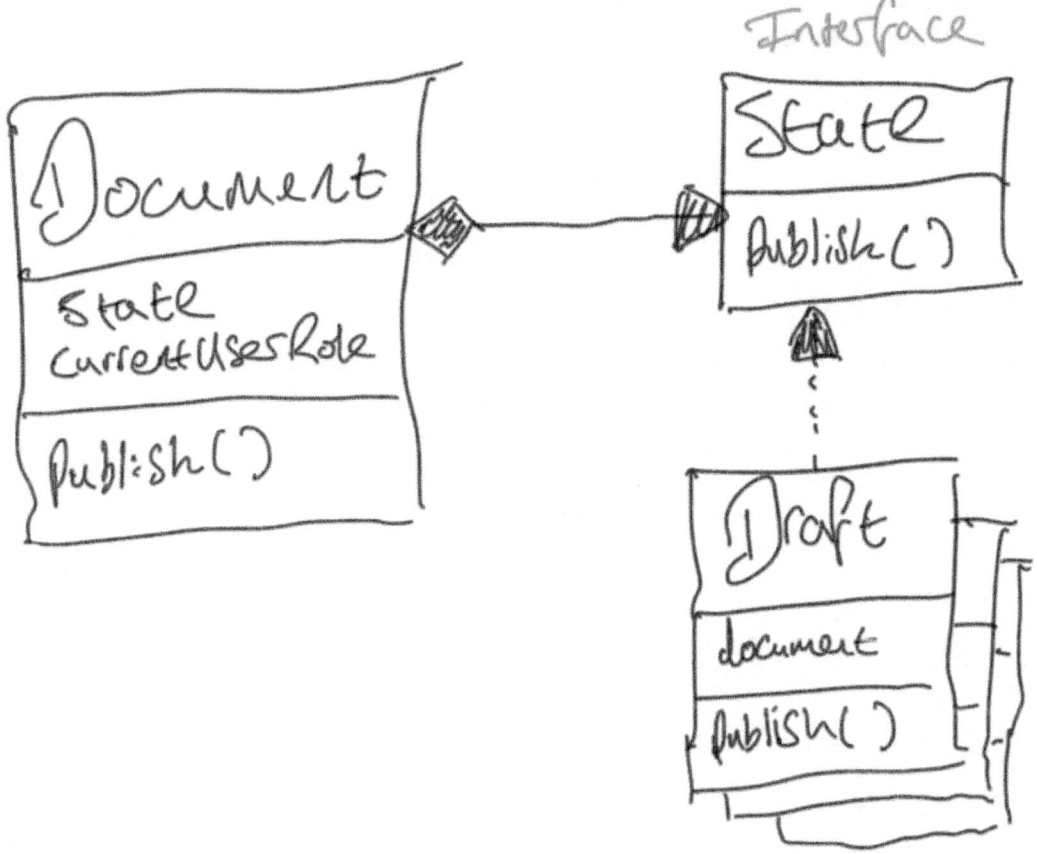

Above, Document keeps reference to (is composed of) a State object. Notice that we are using polymorphism, as the state field can be any one of the concrete state classes (Draft, Moderation, Published), as we are coding to an interface, not concrete classes.

In Document, the publish() method calls state.publish() – it delegates the work to the concrete state object. Why is this good? Because our solution now satisfies the Open/Closed Principle: if we want to add a new state, we create a new concrete state class that implements the State interface – we extend our codebase (add new classes) without having to modify any current classes (Document in our case).

Here's how the State Pattern is represented in GoF:

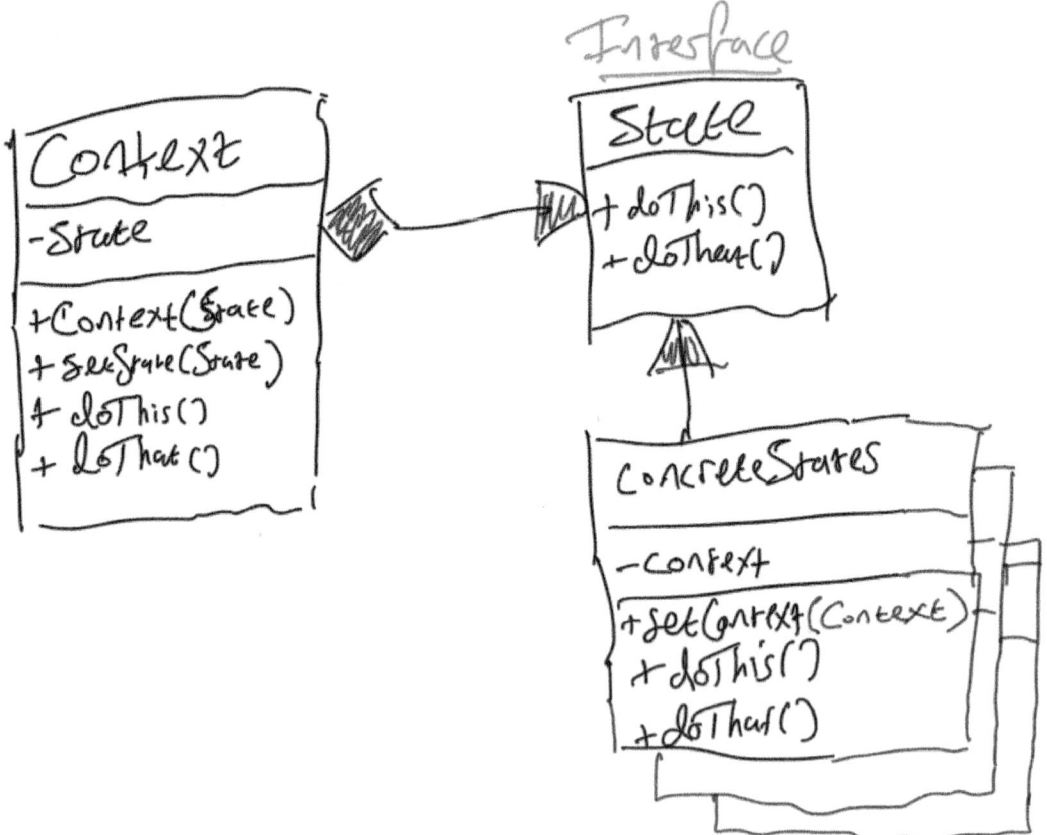

In our case, Document is the context.

Let's implement this in code:

```
public class Document
{
```

```csharp
    public State State { get; set; }
    public UserRoles CurrentUserRole { get; set; }

    public Document(UserRoles currentUserRole)
    {
       State = new DraftState(this); // New documents have draft state by default
       CurrentUserRole = currentUserRole;
    }

    public void Publish()
    {
       State.Publish();
    }
}

public interface State
{
 void Publish();

 // A real Document would have more state-dependent methods, such
 as Render() -- but we'll keep it simple with one method for this
 example.
}

public class DraftState : State
{
 private Document _document;

 public DraftState(Document document)
 {
    _document = document;
 }

 public void Publish()
```

```csharp
    {
        _document.State = new ModerationState(_document);
    }
}

public class ModerationState : State
{
    private Document _document;

    public ModerationState(Document document)
    {
        _document = document;
    }

    public void Publish()
    {
        if (_document.CurrentUserRole == UserRoles.ADMIN)
        {
            _document.State = new PublishedState(_document);
        }
    }
}

public class PublishedState : State
{
    private Document _document;

    public PublishedState(Document document)
    {
        _document = document;
    }

    public void Publish()
    {
        // do nothing
```

```
    }
}
```

The client can then use this State Pattern solution like so:

```
class Program
{
  static void Main(string[] args)
  {
    Document doc = new Document(UserRoles.EDITOR);
    System.Console.WriteLine(doc.State);  // DraftState

    doc.Publish();
    System.Console.WriteLine(doc.State);  // ModerationState

    doc.Publish();
    System.Console.WriteLine(doc.State);  // ModerationState --
editors can't create published documents

    // Simulate Admin logging in and publishing the document
    doc.CurrentUserRole = UserRoles.ADMIN;
    doc.Publish();
    System.Console.WriteLine(doc.State);  // PublishedState

    // Can also switch to any state like so:
    doc.State = new DraftState(doc);
    System.Console.WriteLine(doc.State);  // DraftState
  }
}
```

Now, if we create new states, we don't have to modify the Document class, as its publish() method is coded to an interface, and so delegates the work to a concrete class.

However, using the State Pattern can be overkill/overengineering. For example, consider a simple stopwatch that has two states:

```csharp
public class Stopwatch
{
  private bool IsRunning { get; set; } = false;

  public void click()
  {
    if (IsRunning)
    {
      IsRunning = false;
      System.Console.WriteLine("Stopped");
    }
    else
    {
      IsRunning = true;
      System.Console.WriteLine("Running");
    }
  }
}

class Program
{
  static void Main(string[] args)
  {
    Stopwatch stopwatch = new Stopwatch();
    stopwatch.click(); // Running
    stopwatch.click(); // Stopped
    stopwatch.click(); // Running
  }
}
```

Pretty simple. We can be pretty certain that the stopwatch isn't going to get more complex than this, and so using the State Pattern and creating more classes adds unnecessary complexity.

When to use the State Pattern:

A good indication that you should use the State Pattern is if you have a class that behaves differently depending on its state, and you have a large number of conditionals (if/else statements).

The state pattern can also be used with abstract classes to reduce duplication. You can create a hierarchy of state classes and abstract common code into the abstract base classes.

Pros and Cons of the State Pattern:

- \+ Improve readability and simplicity of the context class by eliminating conditionals.
- \+ Satisfies the Single Responsibility Principle by abstracting state-specific logic into separate classes.
- \+ Satisfies the Open/Closed Principle: we can introduce new states without modifying existing classes.

- \- This pattern can be overkill if there are only a few states or if state logic rarely changes (e.g. our Stopwatch example above)

Strategy Pattern

The Strategy Pattern is used to pass different algorithms, or behaviors, to an object.

First, let's consider an application that stores videos. Before storing a video, the video needs to be compressed using a specific compression algorithm, such as MOV or MP4, then, if necessary, apply an overlay to the video, such as black and white or blur.

Let's create a `VideoStorage` class to handle all of this. We'll also create some enums for the different types of compression algorithms and overlays, as it's good practice to use enums instead of hard-coding literal values in conditionals, i.e. "magic values" (e.g. `if(_compressor == "MOV")`):

```
public enum Compressors
{
 MOV,
 MP4,
 WEBM
}

public enum Overlays
{
 NONE,
 BLACK_AND_WHITE,
 BLUR
}

public class VideoStorage
{
 private Compressors _compressor;
 private Overlays _overlay;

 public VideoStorage(Compressors compressor, Overlays overlay = Overlays.NONE)
   {
     _compressor = compressor;
     _overlay = overlay;
   }

 public void SetCompressor(Compressors compressor)
   {
     _compressor = compressor;
   }

 public void SetOverlay(Overlays overlay)
   {
     _overlay = overlay;
```

```csharp
    }

    public void Store(string fileName)
    {
       if (_compressor == Compressors.MOV)
       {
          System.Console.WriteLine("Compressing using MOV");
       }
       else if (_compressor == Compressors.MP4)
       {
          System.Console.WriteLine("Compressing using MP4");
       }
       else if (_compressor == Compressors.WEBM)
       {
          System.Console.WriteLine("Compressing using WEBM");
       }

       if (_overlay == Overlays.BLACK_AND_WHITE)
       {
          System.Console.WriteLine("Applying black and white overlay");
       }
       else if (_overlay == Overlays.BLUR)
       {
          System.Console.WriteLine("Applying blur overlay");
       }
       else if (_overlay == Overlays.NONE)
       {
          System.Console.WriteLine("Not applying an overlay");
       }

       System.Console.WriteLine("Storing video to " + fileName);
    }
}
```

(Note that we are not concerned with the actual logic to compress videos or apply overlays; we are keeping things simple to make it easy to understand how we can improve the design of this code).

Problems with this Solution

- It violates the Open/closed Principle: adding new compression algorithms or overlays means that we have to *modify* the existing `VideoStorage` class. This working and tested code has to be modified, risking introducing bugs to working code. Also, developers could get lots of merge conflicts, as multiple developers may have to edit one big class – e.g. if one developer is working on compression algorithms, and another on overlays, then both developers will be editing `VideoStorage`.
- Single Responsibility Principle is violated: `VideoStorage` is responsible for compressing videos, applying overlays, and storing the video.
- This class will quickly become very bloated with lots of conditionals. Hard to read, hard to maintain – it easily becomes a maintenance nightmare!

Solution with Strategy Pattern

The UML below shows that when we create a `VideoStorage` object, we pass it the concrete compressor and overlay objects that we want it to use. This is polymorphism: `VideoStorage` can accept many different forms of `Compressor` and `Overlay` objects. `VideoStorage` is composed of `Compressor` and `Overlay` objects (remember: arrow with diamond represents composition). And there are multiple concrete compressor and overlay implementations that extend `Compressor` and `Filter` respectively.

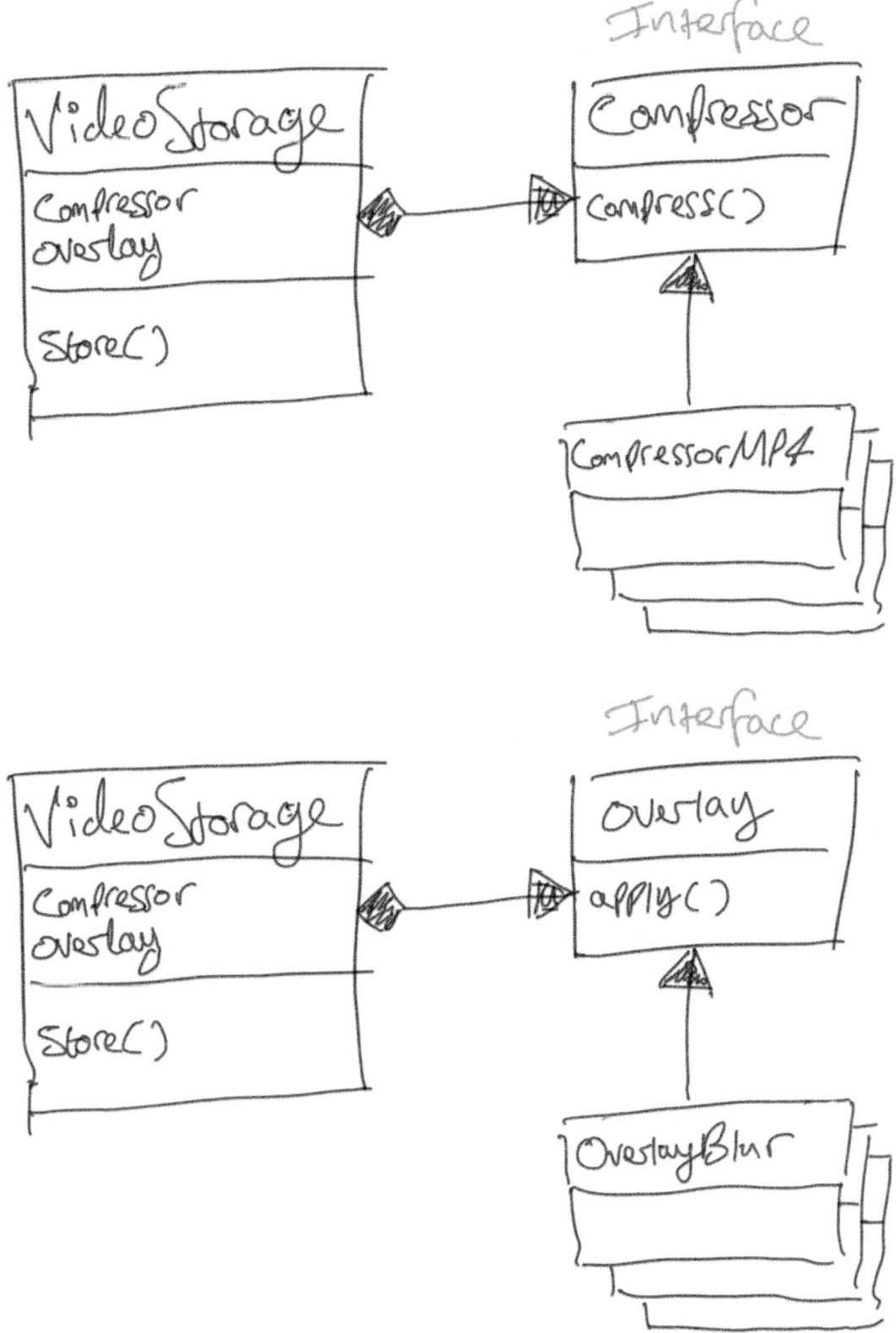

This is the Strategy Pattern. Here's how it looks, with its abstract class names, in GoF:

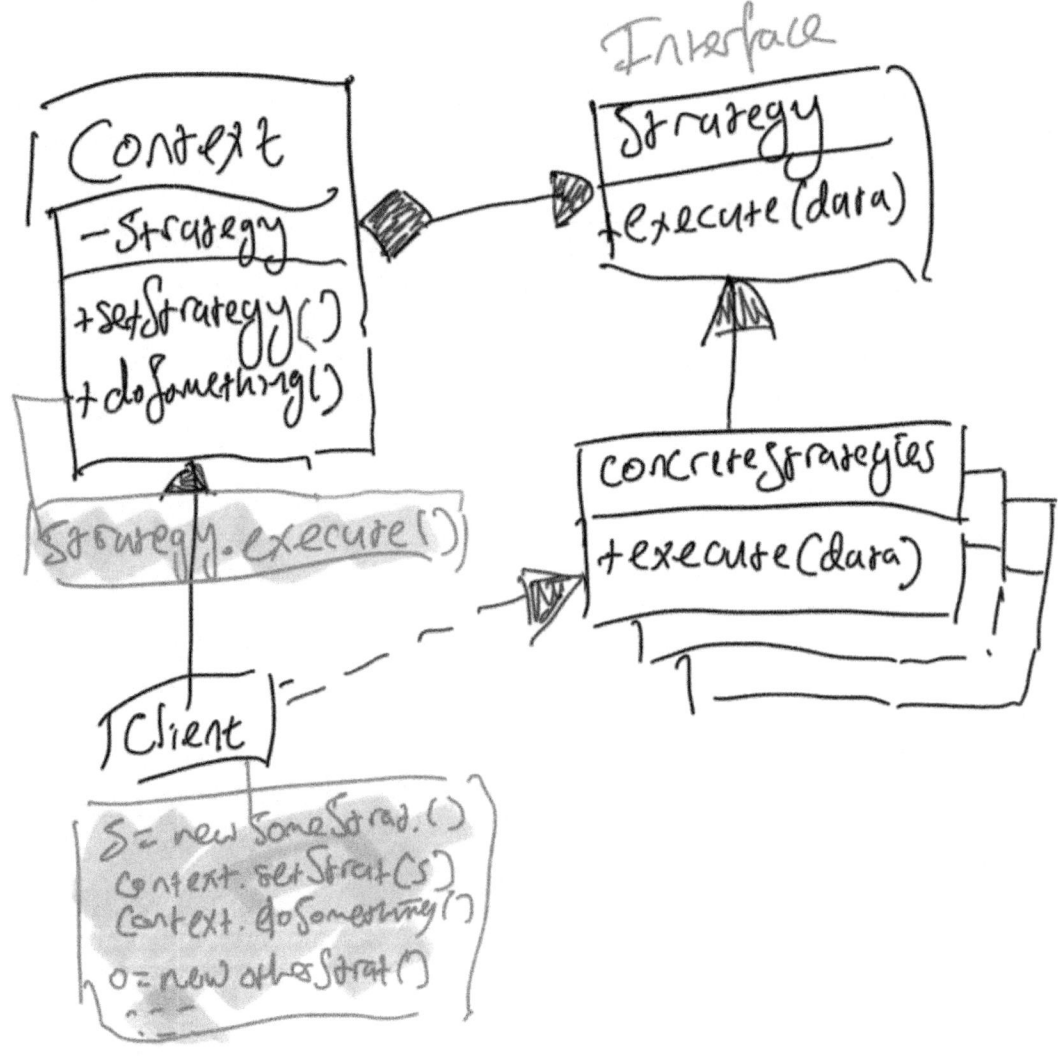

Let's implement this in code:

First, let's create the interfaces for our two strategies:

```csharp
public interface ICompressor
{
  void Compress();
}

public interface IOverlay
{
  void Apply();
}
```

Create the concrete compressor strategies:

```csharp
public class CompressorMOV : ICompressor
{
  public void Compress()
  {
     System.Console.WriteLine("Compressing video using MOV");
  }
}

public class CompressorMP4 : ICompressor
{
  public void Compress()
  {
     System.Console.WriteLine("Compressing video using MP4");
  }
}

public class CompressorWebM : ICompressor
{
  public void Compress()
  {
     System.Console.WriteLine("Compressing video using WebM");
  }
}
```

}

Create the concrete overlay strategies:

```csharp
public class OverlayBlackAndWhite : IOverlay
{
 public void Apply()
 {
    System.Console.WriteLine("Applying black and white overlay");
 }
}

public class OverlayBlur : IOverlay
{
 public void Apply()
 {
    System.Console.WriteLine("Applying blur overlay");
 }
}

public class OverlayNone : IOverlay
{
 public void Apply()
 {
    System.Console.WriteLine("Not applying an overlay");
 }
}
```

Finally, the video storage class that is composed of strategies, and delegates the work to the concrete strategies:

```csharp
public class VideoStorage
{
 // Store references to the strategies, coding to interfaces for polymorphism/flexibility
 private ICompressor _compressor;
```

```csharp
  private IOverlay _overlay;

  // It's common to pass the strategies via constructor
  public VideoStorage(ICompressor compressor, IOverlay overlay)
  {
     _compressor = compressor;
     _overlay = overlay;
  }

  // Provide setters so strategies can be changed at runtime
  public void SetCompressor(ICompressor compressor)
  {
     _compressor = compressor;
  }

  public void SetOverlay(IOverlay overlay)
  {
     _overlay = overlay;
  }

  public void Store(string fileName)
  {
     // Work is now delegated to the concrete compressor and
     // overlay objects. VideoStorage now has no knowledge of the
     // implementation details of each compression and overlay algorithm.
     _compressor.Compress();
     _overlay.Apply();

     System.Console.WriteLine("Storing video to " + fileName);
  }
}
```

Here's how a client would use this solution, passing strategies, and easily swapping between strategies at runtime:

```
class Program
{
  static void Main(string[] args)
  {
    VideoStorage videoStorage = new VideoStorage(new
CompressorMOV(), new OverlayBlackAndWhite());
    videoStorage.Store("/videos/dannys-movies");

    videoStorage.SetOverlay(new OverlayNone());
    videoStorage.Store("/videos/dannys-movies");

    // Logs:
    // Compressing video using MOV
    // Applying black and white overlay
    // Storing video to /videos/dannys-movies
    // Compressing video using MOV
    // Not applying an overlay
    // Storing video to /videos/dannys-movies
  }
}
```

Beautiful: this solution follows the Open-closed SOLID principle, e.g. to create a new compressor, we simply create a new class that extends the `ICompressor` interface -- our code is extended (new class) not modified (no existing classes have to change).

Difference between Strategy and State:

The two patterns are similar in practice, and the difference between them varies depending on who you ask. Some popular choices are:

- States store a reference to the context object that contains them. Strategies do not.
- States are allowed to replace themselves (IE: to change the state of the context object to something else), while Strategies are not.

- Strategies only handle a single, specific task, while States provide the underlying implementation for everything (or almost everything) the context object does.

When to use

A good rule of thumb for when it might be a good time to reach for the Strategy Pattern is when you have a class with a large number of conditional statements that switch between variants of the same algorithm. The algorithm logic can be extracted into separate classes that implement the same interface. The context object then delegates the work to these classes, instead of implementing all of the algorithms itself.

Pros and cons

+ Satisfies open/closed principle: can add new strategies without modifying the context.
+ Can swap algorithms used inside an object at runtime.

- Clients have to be aware of the different algorithms and select the appropriate one.
- If you only have a few algorithms that rarely change, then using the Strategy Pattern may be over-engineering.

Iterator Pattern

The Iterator Pattern provides a way of iterating over an object without having to expose the object's internal structure, which may change in the future. Changing the internals of an object should not affect its consumers.

What does this mean? Let me show you with an example:

Let's say that we have a shopping list of items, and we need to iterate over each of them and display each item in the list:

```
public class ShoppingList
{
  private List<string> _list = new List<string>();
```

```csharp
public void Push(string itemName)
{
   _list.Add(itemName);
}

public string Pop()
{
   var last = _list.Last();
   _list.Remove(last);
   return last;
}

public List<string> GetList()
{
   return _list;
}
}
```

The client can then create a shopping list, iterate through each item in the list, and output it in the console:

```csharp
class Program
{
 static void Main(string[] args)
 {
    ShoppingList shoppingList = new ShoppingList();
    shoppingList.Push("Milk");
    shoppingList.Push("Bread");
    shoppingList.Push("Steak");

    for (int i = 0; i < shoppingList.GetList().Count; i++)
    {
      var item = shoppingList.GetList()[i];
      System.Console.WriteLine(item);
    }
```

```
    // Log:
    // Milk
    // Bread
    // Steak
  }
}
```

Can you spot the problem with this solution?

Remember: "Changing the internals of an object should not affect its consumers."

Above, the client (`Program.cs`) is the consumer (it's consuming `ShoppingList`). However, the consumer needs knowledge of the data structure used to store items, if it wants to loop over the list.

What if we changed the data structure to a fixed-length array:

```
public class ShoppingList
{
  public string[] _list = new string[50];

// ...
```

This would create errors in all consumers that iterate over the list, because fixed-length arrays don't have a `Count` field:

```
shoppingList.GetList().Count;
```

We can use the Iterator Pattern to ensure that changing the internals (e.g. changing the list data structure) doesn't affect consumers. We can add some methods to `ShoppingList` to allow iterating over a shopping list object, without knowing its internal representation:

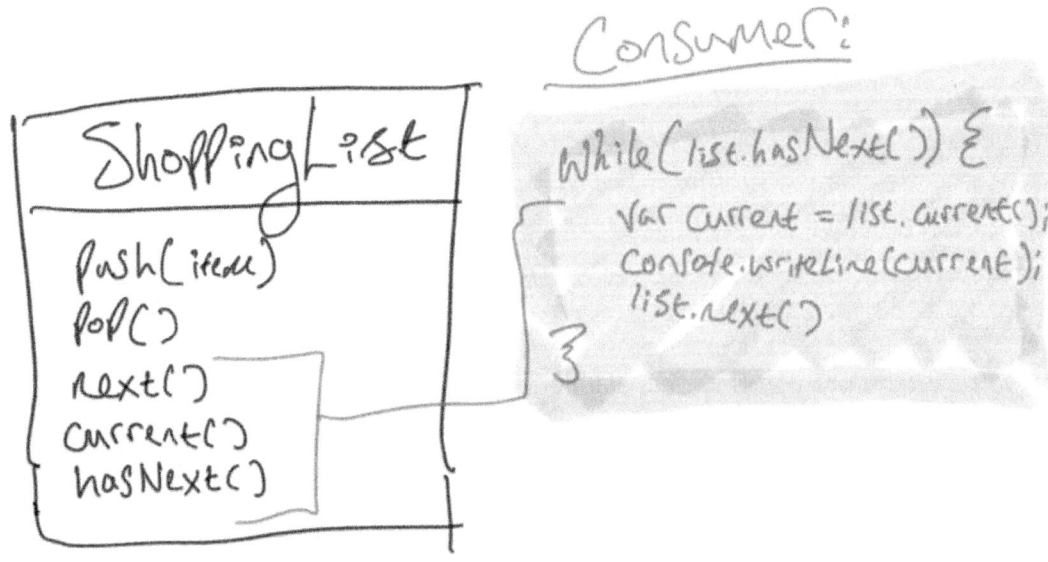

We've added three new methods to help consumers to iterate over the object, without knowledge of the internal data structures: next() goes to the next item, current() returns the current item, hasNext() checks if there is another item. With this structure, we don't know the internal representation of the list object, so if we changed the data structure used in ShoppingList to store items, its consumers wouldn't break or need to be changed. We'd just have to perhaps update the iterator methods to account for the new data structure.

PROBLEM: the above class violates the SOLID Single Responsibility Principle:

1. It's responsible for list management, using push() and pop()
2. It's responsible for iteration, using next(), current() and hasNext()

To follow the SRP, we can put the iterator methods into a new class:

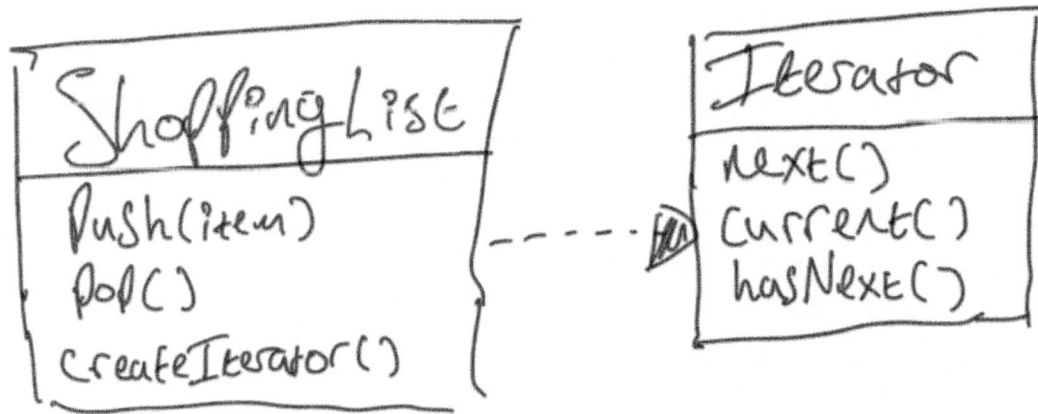

The `createIterator()` method returns an instance of `Iterator` that allows consumers to iterate over shopping lists without knowing internal details.

PROBLEM: if the data structure in `ShoppingList` changes, then we will need a different Iterator to manage it. So, `Iterator` needs to be an interface, and then we can have concrete classes for each data structure that implement `Iterator` to ensure they contain the iterator methods. The interface determines the capabilities we need from a real concrete iterator. The data structures could be `Array`, `List`, `Stack`, etc.

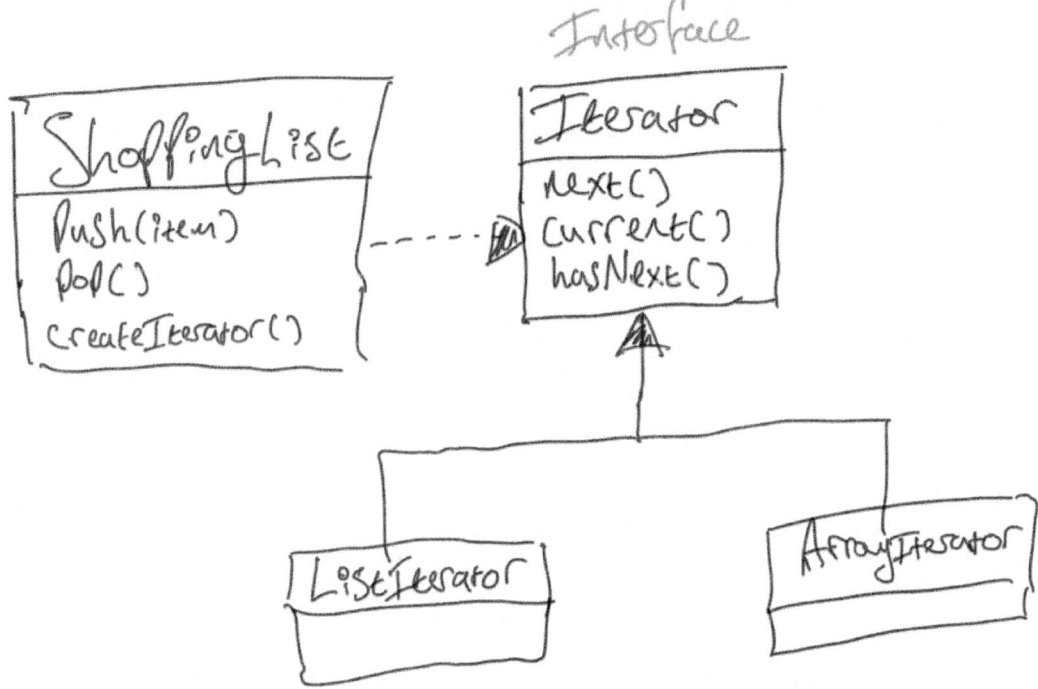

`ShoppingList` has a dependency to the `Iterator` interface, as `createIterator()` returns an object of type `Iterator`. The concrete iterator classes extend `Iterator` and implement its methods.

Here's how our solution looks when using the GoF abstract class names:

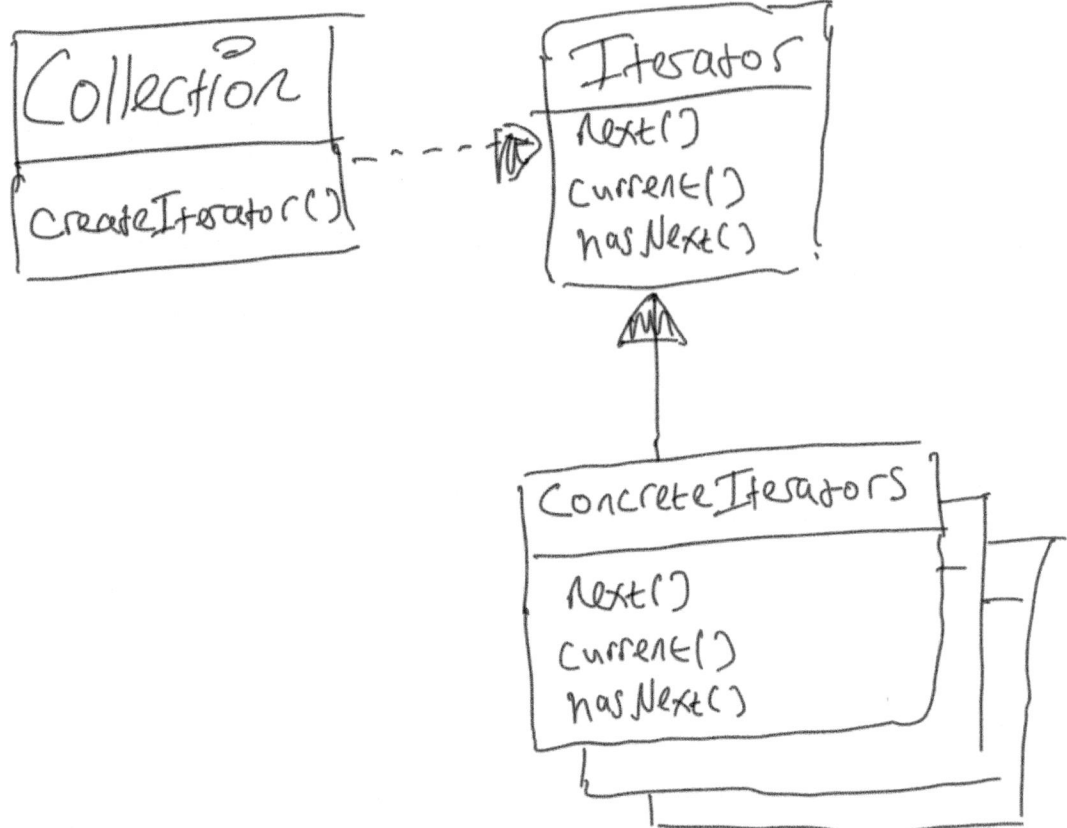

Let's implement this in code:

The interface (note how we use a generic type to make the iterator interface more flexible, so that it can iterate over different types – not just strings):

```
public interface IIterator<T>
{
  void Next();
  bool HasNext();
```

```csharp
// String Current(); // PROBLEM: what if you don't always want
to iterate over strings? E.g. iterate over Customers or integers.
 T Current(); // SOLUTION: Use a Generic type
}
```

The concrete iterator classes will be *nested classes* inside of the `ShoppingList` class. Why? Because these concrete classes are only concerned with iterating over `ShoppingList` objects, it makes sense to nest them so that they can only be used to iterate over shopping list objects, and not be used in other classes throughout our codebase. This is because the nested class is `private`, making it invisible to all other classes.

```csharp
public class ShoppingList
{
  private List<string> _list = new List<string>();

  public void Push(string itemName)
  {
    _list.Add(itemName);
  }

  public string Pop()
  {
    var last = _list.Last();
    _list.Remove(last);
    return last;
  }

  public IIterator<String> CreateIterator()
  {
    return new ListIterator(this);
  }

  private class ListIterator : IIterator<String>
  {
    private ShoppingList _shoppingList;
```

```csharp
    private int _index;

    public ListIterator(ShoppingList shoppingList)
    {
       _shoppingList = shoppingList;
    }

    public string Current()
    {
       return _shoppingList._list[_index];
    }

    public void Next()
    {
       _index++;
    }

    public bool HasNext()
    {
       return _index < _shoppingList._list.Count;
    }

  }
}
```

Our consumers now no longer need any knowledge of the internal data structure used to store shopping list items:

```csharp
class Program
{
 static void Main(string[] args)
 {
    ShoppingList shoppingList = new ShoppingList();
    shoppingList.Push("Milk");
    shoppingList.Push("Bread");
```

```
    shoppingList.Push("Steak");

    IIterator<string> iterator = shoppingList.CreateIterator();

    while (iterator.HasNext())
    {
      System.Console.WriteLine(iterator.Current());
      iterator.Next();
    }

    // // Log:
    // // Milk
    // // Bread
    // // Steak
  }
}
```

We can now safely change the data structure in `ShoppingList` and the code in our consumer will still run. Awesome!

When to use the Iterator Pattern

Employ the Iterator pattern when your collection possesses a complex internal data structure, or a data structure that is likely to change, so that clients can iterate over the collection without any knowledge of the data structure.

Pros and cons

- \+ Satisfies SRP: traversal logic is abstracted into separate classes.
- \+ Satisfied Open/closed principle: you can create new collections and iterators without breaking the code that uses them.

- \- Can be overengineering if your app only works with simple collections.

Command Pattern

The Command Pattern is a behavioral design pattern that encapsulates a request as an object, allowing you to parameterize clients with queues, requests, or operations. It enables you to decouple the sender from the receiver, providing flexibility in the execution of commands and supporting undoable operations.

That probably makes no sense to you, so let's go through an example.

Let's create a remote control that is connected to a light that can be switched on or off:

```
// "Receiver": the light
public class Light
{
 public void TurnOn()
  {
    System.Console.WriteLine("Light is on");
  }

  public void TurnOff()
  {
    System.Console.WriteLine("Light is off");
  }
}

// "Invoker": the remote control
public class RemoteControl
{
 private Light _light;

  public RemoteControl(Light light)
  {
    _light = light;
  }

  public void PressButton(bool turnOn)
```

```
{
    if (turnOn)
    {
        _light.TurnOn();
    }
    else
    {
        _light.TurnOff();
    }
  }
}
```

Here's how a client would use this solution:

```
class Program
{
  static void Main(string[] args)
  {
    Light light = new Light();
    RemoteControl remoteControl = new RemoteControl(light);

    remoteControl.PressButton(true);  // Light is on
    remoteControl.PressButton(false); // Light is off
  }
}
```

Can you spot the issues with this solution?

In this example, the `RemoteControl` directly calls methods on the concrete `Light` object. This direct coupling can make it challenging to extend the functionality or introduce new commands without modifying the `RemoteControl` class.

For example, suppose we want to add the functionality to dim the light in addition to turning it on and off. If we were to follow the above implementation, we would need to modify the `RemoteControl` class directly, which violates the SOLID

Open/Closed Principle. This would make it challenging to extend the functionality without changing existing code. As you've already seen multiple times by now, this isn't ideal!

```
// RemoteControl

// Adding new functionality requires modifying this class, e.g.:
// New method for dimming the light
public void DimLight()
{
  _light.Dim();
}
```

UML for the current solution:

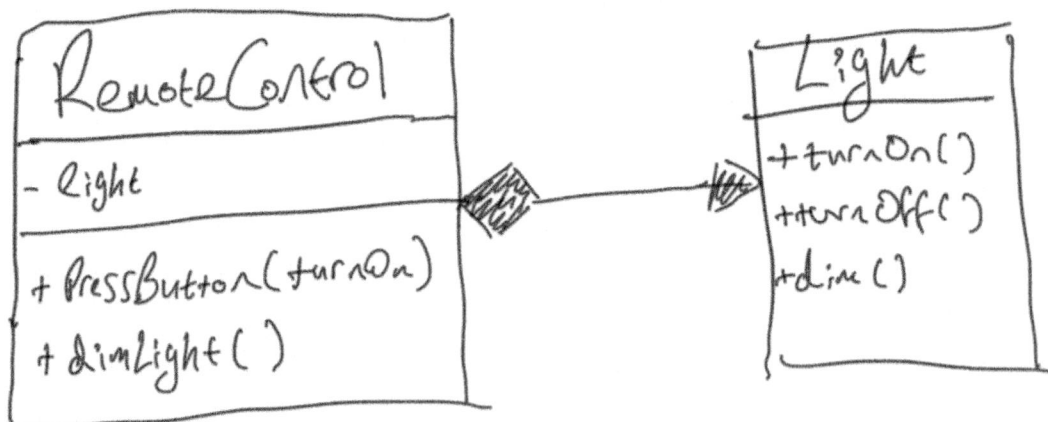

Light is tightly coupled to RemoteControl. If we want to add new features, then we have to modify RemoteControl.

Command Pattern UML:

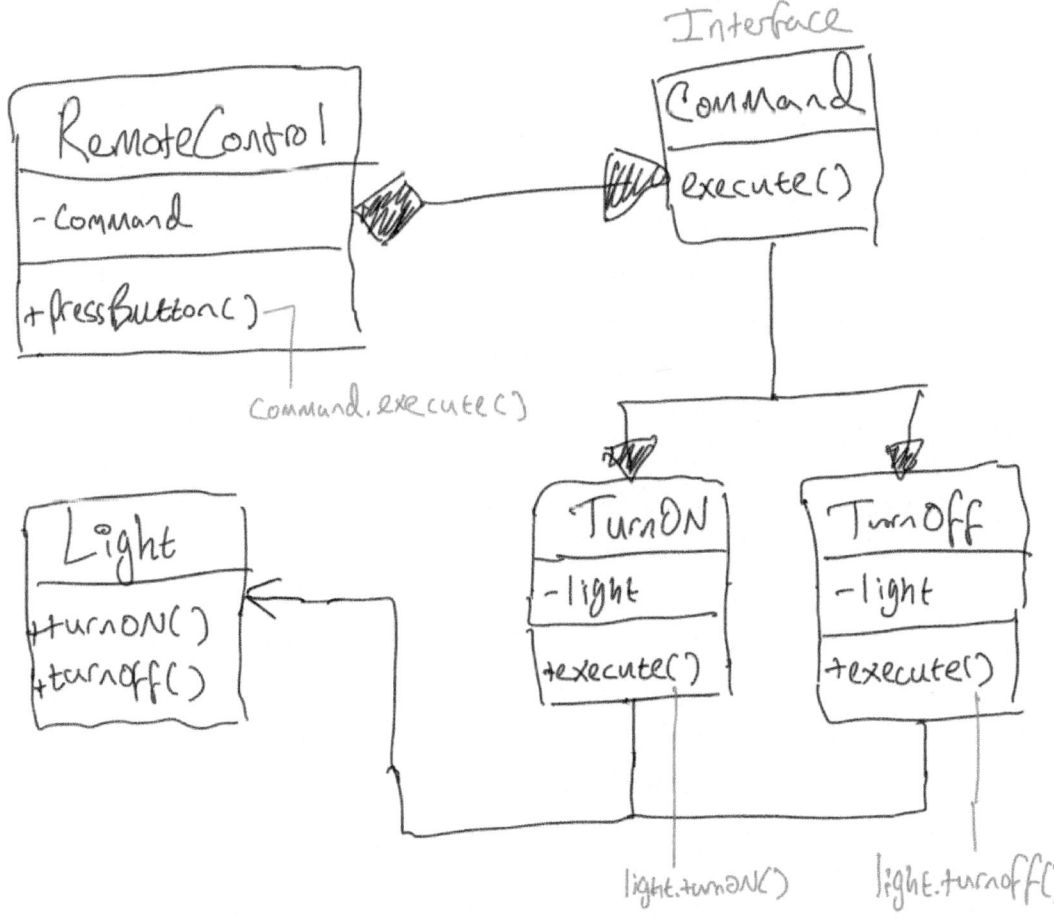

Using the Command Pattern, we can decouple RemoteControl (the "sender") from Light (the "receiver"). Then, to add new functionality, such as dimming the light, we can extend our codebase by adding a new Dim command, without having to modify RemoteControl. The RemoteControl is composed of Command. The concrete commands, TurnOn and TurnOff, implement Command, and store a reference to Light.

Implementing this Command pattern solution in code:

```
public interface ICommand
{
  void Execute();
}

// "Invoker": the remote control
```

```csharp
public class RemoteControl
{
  private ICommand _command;

  public RemoteControl(ICommand command)
  {
    _command = command;
  }

  // Allow ability to swap commands at runtime
  public void SetCommand(ICommand command)
  {
    _command = command;
  }

  public void PressButton()
  {
    _command.Execute();
  }
}

// "Receiver": the light
public class Light
{
  public void TurnOn()
  {
    System.Console.WriteLine("Light is on");
  }

  public void TurnOff()
  {
    System.Console.WriteLine("Light is off");
  }
```

```csharp
    public void Dim()
    {
        System.Console.WriteLine("Light is dim");
    }
}
```

The concrete commands:

```csharp
public class TurnOnCommand : ICommand
{
    private Light _light;

    public TurnOnCommand(Light light)
    {
        _light = light; // _light can only be set in the constructor,
 so the command is immutable (can't be changed once created)
    }

    public void Execute()
    {
        _light.TurnOn(); // business logic is delegated to Light
 object
    }
}

public class TurnOffCommand : ICommand
{
    private Light _light;

    public TurnOffCommand(Light light)
    {
        _light = light;
    }

    public void Execute()
```

```csharp
    {
        _light.TurnOff();
    }
}

public class DimCommand : ICommand
{
    private Light _light;

    public DimCommand(Light light)
    {
        _light = light;
    }

    public void Execute()
    {
        _light.Dim();
    }
}
```

Here's how a client would use this solution:

```csharp
class Program
{
    static void Main(string[] args)
    {
        var light = new Light();
        var remote = new RemoteControl(new TurnOnCommand(light));
        remote.PressButton(); // Light is on

        remote.SetCommand(new DimCommand(light));
        remote.PressButton(); // Light is dim
    }
}
```

The Command Pattern is also commonly used in UI frameworks, especially for handling user interactions with buttons or menu items. Each button or menu item can be associated with a specific command object, allowing the framework to execute the appropriate action when the user interacts with the UI element. This decouples the UI components from the actual operations they perform, providing flexibility and maintainability in UI development. Additionally, the Command Pattern facilitates features such as undo/redo functionality and event logging in UI applications.

Here's how a UI framework that implements the Command Pattern might look:

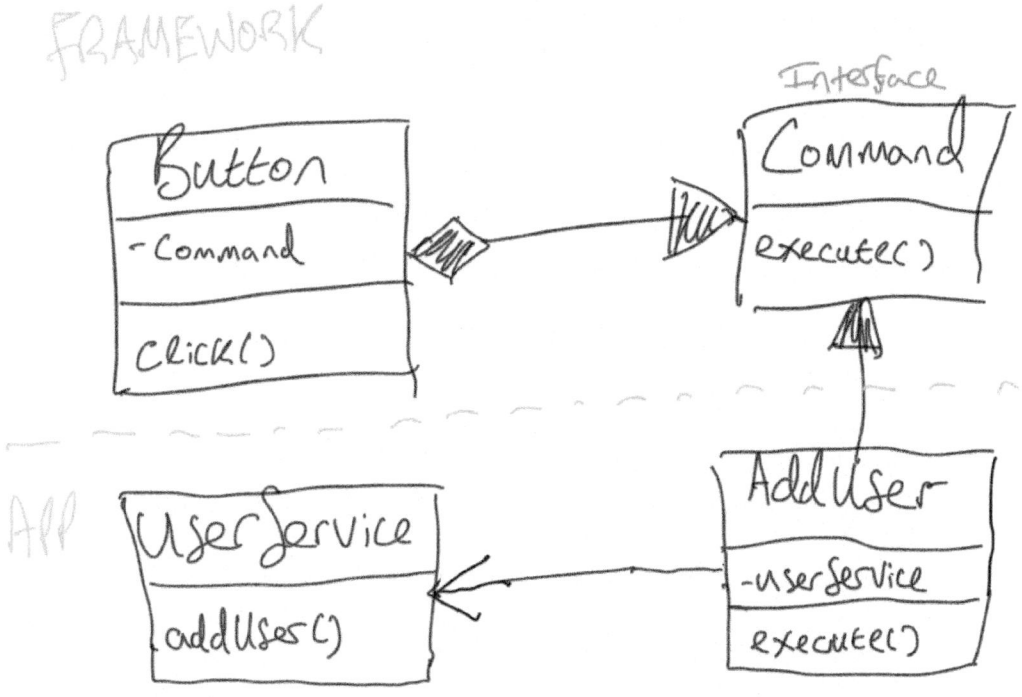

The framework would be code that you couldn't edit, i.e. some UI package. The app is the part that you, the developer, would create. You would create concrete commands that extend the Command interface found in the UI package. Your concrete commands keep a reference to a class that contains the business logic, such as UserService, which contains methods related to adding, updating, deleting and getting users.

A simpler solution, without the Command Pattern, would be to create a load of Button subclasses for each place where a button is used. These subclasses would contain the code for what should happen when that button is clicked:

101

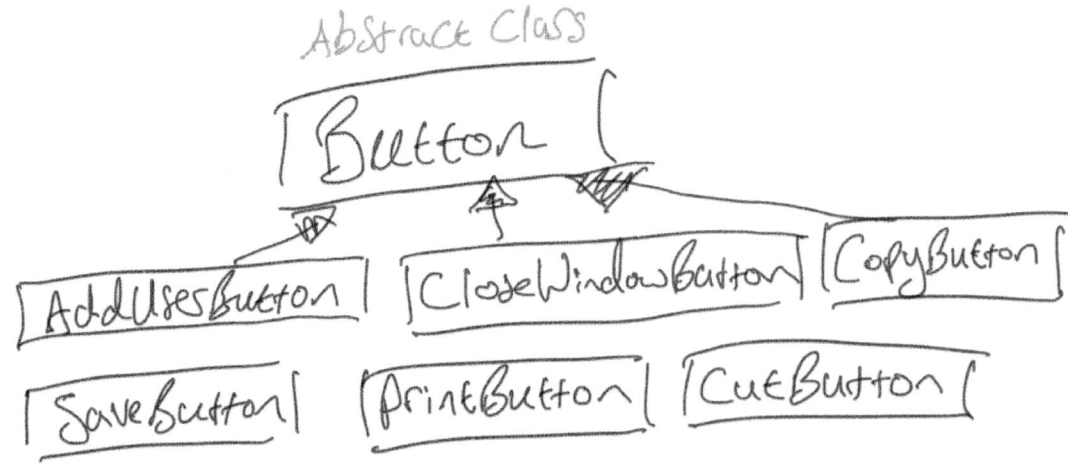

Problems:
- Could end up with a huge number of subclasses. This would be OK if there was no risk of breaking the code in these subclasses every time the base `Button` class is modified – but if we update our UI library and it includes a breaking change to the button class, then it could break all of our button subclasses. This is a fragile solution.
- Some operations, such as "Copy" need to be called from multiple places. E.g., a user can click the copy button, press "Ctrl + C" or right-click and select "copy" from the context menu. With this solution, we'd either have to duplicate the copy logic in multiple classes, or make shortcuts and context menus dependent on buttons, which is a very bad solution.

The Command Pattern solves this issue by breaking the app into layers, following the good software design principle called "principle of separation of concerns". The Command Pattern broke the app into two layers: the GUI and the business logic. The GUI is responsible for rendering things on the screen, capturing user input, and showing results. Then, when it comes to the important stuff, such as validating the info from a contact form and sending an email, the GUI delegates that task to the underlying layer of business logic.

GoF UML:

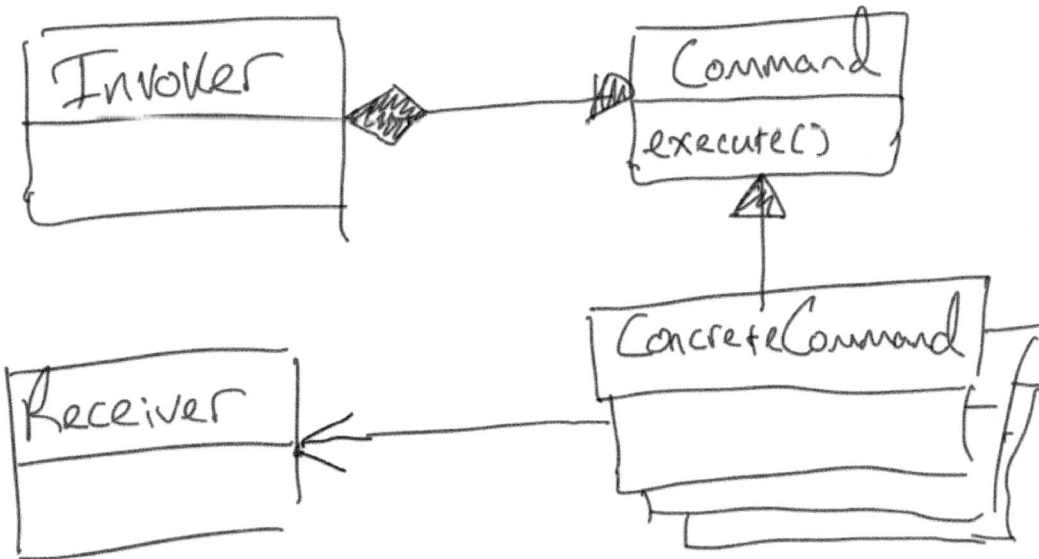

Command Pattern with Undo

Another advantage of the Command Pattern is that it gives us the ability to implement undo functionality.

Say we have a text editor, like VS Code, that allows the user to highlight some text, then click a button that makes the text in an HTML document *italics.*

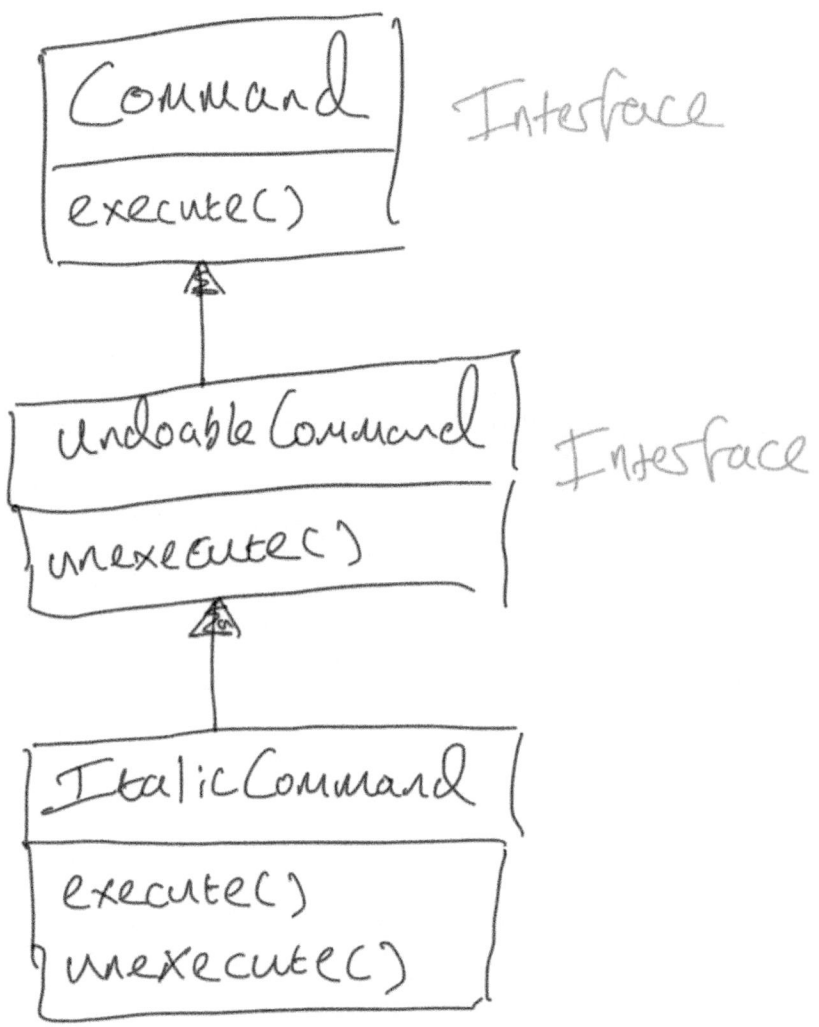

Above, we create a new interface called UndoableCommand, which extends Command; this is because undoable commands are still commands (they can execute forwards and backwards). Why not add the unexecute() method to Command? Because not every command is undoable -- e.g. making text *italics* is undoable, but saving a document, or zooming in/out isn't.

We then implement the methods in a concrete command class, e.g. ItalicCommand.

We can also use the Memento Pattern to implement undo mechanisms. What's the difference between Memento and Command Patterns when it comes to undo operations? With Memento, we store the changes in the state of an object, i.e. we store multiple snapshots over time. Sometimes, storing these snapshots can be expensive, e.g. videos are large files and take up lots of memory.

In those situations, it's better to use the Command Pattern, because every command knows how to undo itself, so we don't have to store multiple snapshots of an object. For example, think of the resize operation: if a user resizes a video, we only have to store the previous dimension of the video; not the entire snapshot of the video object.

Here's how we will implement the Command Pattern with undo capability:

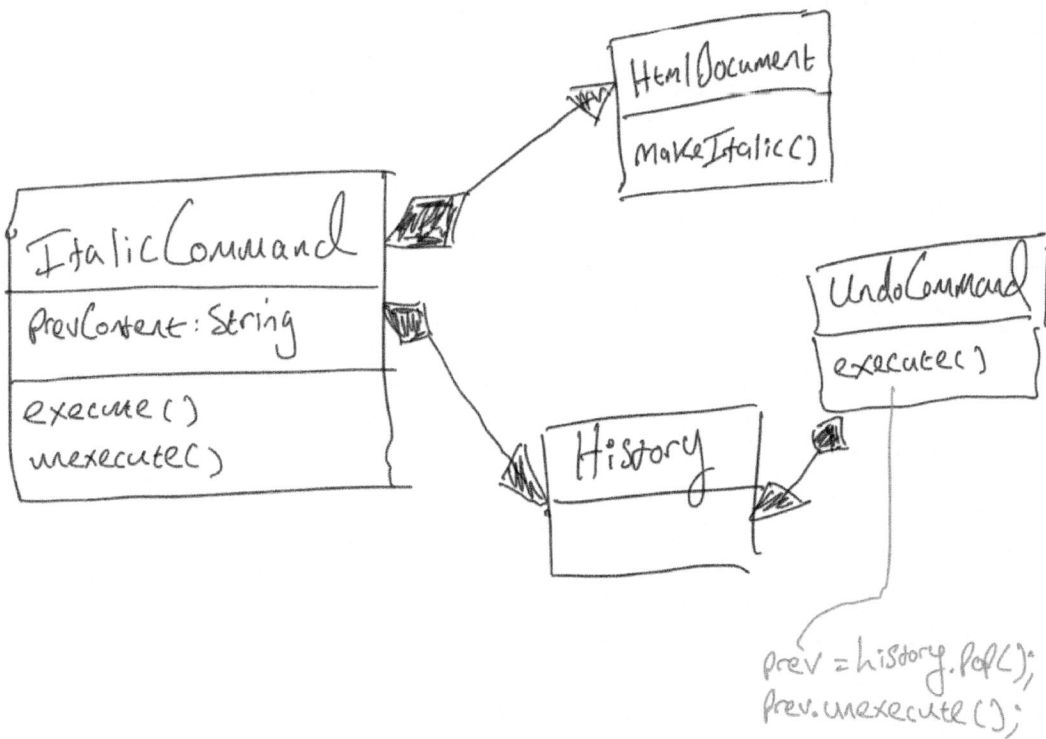

A new class, `UndoCommand` has been created to handle all undo operations. It pops the last command from `History`, then calls `unexecute()` on that command, as all commands know how to unexecute themselves. This will make more sense as we go through the code solution, so let's do that…

Html document class:

```
// This is where we implement our business logic. This class
knows nothing about commands.
```

```csharp
// This is part of the "business layer" of an application.
// Commands are the link between user interface object, and
business objects.
public class HtmlDocument
{
 public string Content { get; set; }

 public void MakeItalic()
 {
    Content = "<i>" + Content + "</i>"; // business logic --
HtmlDocument knows how to make itself bold
 }
}
```

Command interface:

```csharp
public interface Command
{
 void Execute();
}
```

Undoable command interface:

```csharp
// UndoableCommand extends Command, so every UndoableCommand
object is a Command object.
public interface UndoableCommand : Command
{
 void Unexecute();
}
```

Command history class:

```csharp
// Class to keep track of the commands that we've applied.
public class History
{
```

```csharp
private List<UndoableCommand> commands = new
List<UndoableCommand>();

public void Push(UndoableCommand command)
{
    commands.Add(command);
}

public UndoableCommand Pop()
{
    var last = commands.Last();
    commands.Remove(last);
    return last;
}

public int Size()
{
    return commands.Count;
}
}
```

The concrete italic command:

```csharp
public class ItalicCommand : UndoableCommand
{
private HtmlDocument _doc;
private string _prevContent = "";
private History _history;

public ItalicCommand(HtmlDocument doc, History history)
{
    _doc = doc;
    _history = history;
}
```

```
public void Execute()
{
   _prevContent = _doc.Content;
   _doc.MakeItalic(); // delegate the work to the doc business object
   _history.Push(this);
}

public void Unexecute()
{
   _doc.Content = _prevContent;
}
}
```

The class to undo commands:

```
public class UndoCommand : Command
{
 private History _history;

 public UndoCommand(History history)
 {
    _history = history;
 }

 public void Execute()
 {
    if (_history.Size() > 0)
    {
      var lastCommand = _history.Pop(); // remove from history
      lastCommand.Unexecute(); // delegate the undo logic to the UndoableCommand object
    }
 }
}
```

Here's how this solution would be used:

```
class Program
{
  static void Main(string[] args)
  {
     var htmlDoc = new HtmlDocument();
     var history = new History();
     htmlDoc.Content = "Hello world";
     System.Console.WriteLine(htmlDoc.Content); // Hello world

     var italicCommand = new ItalicCommand(htmlDoc, history);
     italicCommand.Execute();
     System.Console.WriteLine(htmlDoc.Content); // <i>Hello world</i>

     var undoCommand = new UndoCommand(history);
     undoCommand.Execute();
     System.Console.WriteLine(htmlDoc.Content); // Hello world
  }
}
```

Nice!

When to use the Command Pattern

Use the Command Pattern when you want to implement reversible operations. The Command Pattern is probably the most popular pattern for implementing undo/redo, and it uses less RAM than the Memento Pattern, which has to backup the whole state of the object.

The Command Pattern is great when you want to queue operations, or schedule their execution, as command objects can be serialized (converted into strings) and stored in databases or sent over networks, then, at a later time, they can be converted back into objects and executed.

Pros and cons

- \+ Satisfies SRP: classes that invoke operations are decoupled from classes that perform these operations.
- \+ Satisfies Open/closed principle: new commands can be added to the codebase without having to modify existing code.

- \- Code may become more complex as you're adding a new layer between senders and receivers.

Template Method Pattern

The Template Method pattern allows you to define a template method, or skeleton, for an operation. The specific steps can then be implemented in subclasses.

Suppose we are designing some software that will be installed on a machine that makes hot beverages. At the beginning we just had tea and coffee. But after some feedback from customers, we needed to add some more beverages, such as camomile tea:

[Diagram: Three classes — Tea, Coffee, Camomile — each with a MakeBeverage() method. Tea's MakeBeverage() is broken down into: BoilWater(), PourIntoCup(), Brew(), AddCondiments(). Annotations: "Same for all beverages" (for BoilWater and PourIntoCup); "Differ, e.g. brewing time may differ" (for Brew and AddCondiments).]

We started out simple, making a separate class for each hot beverage. But as the number of beverages grows, we see a lot of code duplication. We also have no way of ensuring that each class follows a particular structure, which means that the client code will have lots of conditionals to pick the proper course of action depending on the particular beverage class.

Example of a beverage class:

```csharp
public class Tea
{
 public void MakeBeverage()
 {
    BoilWater();
    PourWaterIntoCup();
    Brew();
    AddCondiments();
 }

 private void BoilWater()
 {
    System.Console.WriteLine("Boiling water");
 }

 private void PourWaterIntoCup()
 {
    System.Console.WriteLine("Pouring water into cup");
 }

 private void Brew()
 {
    System.Console.WriteLine("Brewing tea for 3 minutes");
 }

 private void AddCondiments()
 {
    if (CustomerWantsCondiments())
      System.Console.WriteLine("Adding lemon to tea");
```

```csharp
    }

    private bool CustomerWantsCondiments()
    {
        Console.WriteLine("Would you like lemon with your tea? (y/n)");
        string input = Console.ReadLine();
        return input.ToLower() == "y";
    }
}

class Program
{
  static void Main(string[] args)
  {
    var tea = new Tea();
    tea.MakeBeverage();

    // Logs:
    // Boiling water
    // Pouring water into cup
    // Brewing tea for 3 minutes
    // Would you like lemon with your tea? (y/n)
    // "y"
    // Adding lemon to tea
  }
}
```

There are two good ways to solve this issue of code duplication: polymorphism and inheritance. First, we'll use polymorphism, which actually leads to a design pattern that we covered earlier (see if you can spot which one!):

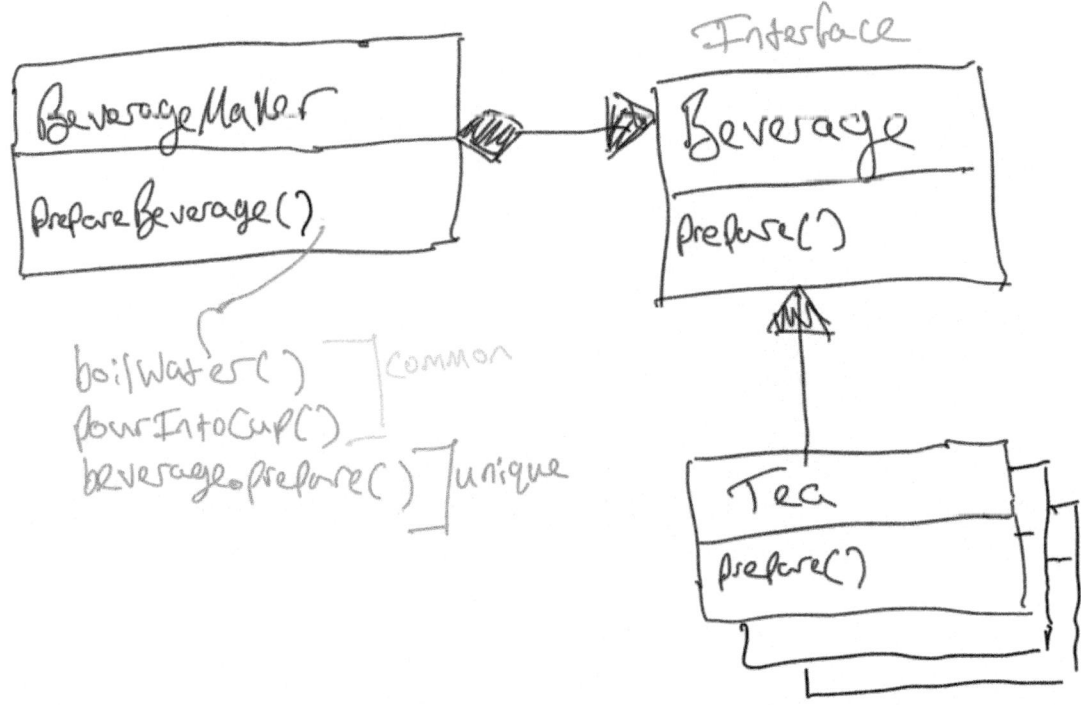

Above, we provide a common Beverage interface to force all beverages to follow a specific structure. We then have a BeverageMaker class that manages preparing different beverages. This class includes the common operations for making all beverages, such as boiling water and pouring it into a cup, and also calls the operations specific to each beverage, which is delegated to Beverage. Now when we create a new beverage, we only have to include code specific/unique to that beverage.

By using polymorphism, we have inadvertently used the Strategy Pattern:

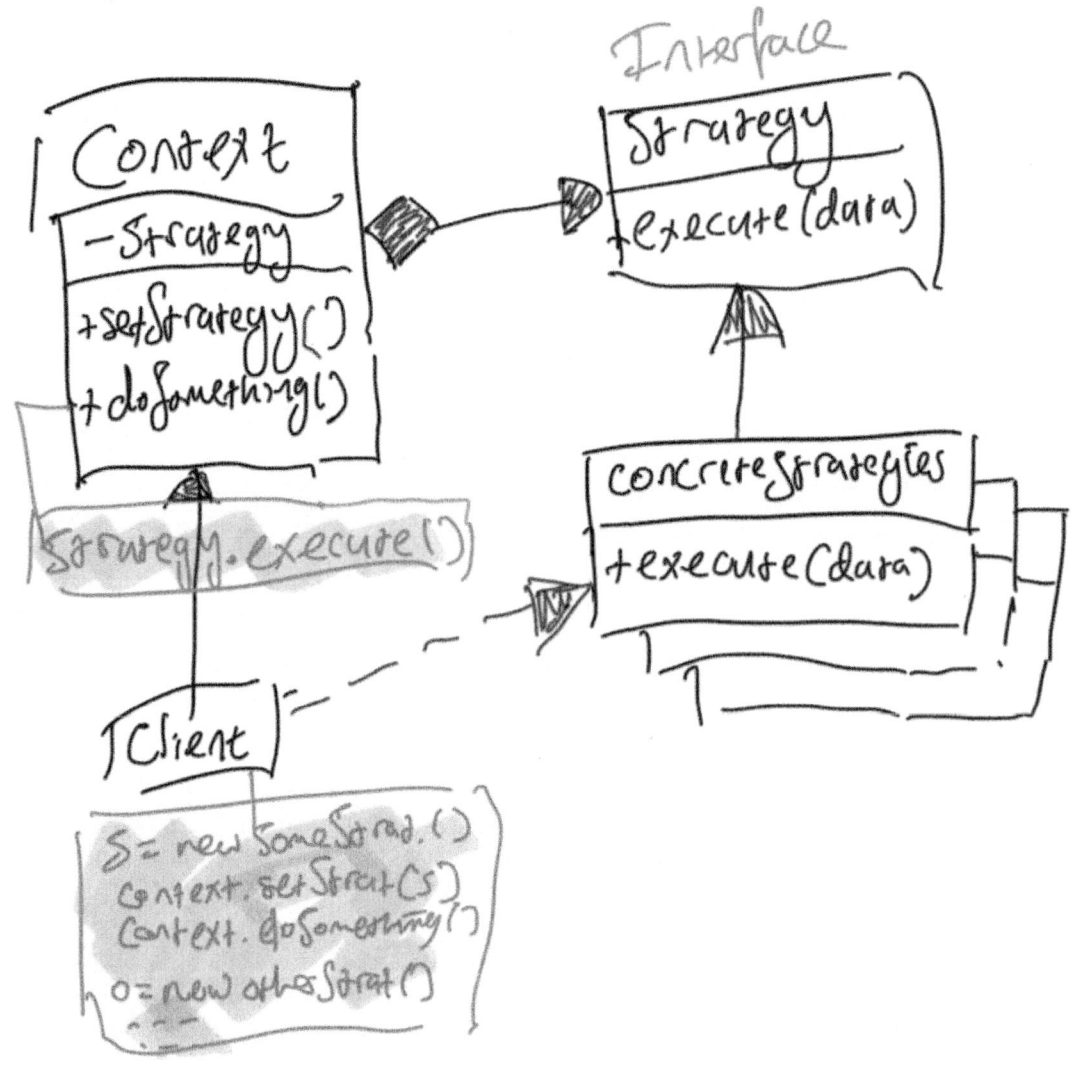

Strategy Pattern (polymorphism) code solution:

```
public interface Beverage
{
  void Prepare();
}

public class Tea : Beverage
{
  public void Prepare()
  {
```

```csharp
    Brew();
    AddCondiments();
  }

  private void Brew()
  {
    System.Console.WriteLine("Brewing tea for 3 minutes");
  }

  private void AddCondiments()
  {
    if (CustomerWantsCondiments())
      System.Console.WriteLine("Adding lemon to tea");
  }

  private bool CustomerWantsCondiments()
  {
    Console.WriteLine("Would you like lemon with your tea? (y/n)");
    string input = Console.ReadLine();
    return input.ToLower() == "y";
  }
}

public class Coffee : Beverage
{
 public void Prepare()
 {
    Brew();
    AddCondiments();
 }

 private void Brew()
 {
```

```csharp
      System.Console.WriteLine("Brewing coffee for 5 minutes");
   }

   private void AddCondiments()
   {
      if (CustomerWantsCondiments())
         System.Console.WriteLine("Adding cream to coffee");
   }

   private bool CustomerWantsCondiments()
   {
      Console.WriteLine("Would you like cream with your coffee? (y/n)");
      string input = Console.ReadLine();
      return input.ToLower() == "y";
   }
}

public class Camomile : Beverage
{
 public void Prepare()
 {
    Brew();
 }

 public void Brew()
 {
    System.Console.WriteLine("Brewing for 3 mins");
 }
}

public class BeverageMaker
{
 private Beverage _beverage;
```

```csharp
public BeverageMaker(Beverage beverage)
{
    _beverage = beverage;
}

public void SetBeverage(Beverage beverage)
{
    _beverage = beverage;
}

public void MakeBeverage()
{
    // Common operations
    BoilWater();
    PourIntoCup();

    // Unique operations
    _beverage.Prepare();
}

private void BoilWater()
{
    System.Console.WriteLine("Boiling water");
}

private void PourIntoCup()
{
    System.Console.WriteLine("Pouring boiled water into cup");
}
}
```

Client:

```csharp
class Program
```

```
{
    static void Main(string[] args)
    {
        var beverageMaker = new BeverageMaker(new Tea());
        beverageMaker.MakeBeverage();

        // Tea Logs:
        // Boiling water
        // Pouring water into cup
        // Brewing tea for 3 minutes
        // Would you like lemon with your tea? (y/n)
        // "y"
        // Adding lemon to tea

        beverageMaker.SetBeverage(new Coffee());
        beverageMaker.MakeBeverage();

        // Coffee Logs:
        // Boiling water
        // Pouring boiled water into cup
        // Brewing coffee for 5 minutes
        // Would you like cream with your coffee? (y/n)
        // "n"
    }
}
```

In `BeverageMaker`, we define the common behavior for making a beverage. We have an interface called `Beverage`, with concrete implementations. From `BeverageMaker`, we specify the beverage, then we are delegating, or forwarding, the execution of tasks related to making a specific beverage to a beverage object. This is the Strategy Pattern.

Solving with inheritance

We can also solve this problem using inheritance:

`Tea`, `Coffee` and `Camomile` have things in common, so we can create an abstract `Beverage` class to implement the `prepare()` method. But, after the water is boiled and then poured into a cup, what happens next is unknown in the abstract `Beverage` class, as it depends on the specific beverage. These beverage-specific steps will be determined later on, when the `Beverage` class is extended.

We can provide a base abstract class called `Beverage` that contains all common operations for making a beverage, and provide methods, `brew()` and `addCondiments()`, which can be implemented/overridden in the concrete beverage classes.

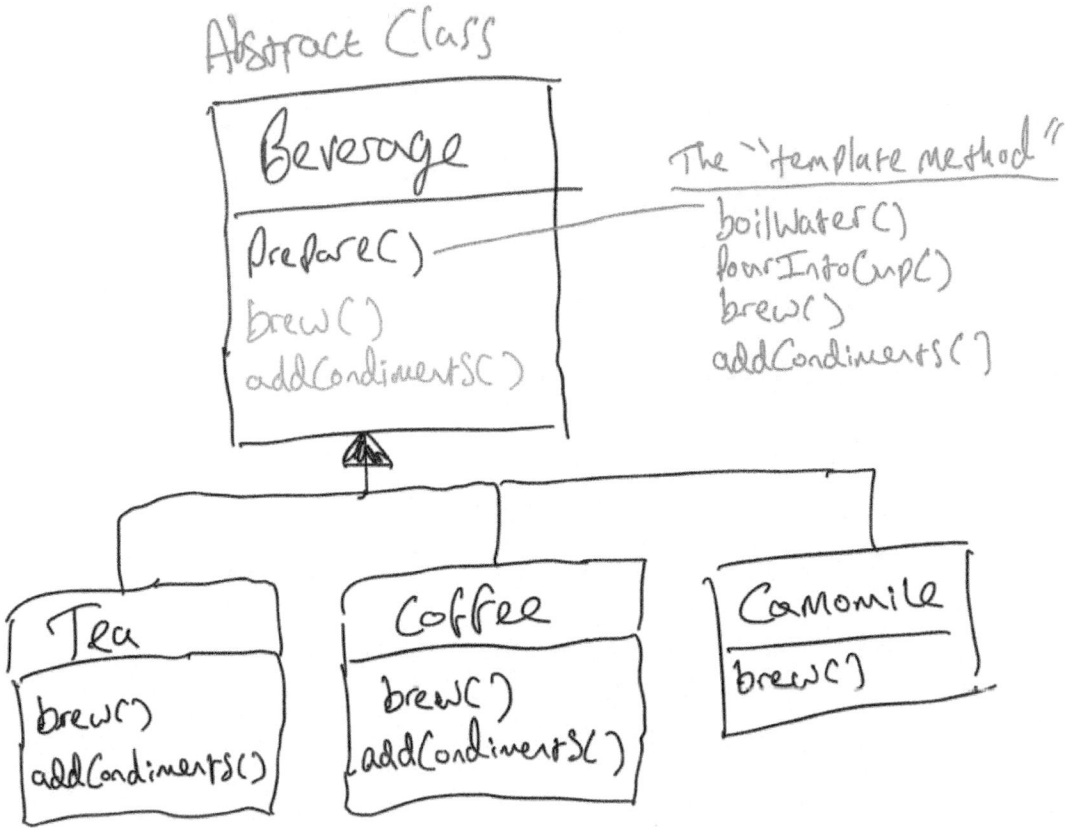

This is the Template Method Pattern: the `Beverage` class has a template method that provides the common setup and structure for preparing a beverage.

Here is how the template method pattern is shown in the Gang of Four book:

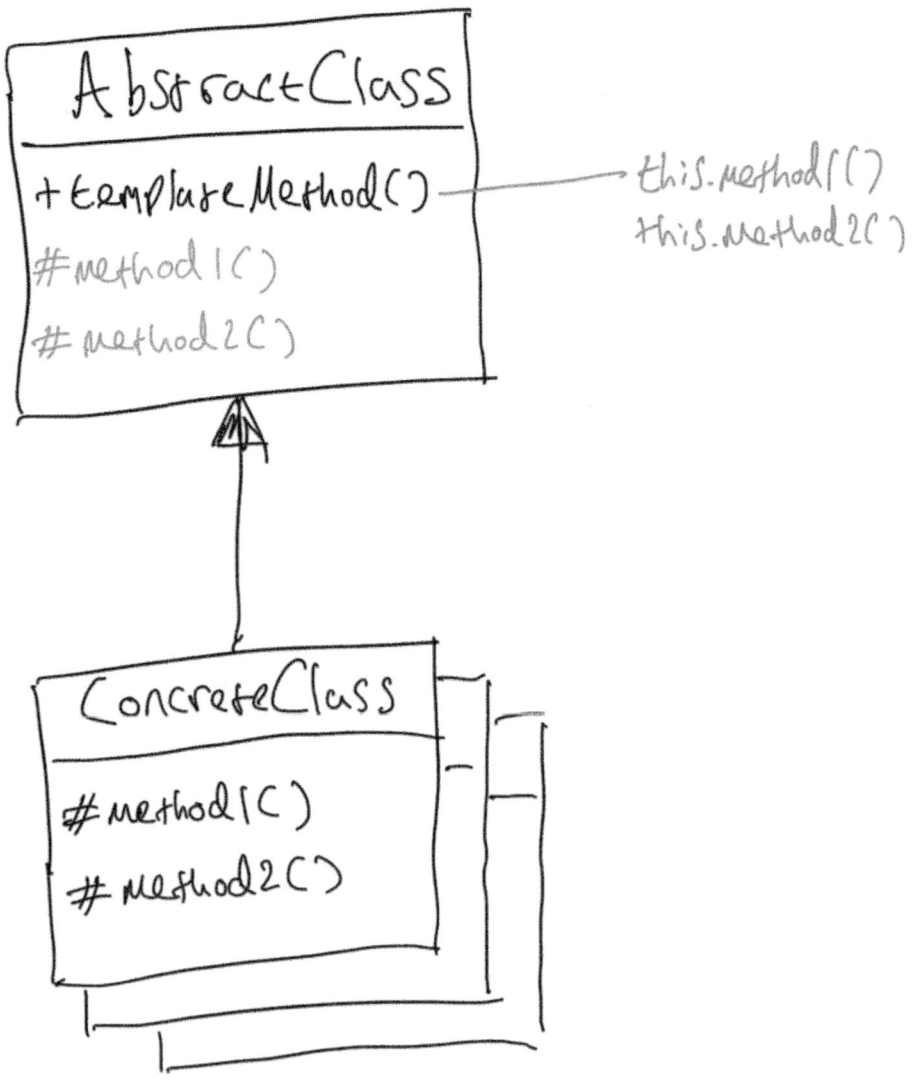

We have an abstract class with a concrete implementation of the common/shared `templateMethod()`. The abstract methods that will be implemented within the concrete classes can be used to alter the behavior of the template method.

We can also give the template methods a default implementation, and leave it up to the subclasses to either take them as they are, or override them. If the template methods have a default implementation, we refer to these methods as "hooks", or "hook operations":

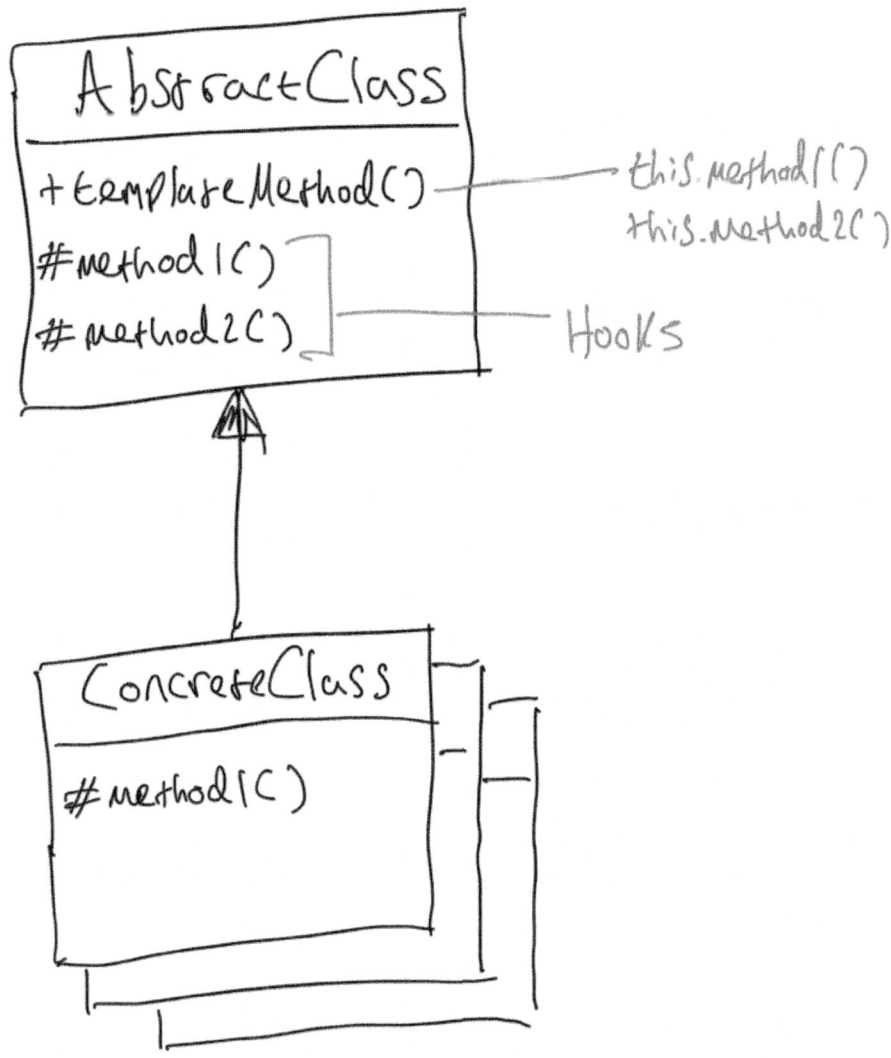

Let's implement the Template Method pattern in code:

The base Beverage class, in our case, doesn't require any abstract methods, as it isn't *required* that they are overridden in subclasses. Instead, we have a normal class with a few virtual methods, which in C# means that they can be optionally overridden in derived classes.

```
public class Beverage
{
  public void Prepare()
  {
```

```csharp
    BoilWater();
    PourIntoCup();
    Brew();
    AddCondiments();
}

private void BoilWater()
{
    System.Console.WriteLine("Boiling water");
}

private void PourIntoCup()
{
    System.Console.WriteLine("Pouring into cup");
}

// Protected, so only available to this class and subclasses
protected virtual void Brew()
{
    // provide a default implementation, so, if not overridden, beverage is brewed for 3 mins
    System.Console.WriteLine("Brewing for 3 mins");
}

// Empty body, as no condiments by default
protected virtual void AddCondiments() { }
}

public class Tea : Beverage
{

    // Tea is brewed for 3 mins, so no need to override the default implementation, Beverage.Brew()
```

```csharp
  protected override void AddCondiments()
  {
    if (CustomerWantsCondiments())
      System.Console.WriteLine("Adding lemon to tea");
  }

  private bool CustomerWantsCondiments()
  {
    Console.WriteLine("Would you like lemon with your tea? (y/n)");
    string input = Console.ReadLine();
    return input.ToLower() == "y";
  }
}

public class Coffee : Beverage
{
  protected override void Brew()
  {
    System.Console.WriteLine("Brewing coffee for 5 mins");
  }

  protected override void AddCondiments()
  {
    if (CustomerWantsCondiments())
      System.Console.WriteLine("Adding cream to coffee");
  }

  private bool CustomerWantsCondiments()
  {
    Console.WriteLine("Would you like cream with your coffee? (y/n)");
    string input = Console.ReadLine();
    return input.ToLower() == "y";
```

```
    }
}
```

Camomile needs to be brewed for 3 mins and requires no condiments, so the default implementations of `Brew()` and `AddCondiments()` don't need to be overridden from `Beverage`.

```
public class Camomile : Beverage
{

}
```

Here's how a client would use this to make different beverages:

```
class Program
{
  static void Main(string[] args)
  {
    var tea = new Tea();
    tea.Prepare();

    // Tea logs:
    // Boiling water
    // Pouring into cup
    // Brewing for 3 mins
    // Would you like lemon with your tea? (y/n)
    // n

    var coffee = new Coffee();
    coffee.Prepare();

    // Coffee logs:
    // Boiling water
    // Pouring into cup
    // Brewing coffee for 5 mins
```

```
        // Would you like cream with your coffee? (y/n)
        // y
        // Adding cream to coffee

        var camomile = new Camomile();
        camomile.Prepare();

        // Camomile logs:
        // Boiling water
        // Pouring into cup
        // Brewing for 3 mins
    }
}
```

It's nice and simple for clients to make beverages. All beverages provide a simple api with a `Prepare()` method, and the rest of the complexities are abstracted away, as the client requires no knowledge of them.

Template Method vs Strategy Pattern

- If you primarily need to customize or override specific steps of an algorithm while keeping the overall structure intact, the Template Method Pattern is a good choice.
- If you need to encapsulate entire algorithms or behaviors as interchangeable components that can be dynamically selected or replaced, the Strategy Pattern is more appropriate.

Both patterns have their strengths and are used to address different design scenarios. The choice between them depends on the specific requirements and design goals of your application.

When to use the Template Method Pattern

Use the Template Method Pattern when you want to allow clients to implement only particular steps in an algorithm, and not the whole algorithm. It's a good pattern to use when you have a bunch of classes with the same logic, or algorithm, but with differences in a few steps. So, if the algorithm changes, it only has to be modified in one place – the base class.

Pros and cons

- + Reduce code duplication
- + Clients are only allowed to modify certain steps in an algorithm, reducing the risk of breaking clients if the algorithm changes

- - Some clients may be limited by the provided template
- - Template methods can be hard to maintain if they have lots of steps

Observer Pattern

The Observer Pattern involves an object, known as the subject, maintaining a list of its dependent objects, called observers, and notifying them automatically of any state changes.

Situation: we have two excel spreadsheets: the first with a table of data and a barchart that depends on that data; the second that calculates a sum from the table in spreadsheet one:

Excel

Spreadsheet 1

Data Source

City	# of dogs
Manchester	1080
London	2004
Stoke	800
Birmingham	1406

Barchart

(bar chart: # of dogs vs Man. Lon. Stk. Birm.)

Spreadsheet 2

Total Dogs

1080 + 2004 + 800 + 1406 = **5290**

Naive solution

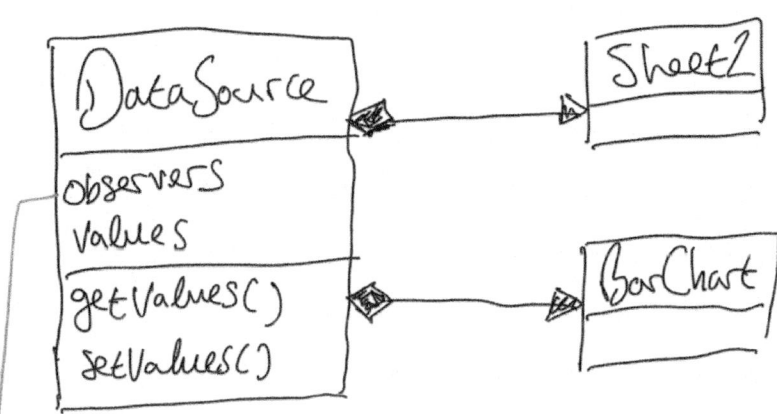

PROBLEM: tight coupling to concrete observers means that we need conditionals to check the object type before updating

Let's implement this naive solution in code to show it's weaknesses:

Sheet 2 loops through the values and sums them up:

```csharp
public class Sheet2
{
  private int _total;

  public int GetTotal()
  {
    return _total;
  }

  public int CalculateTotal(List<int> values)
  {
    var sum = 0;
    foreach (var value in values)
    {
      sum += value;
    }
    System.Console.WriteLine("Total: " + sum);
    return sum;
  }
}

public class BarChart
{
  public void Render(List<int> values)
  {
    System.Console.WriteLine("Rendering bar chart with new values");
  }
}
```

`DataSource` stores a list of dependent objects, so that when it's values are changed, it can update those dependent objects:

```csharp
public class DataSource
{
  private List<int> _values = new List<int>();
  private List<Object> _dependents = new List<Object>();

  public List<int> GetValues()
  {
    return _values;
  }

  public void SetValues(List<int> values)
  {
    _values = values;

    // We now need to update our dependent object
    foreach (var dependent in _dependents)
    {
      // This is gonna be VERY messy if we end up with lots of dependents!!
      if (dependent is Sheet2)
      {
        (dependent as Sheet2).CalculateTotal(_values);
      }
      else if (dependent is BarChart)
      {
        (dependent as BarChart).Render(_values);
      }
    }
  }

  public void AddDependent(Object dependent)
```

```
  {
    _dependents.Add(dependent);
  }

  public void RemoveDependent(Object dependent)
  {
    _dependents.Remove(dependent);
  }
}
```

Using this solution:

```
class Program
{
  static void Main(string[] args)
  {
    DataSource dataSource = new DataSource();

    Sheet2 sheet2 = new Sheet2();
    BarChart barChart = new BarChart();

    dataSource.AddDependent(sheet2);
    dataSource.AddDependent(barChart);

    // Calling SetValues() triggers the total and bar chart to
    also be updated:
    dataSource.SetValues([5, 5, 1, 10]);
    // Logs:
    // Total: 21
    // Rendering bar chart with new values

    dataSource.SetValues([1, 2, 3]);
    // Logs:
    // Total: 21
    // Rendering bar chart with new values
```

```
}
}
```

Can you spot the issues with this solution? What SOLID principles are we violating? The two most obvious issues:

- SRP: `DataSource` has two responsibilities: storing data and managing dependent, observer objects.
- OCP: every time we create a new observer object, we have to *modify* `DataSource`. This is because we are programming to concrete objects, rather than to a generic interface.

How do we solve this?

- To solve the SRP violation, we could create a separate class for managing the dependent observer objects.
- To solve the OCP violation, we can ensure that all observer objects (e.g. `Sheet2` and `BarChart`) implement a common interface so that they provide consistent methods, allowing us to use polymorphism in `DataSource`.

Introducing the Observer Pattern

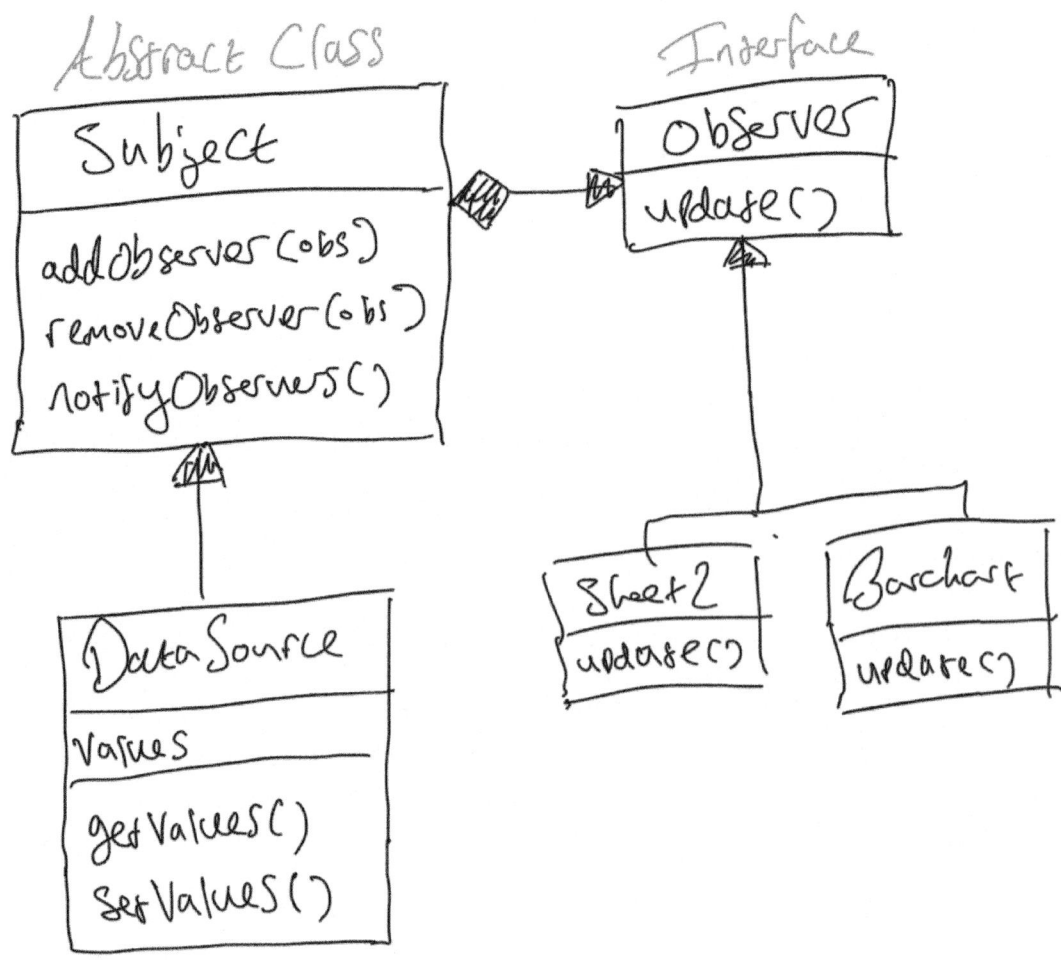

Above, `Sheet2` and `Barchart` implement a common interface, so `DataSource` can now talk to that one interface, and not multiple concrete classes. We've also created a `Subject` class to provide the methods for managing observers.

This follows the open-closed SOLID principle, as we can extend our application by adding new observer classes, without having to modify `DataSource`. E.g., tomorrow we may want to add another spreadsheet that finds the average of the data source values -- we can just create a new `Sheet3` class that implements `Observer`, and `DataSource` doesn't care; it just talks to the observer interface.

`setValues(values)` will loop through all of its observers and call `update()` on each. This is polymorphic behavior: a different `update()` method will be called depending on the observer -- but `DataSource` doesn't need to know what the specific concrete observers are. Each concrete implementation figures out how to update themselves.

GoF Observer pattern:

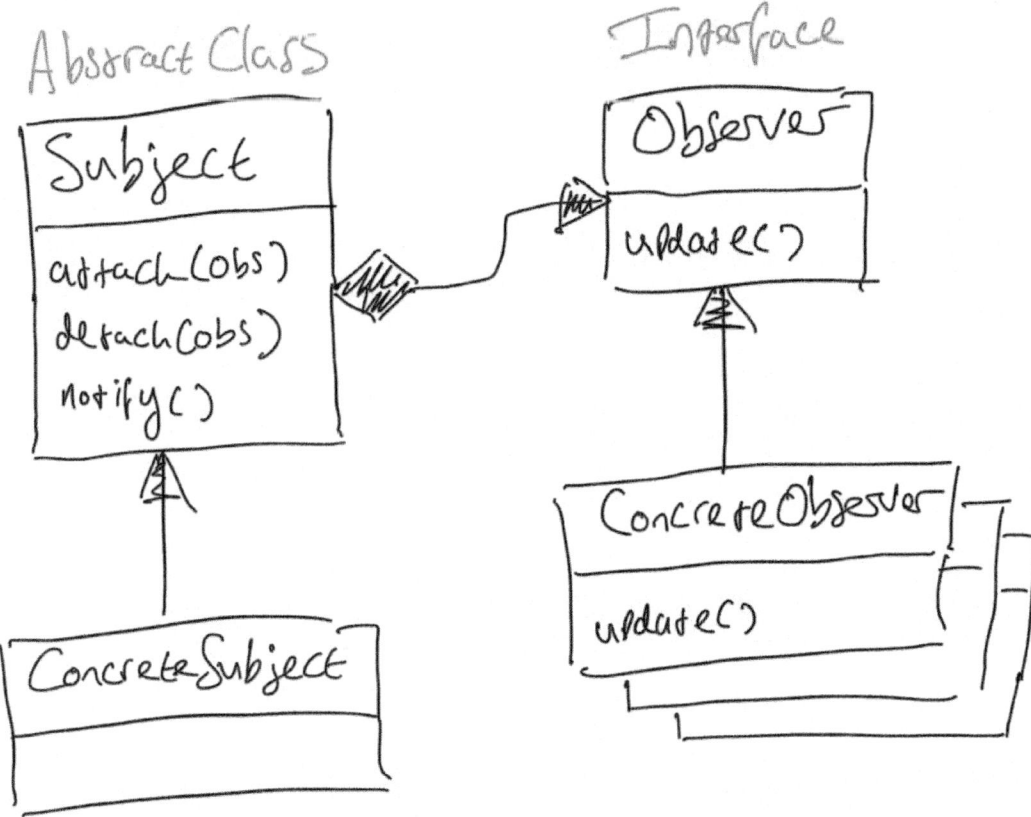

The Observer Pattern is also known as the pub (publish) and sub (subscribe) pattern: the subject (publisher) publishes changes in its state, and the subscribers (observers) subscribe to those events.

Refactoring our code to use the Observer pattern:

The observer interface:

```
public interface Observer
{
  void Update();
}
```

The concrete observers, that implement the observer interface:

```csharp
public class BarChart : Observer
{
  private DataSource _dataSource;

  public BarChart(DataSource dataSource)
  {
     _dataSource = dataSource;
  }

  public void Update()
  {
     System.Console.WriteLine("Rendering bar chart with new values");
  }
}

public class Sheet2 : Observer
{
  private int _total;
  private DataSource _dataSource;

  public Sheet2(DataSource dataSource)
  {
     _dataSource = dataSource;
  }

  public int GetTotal()
  {
     return _total;
  }

  public void Update()
  {
     var sum = CalculateTotal(_dataSource.GetValues());
```

```csharp
      System.Console.WriteLine("Total: " + sum);
      _total = sum;
   }

   private int CalculateTotal(List<int> values)
   {
      var sum = 0;
      foreach (var value in values)
      {
         sum += value;
      }
      return sum;
   }
}
```

The subject class, that can be extended by any class that needs to be observed:

```csharp
public class Subject
{
   private List<Observer> _observers = new List<Observer>();

   public void AddObserver(Observer observer)
   {
      _observers.Add(observer);
   }

   public void RemoveObserver(Observer observer)
   {
      _observers.Remove(observer);
   }

   public void NotifyObservers()
   {
      foreach (Observer observer in _observers)
      {
```

```
      observer.Update();
    }
  }
}
```

The concrete subject class – the class being observed:

```
public class DataSource : Subject
{
  private List<int> _values = new List<int>();

  public List<int> GetValues()
  {
    return _values;
  }

  public void SetValues(List<int> values)
  {
    _values = values;

    NotifyObservers();
  }
}
```

Here's how we'd use this solution:

```
class Program
{
  static void Main(string[] args)
  {
    DataSource dataSource = new DataSource();

    Sheet2 sheet2 = new Sheet2(dataSource);
    BarChart barChart = new BarChart(dataSource);
```

```
    dataSource.AddObserver(sheet2);
    dataSource.AddObserver(barChart);

    // Calling SetValues() triggers the total and bar chart to
also be updated:
    dataSource.SetValues([5, 5, 1, 10]);
    // Logs:
    // Total: 21
    // Rendering bar chart with new values

    dataSource.SetValues([1, 2, 3]);
    // Logs:
    // Total: 6
    // Rendering bar chart with new values
  }
}
```

Communication styles

Above, the observers get notified of a change, but they don't know what has changed. One solution is to add a parameter to the observer `update()` method. This is known as a "push" style of communication, as the Subject pushes the changes to the observers:

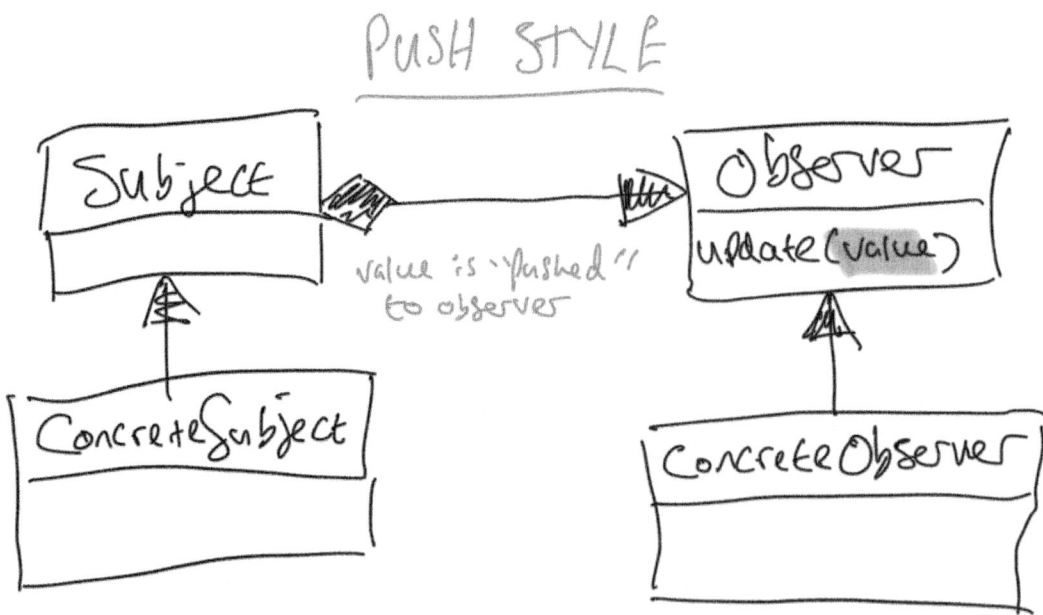

For flexibility, `value` could be any `Object` or generic type.

The push style has the advantage that the Concrete observer doesn't depend on (has no knowledge or "coupling" to) the concrete subject.

Problem: what if each observer needs a different set of values? This is where we could use a Pull style of communication, where the observer stores a reference to the concrete subject, then whenever it is notified of a change, it pulls, or queries, the data it needs from the concrete subject:

PULL STYLE

```
┌─────────────┐                    ┌─────────────┐
│  Subject    │◇──────────────────▶│  Observer   │
│             │                    │  update()   │
└─────────────┘                    └─────────────┘
       △                                  △
       │                                  │
┌─────────────┐                    ┌─────────────────┐
│ConcreteSubject│◀─ ─ ─ ─ ─ ─ ─ ─ ─│ConcreteObserver │
│ getValue()  │                    │                 │
└─────────────┘                    └─────────────────┘
                Value is
              "pulled" from
             concrete subject
```

The concrete observer stores a reference to the concrete subject. We give concrete subjects a `getValue()` method, so a concrete observer can get the data it needs. This gives more flexibility; however, we have coupling between the concrete classes. But this is not a bad type of coupling. A bad coupling would be between `ConcreteSubject` and `ConcreteObserver`, because these observers could change in the future, and we may introduce more observers -- and `ConcreteSubject` would have to keep reference to them all. We don't want to change our concrete subject class (`DataSource` in our example) every time there is a new observer.

In reality, we never have zero coupling in software. What matters is the direction of the relationship.

With Pull style communication, we pass the concrete subject (`dataSource`) to the observer objects constructors – just like we did when implementing the Observer pattern for our `DataSource` with the `BarChart` and `Sheet2` observers.

Mediator Pattern

The Mediator pattern defines an object (the Mediator) that describes how a set of objects interact with each other, therefore reducing lots of chaotic dependencies between those objects.

Let's say we have a blog that lists all of your posts, and you can select a post and then edit that post's title:

Select an article from the post container on the left, and the input is populated on the right with the title:

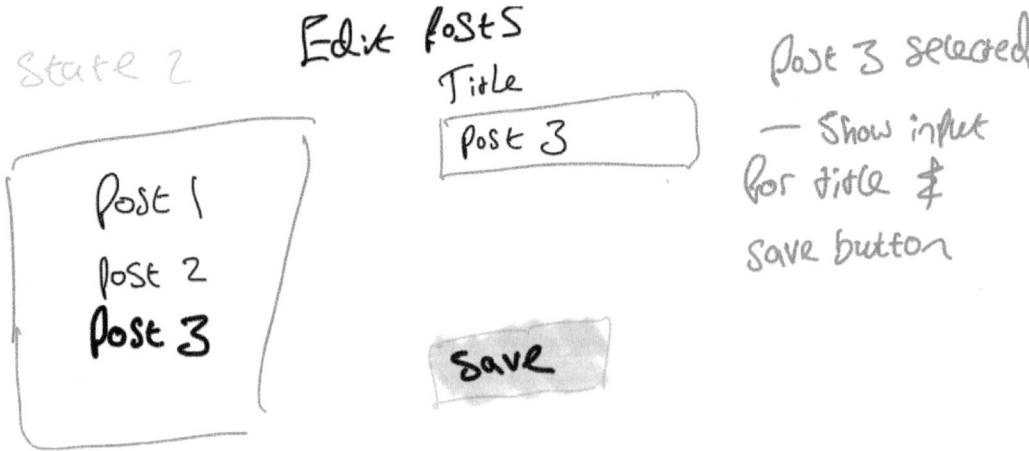

The save button is disabled if no title provided, or no article selected.

Components (classes) that we need:

- ListBox that contains the posts (on left)
- TextBox for editing title
- Button that can be disabled or enabled

The above classes will come from a UI framework, so we do not have access to the source code.

When an article is selected from the list box, the text box should be populated, and the button enabled. When we clear the text box, the button should become disabled.

But how do they talk to each other? They should be able to talk to each other without knowledge of each other.

One solution would be to use inheritance:

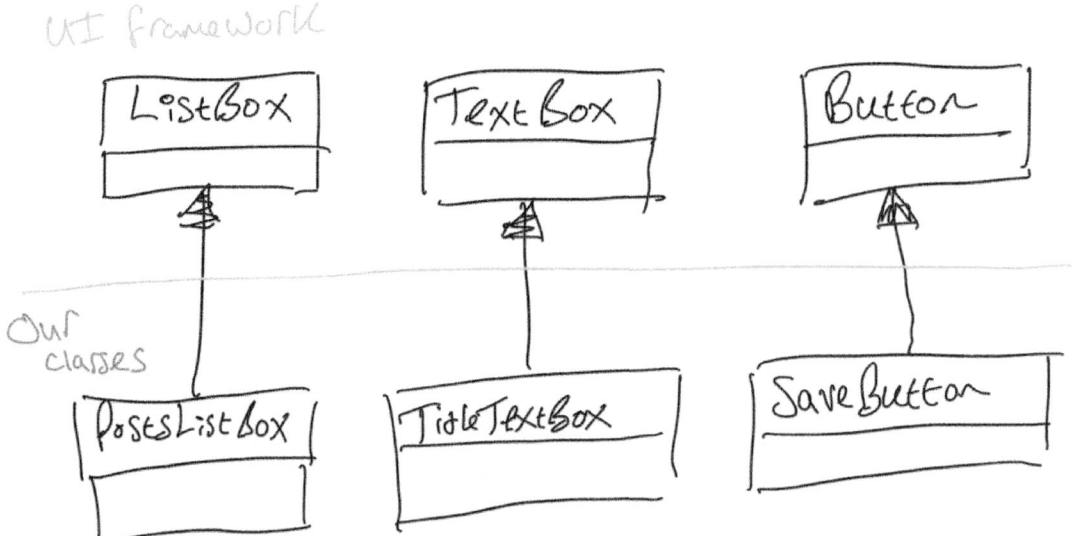

Then they could talk to each other, like so:

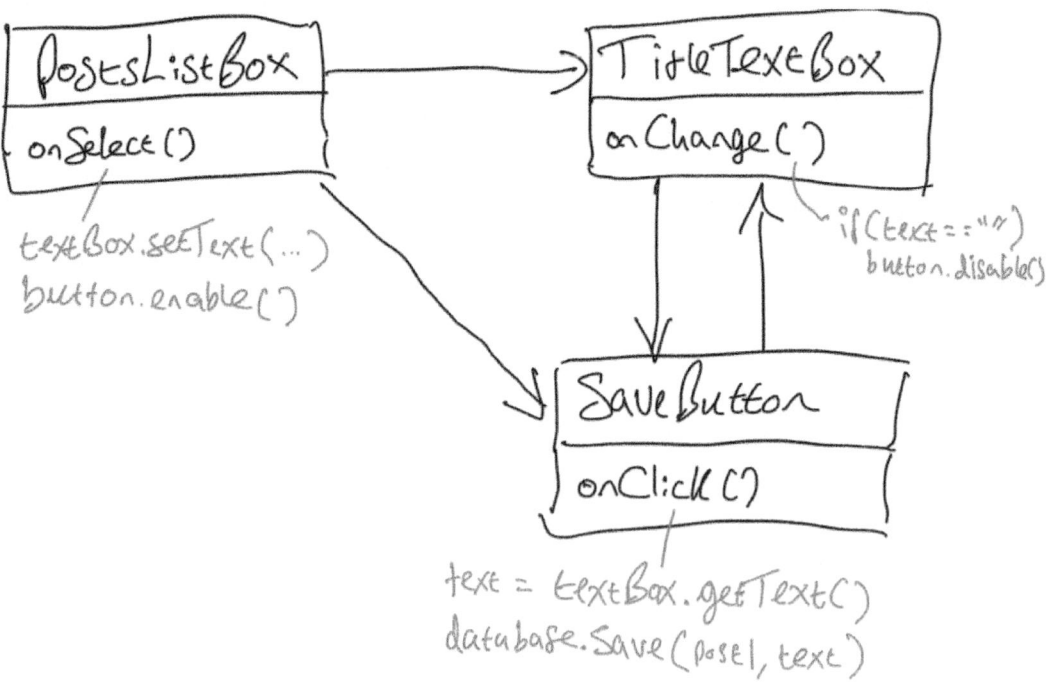

Whenever a post is selected, `PostsListBox` calls its `onChange()` method to populate the title text box and enable the button, etc…

Problem: as our form gets more complex, there becomes lots of dependencies/connections between these classes. Also, the logic for this form is spread all over the place, so to see what's going on in this form, you have to look at multiple classes. It's difficult to understand and maintain.

Using the Mediator pattern, the UI components don't know about each other, and all interaction logic is in the dialogue box ("the Mediator"):

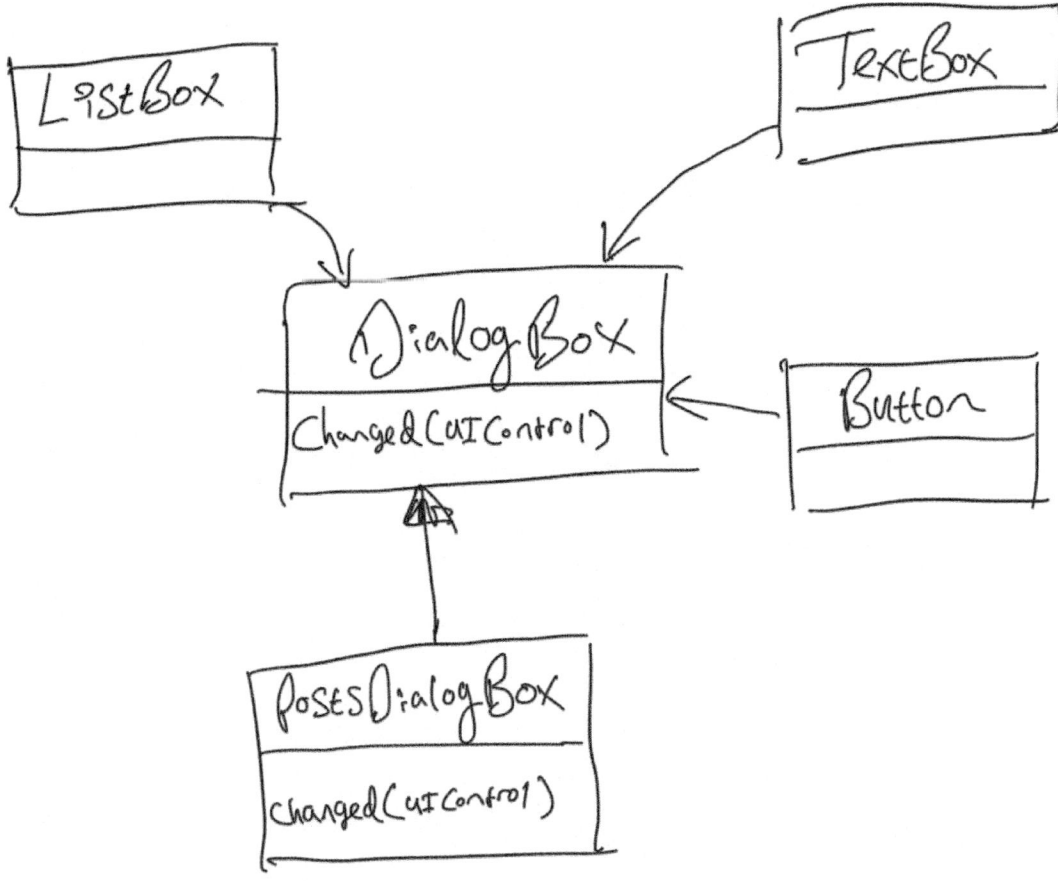

Whenever a UI component changes, it notifies its owner, the dialog box, by calling the changed(UIControl) method and passing itself as argument, which then handles updating other components.

Let's implement this in code so that it makes more sense to you:

The abstract DialogBox class, to ensure that all concrete dialog boxes have a common Changed() method that can be called by UI components, informing the dialog box that it's changed, so that the concrete dialog box can update other ui components accordingly:

```
// This class plays the role of "mediator". Every time a UI
component changes state, it'll call its group's dialogue box.
// Abstract class, not interface, because a real GUI framework
would provide some concrete methods too
public abstract class DialogBox
{
  public abstract void Changed(UIControl uiControl);
}
```

The abstract `UIControl` class ensures that each UI component gets put into a dialog box (group of UI components):

```
public abstract class UIControl
{
  protected DialogBox _owner; // so all UI components can be
grouped into a dialogue box and know & can talk to their owner,
allowing the owner to change other UI components accordingly

  public UIControl(DialogBox owner)
  {
    _owner = owner;
  }
}
```

The UI components extend the `UIControl` class, and put themselves into a dialog box via their constructor:

```
public class ListBox : UIControl
{
  private string _selection = "";

  public ListBox(DialogBox owner) : base(owner)
  {
  }
```

```csharp
  public string GetSelection()
  {
    return _selection;
  }

  public void SetSelection(string selection)
  {
    _selection = selection;
    _owner.Changed(this);
  }
}

public class TextBox : UIControl
{
  private string _text = "";

  public TextBox(DialogBox owner) : base(owner)
  {
  }

  public string GetText()
  {
    return _text;
  }

  public void SetText(string text)
  {
    _text = text;
    _owner.Changed(this);
  }
}

public class Button : UIControl
{
```

```csharp
  private bool _isEnabled;

  public Button(DialogBox owner) : base(owner)
  {
  }

  public bool IsEnabled()
  {
    return _isEnabled;
  }

  public void SetEnabled(bool isEnabled)
  {
    _isEnabled = isEnabled;
    _owner.Changed(this); // tell the mediator that "I, this button object, have changed"
  }
}
```

The `PostsDialogBox` contains all of the UI components for our post title editing app and updates them depending on which component called it's `Changed()` method:

```csharp
public class PostsDialogBox : DialogBox
{
 // fields for all ui components
 private ListBox _postsListBox;
 private TextBox _titleTextBox;
 private Button _saveButton;

 public PostsDialogBox()
 {
   _postsListBox = new ListBox(this);
   _titleTextBox = new TextBox(this);
   _saveButton = new Button(this);
```

```
    _saveButton.SetEnabled(false); // initially disabled
  }

  public override void Changed(UIControl uiControl)
  {
    if (uiControl == _postsListBox)
    {
      handlePostChanged();
    }
    else if (uiControl == _titleTextBox)
    {
      handleTitleChanged();
    }
  }

  private void handlePostChanged()
  {
    _titleTextBox.SetText(_postsListBox.GetSelection());
    _saveButton.SetEnabled(true);
  }

  private void handleTitleChanged()
  {
    bool isTitleEmpty = _titleTextBox.GetText() == "";
    _saveButton.SetEnabled(!isTitleEmpty);
  }
}
```

Notice how clear it is when all of the business logic for our app is centered in this one class, the Mediator, and not spread out over multiple UI components.

Let's create a method inside of `PostsDialogBox` to simulate a user interaction:

```
public void SimulateUserInteraction()
{
```

```
  _postsListBox.SetSelection("Post 2");
  System.Console.WriteLine("Title text box: " +
_titleTextBox.GetText());
  System.Console.WriteLine("Button enabled: " +
_saveButton.IsEnabled());
}
```

Testing it out:

```
class Program
{
  static void Main(string[] args)
  {
    var postsDialogBox = new PostsDialogBox();
    postsDialogBox.SimulateUserInteraction();

    // Logs:
    // Title text box: Post 2
    // Button enabled: True
  }
}
```

Perfect!

What if we enter no title:

```
public void SimulateUserInteraction()
{
  _postsListBox.SetSelection("Post 2");
  _titleTextBox.SetText(""); // add this line
  System.Console.WriteLine("Title text box: " +
_titleTextBox.GetText());
  System.Console.WriteLine("Button enabled: " +
_saveButton.IsEnabled());
}
```

Logs after running:

```
// Title text box:
// Button enabled: False
```

Perfect!

GoF UML

Here's how the Mediator pattern looks with its abstract class names from the GoF book:

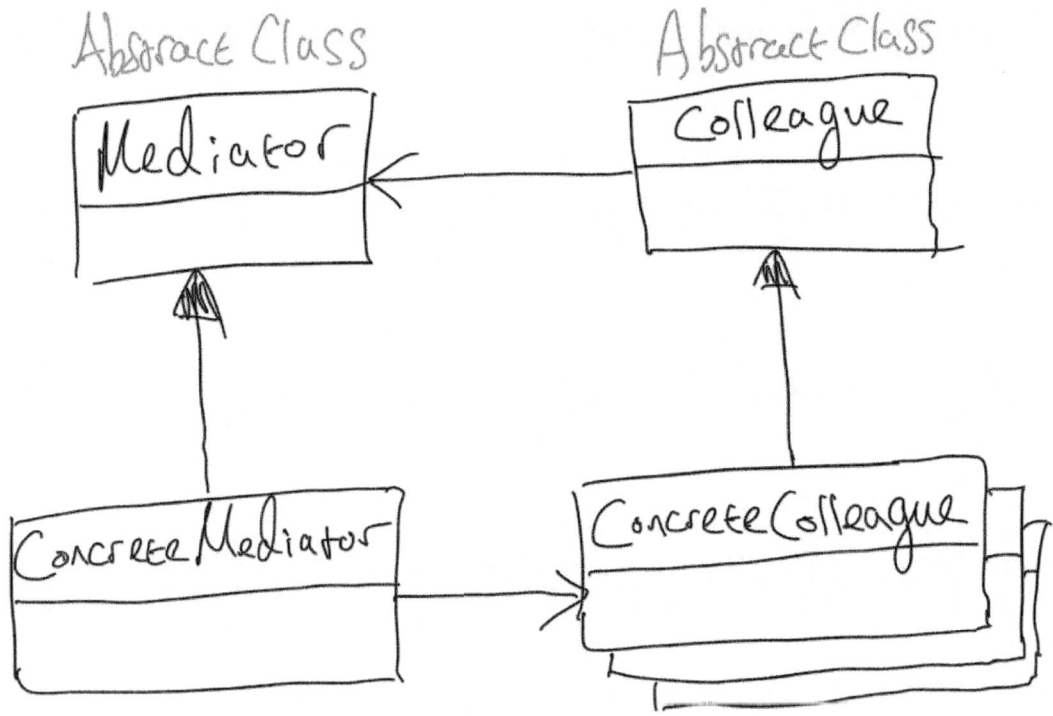

Here are the abstract names for our previous post-title-editing app:

- Mediator = `DialogueBox`
- ConcreteMediator = `PostsDialogueBox`
- Colleague = `UIControl`

- ConcreteColleague(s) = our concrete UI classes (`Button`, `TextBox`, `ListBox`)

The concrete colleagues are all unrelated/uncoupled from each other. They talk to each other indirectly via a mediator, allowing them to be reused in different contexts – e.g., we are not coupling a list box to a text box or button.

The only coupling we have is between `ConcreteMediator` and `ConcreteColleague`. This is fine, because in our example the `PostsDialogueBox` needs to know about all of its UI components so they can interact with each other.

Mediator pattern with Observer pattern

One problem with our previous solution is that the `changed()` method on `PostsDialogueBox` can get bulky as we add more UI components -- lots of if/else to see what component has changed:

```
public override void Changed(UIControl uiControl)
{
  if (uiControl == _postsListBox)
  {
    handlePostChanged();
  }
  else if (uiControl == _titleTextBox)
  {
    handleTitleChanged();
  }
}
```

To solve this, we can implement the Mediator pattern using the Observer pattern. Observer pattern reminder:

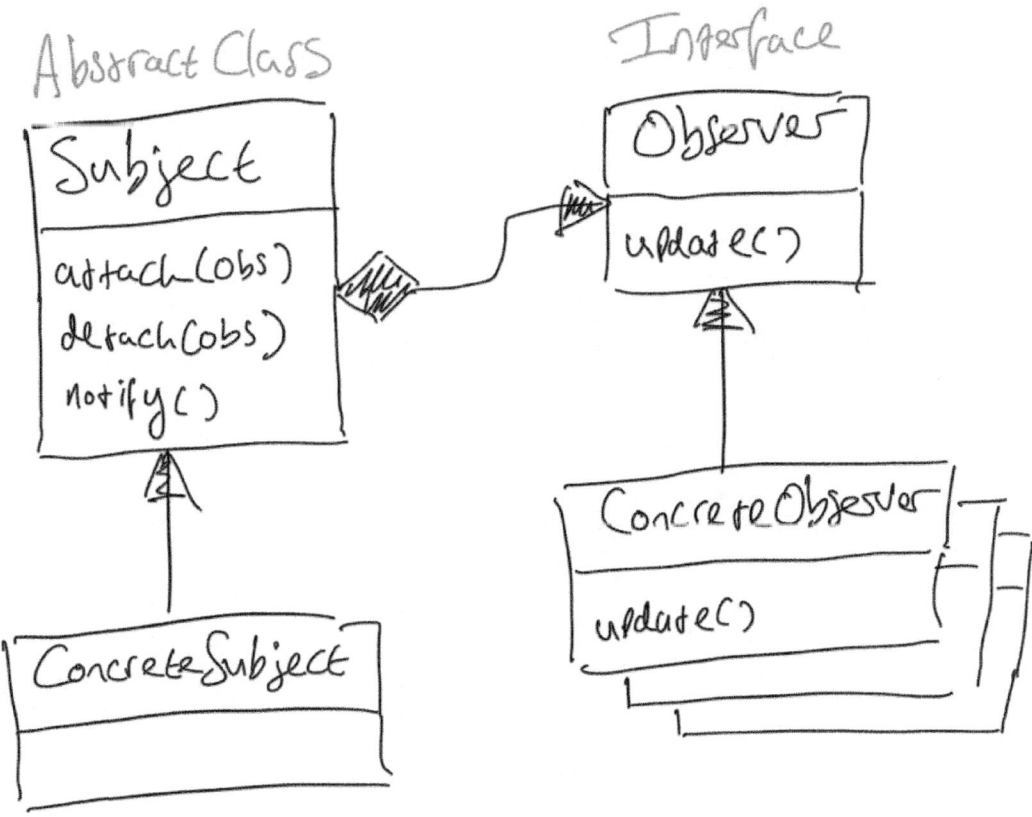

The subject notifies the observer when any change happens.

Below, the UI controls are the subjects, and the `PostsDialogBox` is the observer. When a UI control changes, `PostsDialogBox` gets notified:

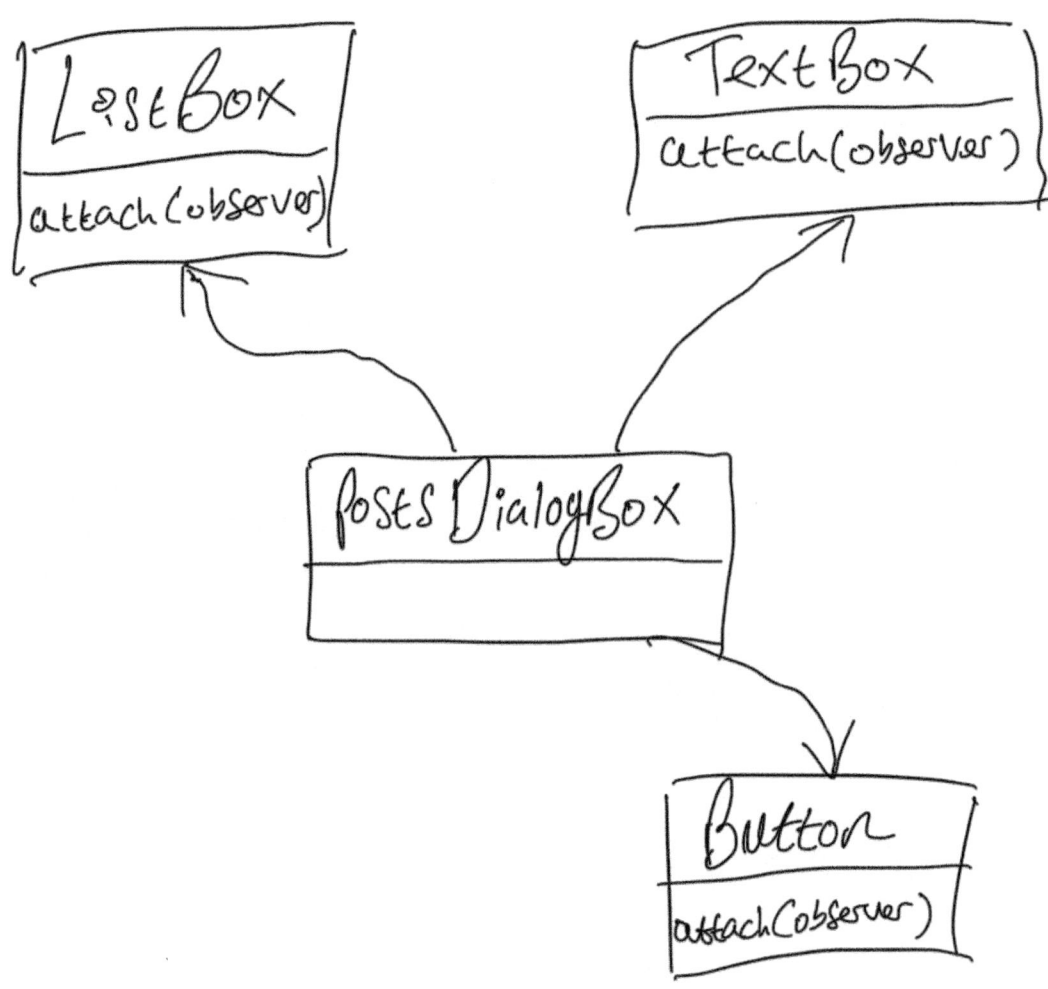

This will make much more sense when implemented in code, so let's do that:

First, we will create the UI framework:

```
// In C#, we can use delegates to specify what an event handler,
// or "callback", function/method should look like. Here, we say
// that EventHandler methods should return void and receive no
// arguments.
public delegate void EventHandler();
```

The `UIControl` class is now the "Subject" class from the Observer pattern, and will be the base class for all UI components so that they can keep a list of callbacks for updating other UI components when a user interacts with it:

```csharp
// This is our "Subject" from the GoF observer pattern.
public class UIControl
{
  private List<EventHandler> _eventHandlers = new List<EventHandler>();

  public void AddEventHandler(EventHandler handler)
  {
    _eventHandlers.Add(handler);
  }

  public void NotifyEventHandlers()
  {
    foreach (var handler in _eventHandlers)
    {
      handler();
    }
  }
}
```

Our UI components:

```csharp
public class ListBox : UIControl
{
  private string _selection = "";

  public string GetSelection()
  {
    return _selection;
  }

  public void SetSelection(string selection)
  {
    _selection = selection;
```

```csharp
    NotifyEventHandlers();
  }
}

public class TextBox : UIControl
{
  private string _text = "";

  public string GetText()
  {
    return _text;
  }

  public void SetText(string text)
  {
    _text = text;
    NotifyEventHandlers();
  }
}

public class Button : UIControl
{
  private bool _isEnabled;

  public bool IsEnabled()
  {
    return _isEnabled;
  }

  public void SetEnabled(bool isEnabled)
  {
    _isEnabled = isEnabled;
    NotifyEventHandlers();
  }
```

}

`PostsDialogBox` is now both a mediator, containing all the business logic for how UI components should interact, and an observer, receiving notice whenever a UI component changes:

```
// The Concrete Observer class
public class PostsDialogBox
{
  // declare fields for UI components
  private ListBox _postsListBox;
  private TextBox _titleTextBox;
  private Button _saveButton;

  public PostsDialogBox()
  {
    // assign ui components
    _postsListBox = new ListBox();
    _titleTextBox = new TextBox();
    _saveButton = new Button();

    // add event handler methods to each ui component
    _postsListBox.AddEventHandler(PostSelected);
    _titleTextBox.AddEventHandler(TitleChanged);
  }

  // event handler methods:
  private void PostSelected()
  {
    _titleTextBox.SetText(_postsListBox.GetSelection());
    _saveButton.SetEnabled(true);
  }

  private void TitleChanged()
  {
```

```
        var isTitleEmpty = _titleTextBox.GetText() == "";
        _saveButton.SetEnabled(!isTitleEmpty);
    }
}
```

Let's add a method to `PostsDialgBox` to simulate a user interaction and test this out:

```
public void SimulateUserInteraction()
{
  _postsListBox.SetSelection("Post 2");
  // _titleTextBox.SetText("");
  System.Console.WriteLine("Title text box: " +
_titleTextBox.GetText());
  System.Console.WriteLine("Button enabled: " +
_saveButton.IsEnabled());
}

class Program
{
  static void Main(string[] args)
  {
    var postsDialogBox = new PostsDialogBox();
    postsDialogBox.SimulateUserInteraction();

    // Logs:
    // Title text box: Post 2
    // Button enabled: True
  }
}
```

Awesome, we've combined the Mediator pattern with the Observer pattern, and reduced the ugly, bulky conditionals in `PostsDialogBox`.

Chain of Responsibility Pattern

The Chain of Responsibility pattern allows building a chain of objects to handle a request. A request is passed through a chain of handlers, each capable of either handling the request or passing it to the next handler in the chain.

To understand this, let's go through an example, where we first create a simple, naive solution, then refactor it into something more maintainable using the Chain of Responsibility pattern.

Let's say we have a web page that contains some information that only admins of the website can access, such as a page that allows an admin to manage the website's users – e.g. create new users, get information, update user information, etc.

Say that a user makes a request to the website's server, but before returning the web page, the user's data must be validated (e.g. trim any whitespace around user-entered data), authenticate the user (e.g. check their username and password is correct), and then log some information onto the server about this request. If any of those steps fail, then "access denied" is returned to the user.

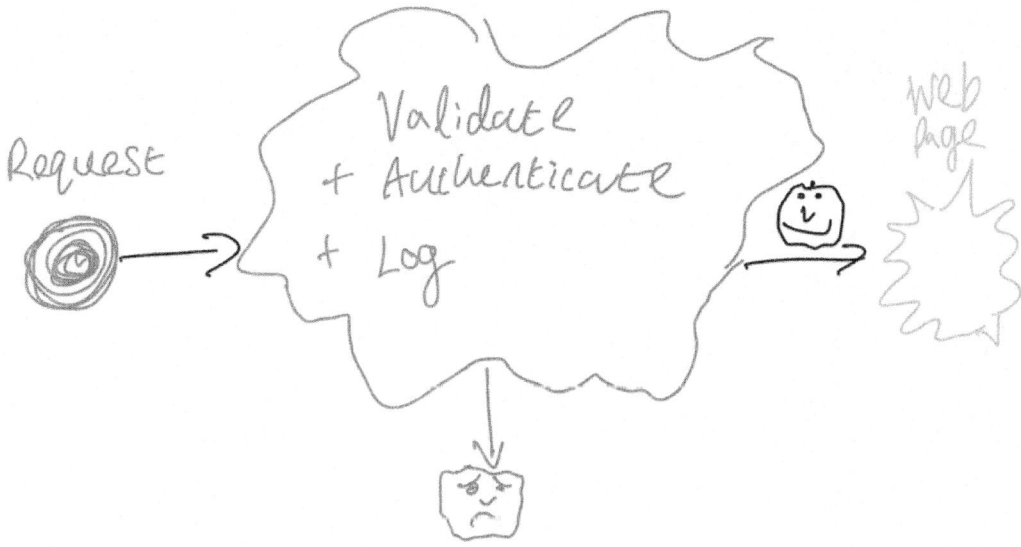

Let's code up a straightforward solution for this example:

```
public class HttpRequest
{
```

```csharp
  private string _username;
  private string _password;
  public string ValidatedUsername { get; set; } = "";
  public string ValidatedPassword { get; set; } = "";

  public HttpRequest(string username, string password)
  {
    _username = username;
    _password = password;
  }

  public string GetUsername()
  {
    return _username;
  }

  public string GetPassword()
  {
    return _password;
  }
}

public class Validator
{
 public void Validate(HttpRequest request)
 {
    var username = request.GetUsername();
    var password = request.GetPassword();

    // Trim whitespace
    request.ValidatedUsername = username.Trim();
    request.ValidatedPassword = password.Trim();
 }
}
```

```csharp
public class Authenticator
{
 public bool Authenticate(HttpRequest request)
 {
    var username = request.GetUsername();
    var password = request.GetPassword();

    return username == "danny" && password == "123";
 }
}

public class Logger
{
 public void Log(HttpRequest request)
 {
    System.Console.WriteLine("Log");
 }
}

public class WebServer
{
 public void Handle(HttpRequest request)
 {
    var validator = new Validator();
    validator.Validate(request);

    var authenticator = new Authenticator();
    authenticator.Authenticate(request);

    var logger = new Logger();
    logger.Log(request);
 }
}
```

Using this solution:

```
class Program
{
  static void Main(string[] args)
  {
    var server = new WebServer();
    var request = new HttpRequest("danny", "123");
    server.Handle(request);
  }
}
```

Problems with this solution:
- With this approach, the order of operations – validate, authorize, log – are hard-coded inside the `WebServer` class. If, in the future, we wanted to disable logging or authentication for certain scenarios/web pages, we cannot do so; we'd have to come back and modify the code in `WebServer`, violating the open/closed principle. The Chain of Responsibility pattern solves this, as we can build a pipeline with a chain of objects for processing a request (the request can be of any type, not just http).
- Because of the `new` keyword inside `WebServer.handle()` when creating validate, authorize and log objects, this `WebServer` class is tightly coupled to the concrete `Validator`, `Authenticator` and `Logger` implementations. To solve this, we could extract interfaces from these classes, and have our `WebServer` talk to `IAuthenticator`, `IValidator` and `ILogger` interfaces.

Chain of Responsibility solution
Instead of having all of our request processing logic inside of the `WebServer.handle()` method, we can create a processing pipeline – a chain of objects:

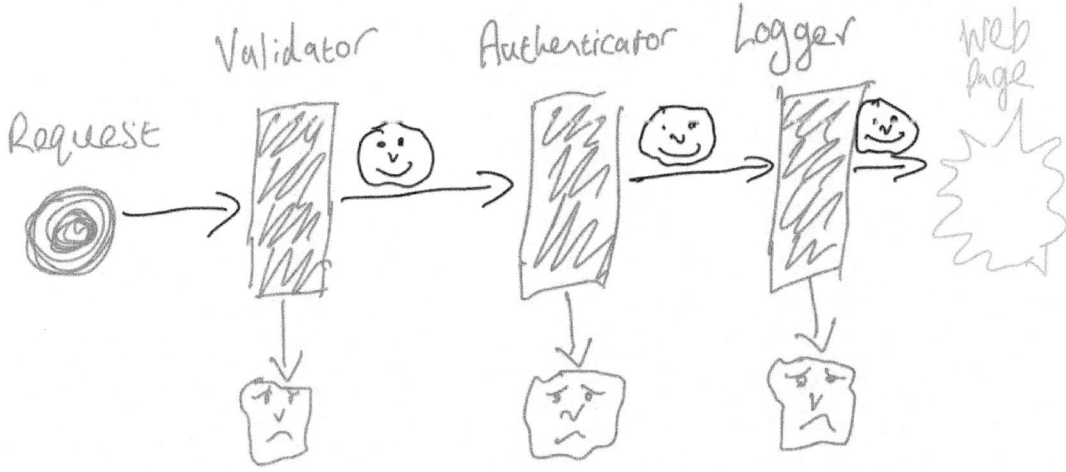

Each object only knows about the next object in the chain. First, a request is passed to the first object in the chain (`Validator`). If this request is successful, it passes the request to the next object in the chain; if not successful, it will stop processing right there, so the other objects aren't used.

Here's the UML for this Chain of Responsibility solution:

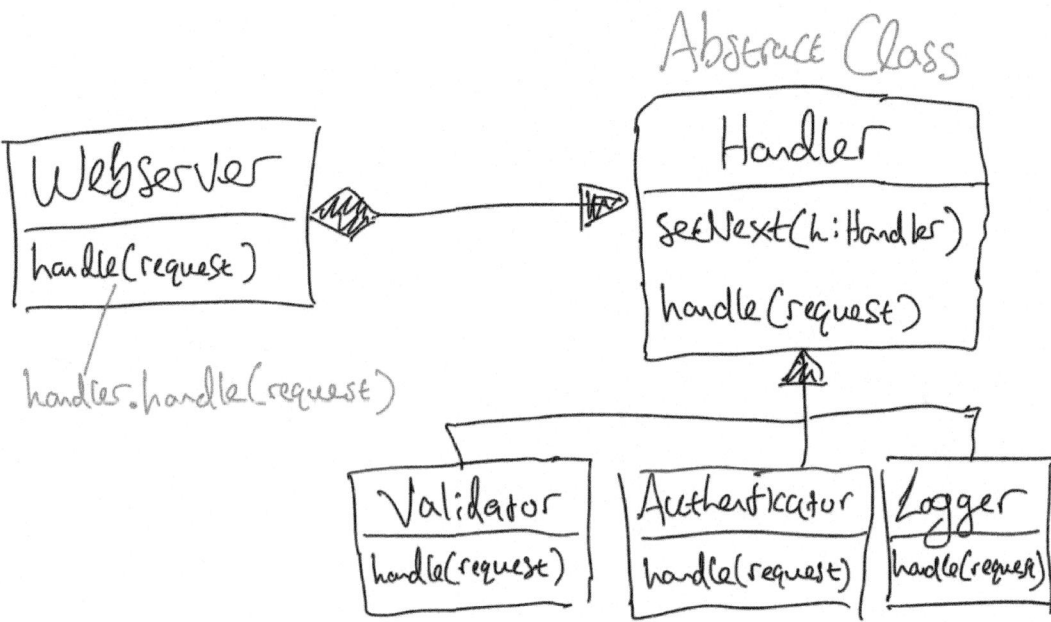

We have an abstract class called `Handler` that has a reference to itself -- it has a field called `next` of type `Hanlder`, so, with this, each handler can know about the next handler in the chain (it's a *linked list* data structure). `handle()` is an abstract method, because at the time of implementing this class we don't know how to handle a request -- we determine/implement this in our concrete handlers (`Validator`, `Authenticator` and `Logger`).

`WebServer` has a reference to the first handler in the chain. Note: `WebServer` is not talking directly to the concrete handlers; it's talking to the handler interface. So, it's completely decoupled from the concrete implementations.

This satisfies the open/closed principle -- if we want to remove logging, we don't have to go to the `handle()` method on `WebServer` and change its implementation. Also, if we want to add a new process, we can create a new class that extends `Hanlder`, then add it to our chain -- we extend the code, but don't modify any existing implementations.

Here is the GoF implementation of the Chain of Responsibility pattern:

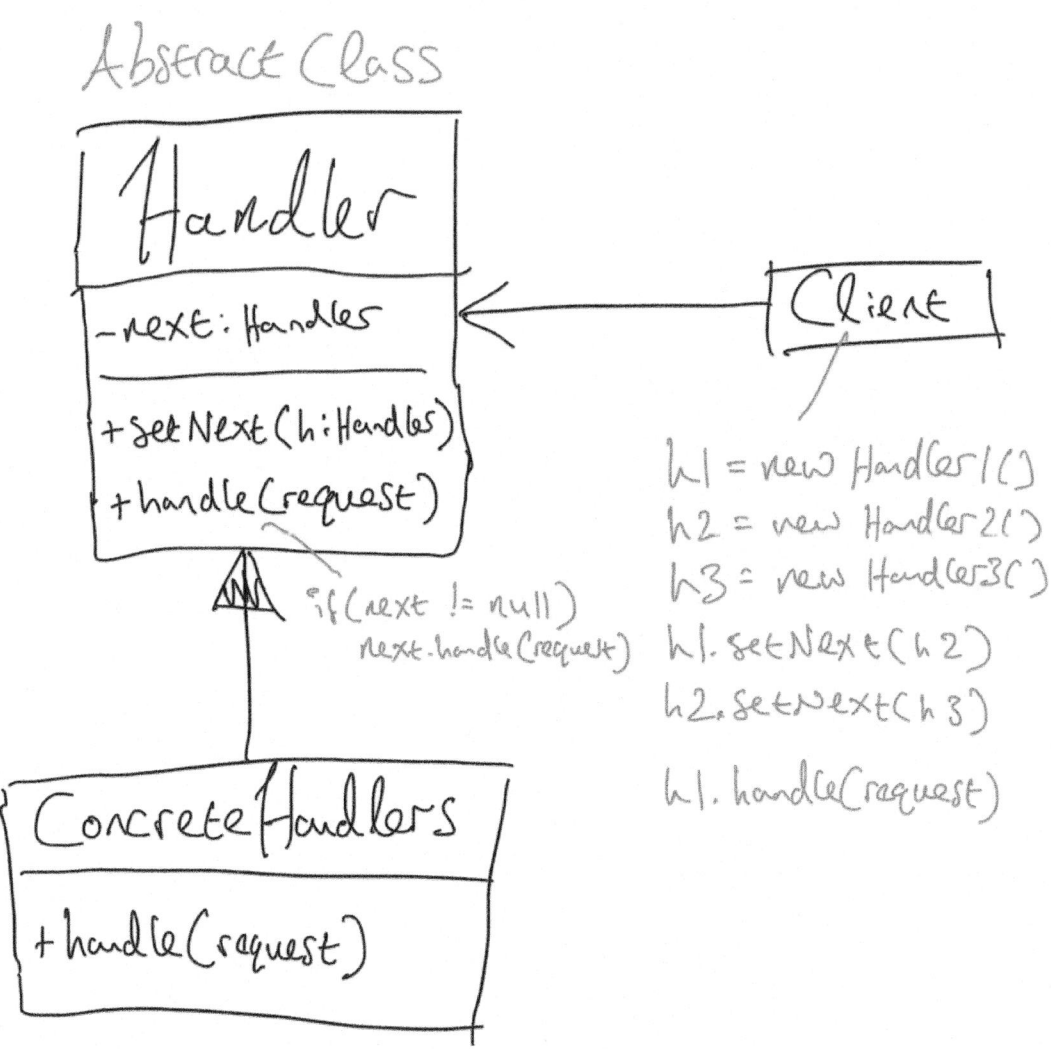

Let's now implement this solution in code:

The `HttpRequest` class remains the same as before.

First, we will create the abstract `Handler` class:

```
public abstract class Handler
{
  private Handler _nextHandler; // the next handler to call in the chain (after this one)

  public Handler SetNext(Handler handler)
```

```csharp
{
    _nextHandler = handler;

    // returning handler allows us to link handlers in a
    convenient way, e.g. handler1.SetNext(handler2).SetNext(handler3)
    return handler;
}

// Handle template method.
public void Handle(HttpRequest request)
{
    // if DoHandle() returns true, we return early and the request processing ends
    if (DoHandle(request))
        return;

    // DoHandle is false, so check if there is a next handler, and if so, call its Handle() method.

    if (_nextHandler != null)
        _nextHandler.Handle(request);
}

public abstract bool DoHandle(HttpRequest request);
}
```

The concrete handlers:

```csharp
public class Validator : Handler
{
    public override bool DoHandle(HttpRequest request)
    {
        System.Console.WriteLine("Validating");
        var username = request.GetUsername();
        var password = request.GetPassword();
```

```csharp
    // Trim whitespace
    request.ValidatedUsername = username.Trim();
    request.ValidatedPassword = password.Trim();

    // returning false means that we are not done processing the
    request, so the next handler in the chain should be called.
    Returning true ends the request processing here.
    return request.ValidatedUsername == "" ||
request.ValidatedPassword == "";
 }
}


public class Authenticator : Handler
{
 public override bool DoHandle(HttpRequest request)
 {
    System.Console.WriteLine("Authenticating");
    var username = request.GetUsername();
    var password = request.GetPassword();
    return !(username == "danny" && password == "123");
 }
}

public class Logger : Handler
{
 public override bool DoHandle(HttpRequest request)
 {
    System.Console.WriteLine("Logging");
    return false;
 }
}
```

The WebServer:

```
public class WebServer
{
  private Handler _handler;

  public WebServer(Handler handler)
  {
    _handler = handler;
  }

  public void Handle(HttpRequest request)
  {
    _handler.Handle(request);
  }
}
```

Using this solution:

```
class Program
{
  static void Main(string[] args)
  {
    var validator = new Validator();
    var authenticator = new Authenticator();
    var logger = new Logger();

    validator.SetNext(authenticator).SetNext(logger);

    var server = new WebServer(validator);

    // Request with valid credentials
    var request1 = new HttpRequest("danny", "123");
    server.Handle(request1);

    // Logs:
```

```
    // Validating
    // Authenticating
    // Logging

    // Request with invalid password
    var request2 = new HttpRequest("danny", "abcde");
    server.Handle(request2);

    // Logs (notice how there is no "Logging" - since
authentication failed, the request chain was cut short and didn't
go to the next link):
    // Validating
    // Authenticating

    // Request with no empty credentials will cause validation to
fail
    var request3 = new HttpRequest("", "");
    server.Handle(request3);

    // Logs:
    // Validating
  }
}
```

We now have a flexible solution that makes it easy to change the order of processes, and add or remove processes, without having to modify existing code – satisfying the open/closed principle.

Visitor Pattern

The Visitor pattern separates the algorithms, or behaviors, from the objects on which they operate.

Say that you are a developer for a marketing agency, that has different types of clients:

- Restaurants
- Law firms
- Retailers

Here's how the code looks:

```csharp
public abstract class Client
{
 protected string _name;
 protected string _email;

 public Client(string name, string email)
 {
    _name = name;
    _email = email;
 }
}

public class Law : Client
{
 public Law(string name, string email) : base(name, email)
 {
 }
}

public class Restaurant : Client
{
 public Restaurant(string name, string email) : base(name, email)
 {
 }
}

public class Retail : Client
{
 public Retail(string name, string email) : base(name, email)
 {
```

    }
}

Everything is just a plane and simple C# object. Simple.

But your manager comes to you and says that they need the ability to send a specialized email with marketing tips for each of the different types of clients. E.g., restaurants need tips on how they can better market their food, but law firms don't.

So, it seems a good idea to add an abstract method, SendEmail(), to Client(), then implement that method in each concrete client:

```
public abstract class Client
{
    protected string _name;
    protected string _email;

    public Client(string name, string email)
    {
        _name = name;
        _email = email;
    }

    public abstract void SendEmail();
}

public class Law : Client
{
    public Law(string name, string email) : base(name, email)
    {
    }

    public override void SendEmail()
    {
```

```csharp
        System.Console.WriteLine("Sending law marketing tips email to
" + _email);
    }
}

public class Restaurant : Client
{
    public Restaurant(string name, string email) : base(name, email)
    {
    }

    public override void SendEmail()
    {
        System.Console.WriteLine("Sending restaurant marketing tips email to " + _email);
    }
}

public class Retail : Client
{
    public Retail(string name, string email) : base(name, email)
    {
    }

    public override void SendEmail()
    {
        System.Console.WriteLine("Sending retail marketing tips email to " + _email);
    }
}
```

Emails can now be sent easily by using polymorphism:

```csharp
class Program
{
```

```csharp
static void Main(string[] args)
{
    // Get list of clients (e.g. from db)
    var clients = new List<Client> {
      new Retail("Debinhams", "team@debinhams.co.uk"),
      new Restaurant("Frankie and Bennys", "frank@fandb.com"),
      new Law("Hamlin McGil Law Firm", "howard@handm.com")
    };

    // Loop through clients and send marketing email
    foreach (var client in clients)
    {
      client.SendEmail(); // polymorphism makes this easy
    }

    // Logs:
    // Sending retail marketing tips email to team@debinhams.co.uk
    // Sending restaurant marketing tips email to frank@fandb.com
    // Sending law marketing tips email to howard@handm.com
}
}
```

This appears to be a nice elegant solution. But the manager comes back to us and says that they need a way to export clients as PDFs and XML. You quickly realize that your manager is going to keep coming to you asking for more and more features.

Following our current design, everytime we want to add new functionality, we have to open up our code for modification, breaking the open/closed principle. We are also violating the SRP, as clients are now responsible for storing client info, sending emails, and exporting.

Also, initially, the clients were simple plain old C# objects, but adding the ability to send email means adding 3rd-party library code into these classes, that calls email clients like Gmail and Outlook. This can easily break our previously working code.

Here is the UML for this solution:

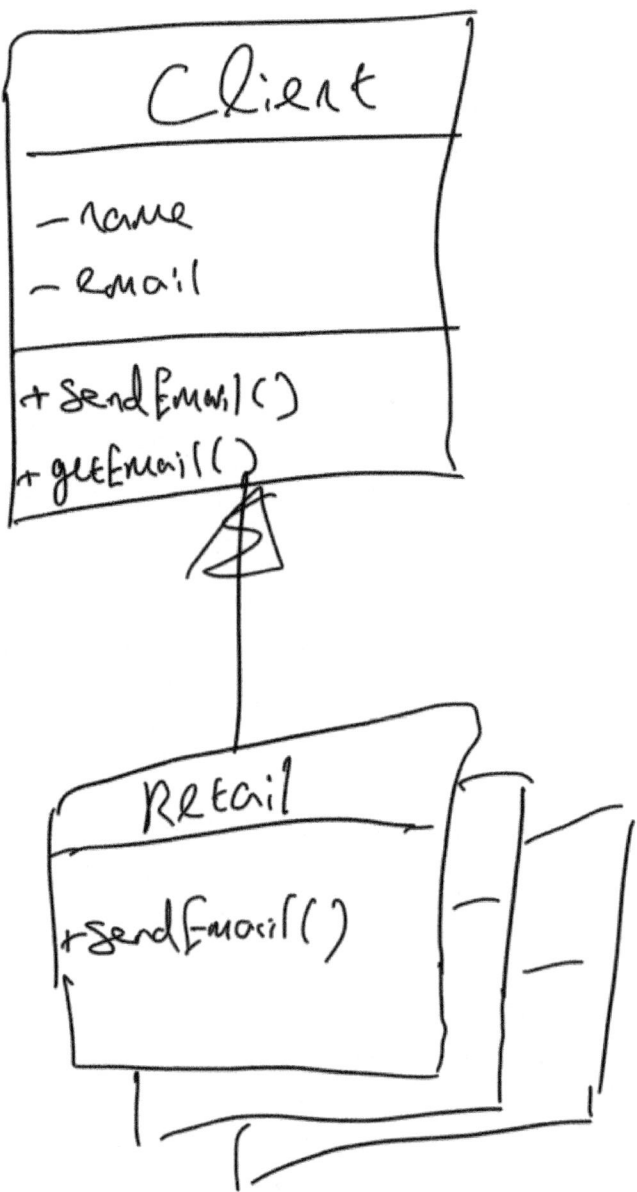

To solve these issues, we need to extract these behaviors outside of the client classes on which they operate. Remember: The Visitor pattern separates the algorithms, or behaviors, from the objects on which they operate. So, let's implement the Visitor pattern.

Here's the UML:

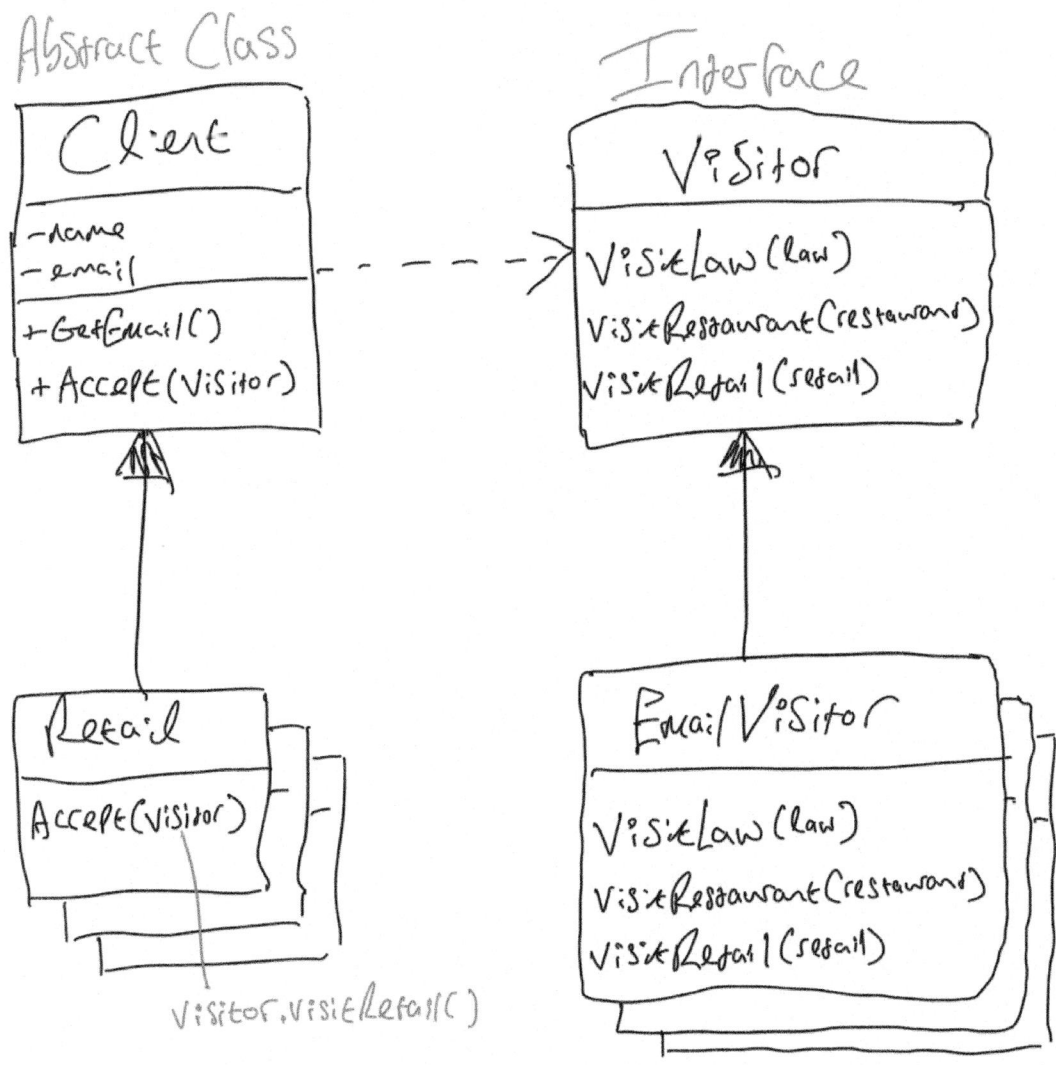

The behaviors have been abstracted into the concrete visitor classes, which can be passed to the objects that they operate on, like so:

```
// Loop through clients and send marketing email
foreach (var client in clients)
{
  client.Accept(new EmailVisitor()); // pass the operation that we
want to do to the client
}
```

GoF UML:

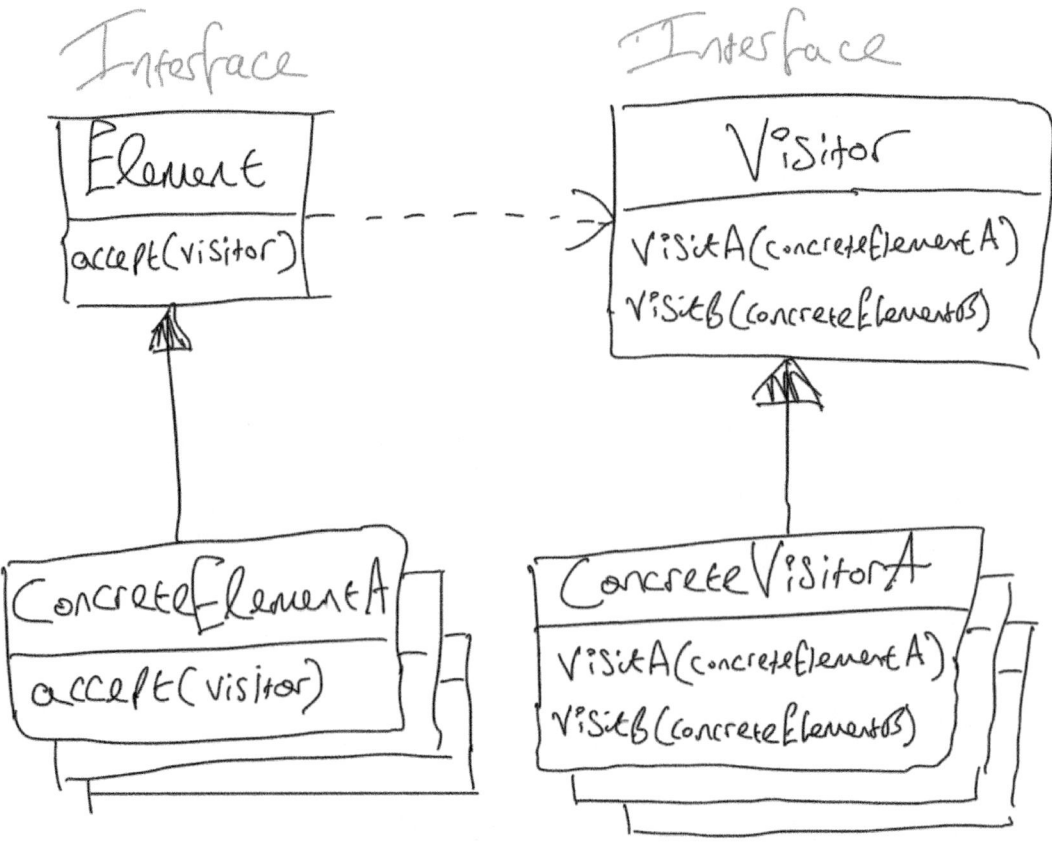

Note that design patterns are not super rigid – e.g. in our case, the Element class is an abstract class and not an interface, because we want to provide some common fields and some methods common to all clients.

OK, lets implement this in code so that it makes more sense:

First, let's create our base Client class with an Accept method that takes a visitor object:

```
public abstract class Client
{
  protected string _name;
  protected string _email;

  public Client(string name, string email)
  {
    _name = name;
```

```csharp
    _email = email;
  }

  public string GetEmail()
  {
    return _email;
  }

  public abstract void Accept(Visitor visitor);
}
```

Next, let's create our visitor interface:

```csharp
public interface Visitor
{
  void VisitRetail(Retail retail);

  void VisitLaw(Law law);

  void VisitRestaurant(Restaurant restaurant);
}
```

Next, the specific client classes. Notice the `Accept()` method calls the appropriate method on the `Visitor`. Also notice how it is talking to the `Visitor` interface, and not concrete objects, allowing any type of `Visitor` object to be passed in:

```csharp
public class Law : Client
{
  public Law(string name, string email) : base(name, email)
  {
  }

  public override void Accept(Visitor visitor)
  {
    visitor.VisitLaw(this);
```

```csharp
    }
}

public class Restaurant : Client
{
  public Restaurant(string name, string email) : base(name, email)
  {
  }

  public override void Accept(Visitor visitor)
  {
     visitor.VisitRestaurant(this);
  }
}

public class Retail : Client
{
  public Retail(string name, string email) : base(name, email)
  {
  }

  public override void Accept(Visitor visitor)
  {
     visitor.VisitRetail(this);
  }
}
```

Next, create a concrete visitor for sending marketing emails for each type of client. The abstract client now includes an abstract `Accept()` method with a `Visitor` parameter. This method will allow certain operations to be passed to clients:

```csharp
public class EmailVisitor : Visitor
{
  public void VisitLaw(Law law)
  {
```

```
            System.Console.WriteLine("Sending law marketing tips email to
" + law.GetEmail());
        }

        public void VisitRestaurant(Restaurant restaurant)
        {
            System.Console.WriteLine("Sending restaurant marketing tips
email to " + restaurant.GetEmail());
        }

        public void VisitRetail(Retail retail)
        {
            System.Console.WriteLine("Sending retail marketing tips email
to " + retail.GetEmail());
        }
}
```

To use this solution, we pass the operation that we want to perform into the client object's `Accept()` method:

```
class Program
{
    static void Main(string[] args)
    {
        // Get list of clients (e.g. from db)
        var clients = new List<Client> {
            new Retail("Debinhams", "team@debinhams.co.uk"),
            new Restaurant("Frankie and Bennys", "frank@fandb.com"),
            new Law("Hamlin McGil Law Firm", "howard@handm.com")
        };

        // Loop through clients and send marketing email
        foreach (var client in clients)
        {
```

```
        client.Accept(new EmailVisitor()); // pass the operation
that we want to do to the client
    }

    // Logs:
    // Sending retail marketing tips email to team@debinhams.co.uk
    // Sending restaurant marketing tips email to frank@fandb.com
    // Sending law marketing tips email to howard@handm.com
  }
}
```

Now, when our manager comes to us asking for new features, we can *extend* our code, and not *modify* it. E.g., to add export-as-pdf functionality, we could do something like this:

```
public class PDFExportVisitor : Visitor
{
 public void VisitLaw(Law law)
 {
    System.Console.WriteLine("Exporting law client as PDF.");
 }

 public void VisitRestaurant(Restaurant restaurant)
 {
    System.Console.WriteLine("Exporting restaurant client as PDF.");
 }

 public void VisitRetail(Retail retail)
 {
    System.Console.WriteLine("Exporting retail client as PDF.");
 }
}
```

Then, to export a list of clients as PDF:

```
// Loop through clients and send marketing email
foreach (var client in clients)
{
  client.Accept(new PDFExportVisitor());
}

// Logs:
// Exporting retail client as PDF.
// Exporting restaurant client as PDF.
// Exporting law client as PDF.
```

Awesome – SRP and open/closed principles are satisfied!

Interpreter Pattern

The Interpreter pattern defines a way to represent and evaluate sentences in a language by using an abstract class for expressions, which concrete subclasses implement to interpret specific parts of the language's grammar.

The interpreter pattern is probably the most complex and least used of the GoF design patterns. Most courses on design patterns that I've seen don't include the Interpreter pattern. However, at the beginning of this course, I promised that I'd teach you all 23 GoF design patterns, so let's have a crack at it! After the example, I'll also discuss why this pattern is rarely used.

Example use-cases:
- Parsing and executing SQL queries, where the Interpreter pattern helps parse the query syntax and execute it against a database.
- Calculators or scientific software that interpret and evaluate complex mathematical formulas entered by users.
- Web frameworks that render HTML templates with embedded expressions or directives – i.e. templates – (e.g., `{{ variable }}` in Django or `<% expression %>` in JSP).

So, let's say that we need to build a calculator app, that takes some user input string, and calculates the result.

User input: "1 + 2 * 3"

An interpreter will convert/parse this input, or "expression", into an Abstract Syntax Tree (AST), or "Expression tree":

```
IExpression expressionTree =
        new AdditionExpression(
          new MultiplicationExpression(
              new NumberExpression("2"),
              new NumberExpression("3")
          ),
          new NumberExpression("1")
        );
```

Essentially, we are converting, or parsing, an input string into a tree of objects according to the grammar rules that we specify.

The result of this expression can be found by calling its interpret method:

```
expressionTree.Interpret()
```

We can use the Interpreter pattern to get from the user input to the AST.

The components of the Interpreter pattern:

- **Abstract Expression**: Establishes the interface for all expressions within the language.
- **Terminal Expression**: Represents the fundamental components of the language, such as numbers or variables. In the above example `NumberExpression` is a terminal expression, or "leaf", that represents integers.
- **Non-terminal Expression**: Represents more complex expressions that are composed of other expressions using operators or functions. Above, `AdditionExpression` and `MultiplicationExpression` are non-terminal, or "composite", expressions.
- **Interpreter**: Implements the logic for interpretation and determines how to evaluate different types of expressions.

OK, I'm fully aware that you have no idea what is going on, so let's go through an example. It will definitely help if you try to code this example out a few times!

The `Context` class contains any global information needed for interpretation. For our simple calculator example, we don't currently need context. But, say that we wanted to interpret English to Spanish. Each Spanish-speaking country speaks Spanish slightly differently. So the context could contain the country and city that we are located in. It could also keep the gender of the person we are speaking to, as that could also affect the interpretation.

```
public class Context
{
  // Any global information needed for interpretation
}
```

The *abstract expression* interface:

```
public interface IExpression
{
  int Interpret(Context context);
}
```

The *terminal expressions* (for this example, we only need one)

```
public class NumberExpression : IExpression
{
  private int _number;

  public NumberExpression(int number)
  {
    _number = number;
  }

  public NumberExpression(string number)
  {
    _number = int.Parse(number);
```

```
  }

  public int Interpret(Context context)
  {
    return _number;
  }
}
```

The *non-terminal* expressions:

```
public class AdditionExpression : IExpression
{
 private IExpression _left;
 private IExpression _right;

  public AdditionExpression(IExpression left, IExpression right)
  {
    _left = left;
    _right = right;
  }

  public int Interpret(Context context)
  {
    return _left.Interpret(context) + _right.Interpret(context);
  }
}

public class SubtractionExpression : IExpression
{
 private IExpression _left;
 private IExpression _right;

  public SubtractionExpression(IExpression left, IExpression right)
  {
```

```
      _left = left;
      _right = right;
   }

   public int Interpret(Context context)
   {
      return _left.Interpret(context) - _right.Interpret(context);
   }
}

public class MultiplicationExpression : IExpression
{
   private IExpression _left;
   private IExpression _right;

   public MultiplicationExpression(IExpression left, IExpression right)
   {
      this._left = left;
      this._right = right;
   }

   public int Interpret(Context context)
   {
      return _left.Interpret(context) * _right.Interpret(context);
   }
}
```

The *interpreter* (or "parser") class needs to convert the input string, e.g. "1 + 2 * 3", into an Abstract Syntax Tree (or "expression tree"). Parsers are complex (as I'll show you shortly) and are easy to get wrong; so, for simplicity, we'll skip building an actual parser and just hard-code in the expression tree for the input "1 + 2 * 3". Of course, in the real world, you'd need a proper parser.

```
public class Interpreter
{
```

```
private Context _context;

public Interpreter(Context context)
{
  _context = context;
}

public int Interpret(string expression)
{
  IExpression expressionTree = BuildExpressionTree(expression);
  return expressionTree.Interpret(_context);
}

private IExpression BuildExpressionTree(string input)
{
  // To demonstrate what this builder should do, we'll hard code
the input and its result:
  input = "1 + 2 * 3"; // result should be 7

  // parser converts this input string into an Abstract Syntax
Tree of objects ("expression tree")...

  // Notice how our tree satisfies BODMAS:
  // 1 + 2 * 3
  // 2 * 3 = 6
  // 1 + 6 = 7
  IExpression expressionTree =
    new AdditionExpression(
        new MultiplicationExpression(
            new NumberExpression("2"),
            new NumberExpression("3")
        ),
        new NumberExpression("1")
    );
```

```
        return expressionTree;
    }
}
```

Here's how a client would use this solution:

```
string input = "1 + 2 * 3";

Context context = new Context();
Interpreter interpreter = new Interpreter(context);
int result = interpreter.Interpret(input);
System.Console.WriteLine("Result: " + result); // 7
```

Let me show you what an interpreter class would look like if it actually parsed the input string into an expression tree. For simplicity (and a little sanity), this interpreter only handles addition and subtraction. Handling multiplication, division and brackets requires more complexity; example: "1 + 3 * 4" requires 3 * 4 to be executed before adding the 1, due to BODMAS. Creating language/grammar parsers is very difficult to get right!

```
// Example of an interpreter that includes an actual parser for
// converting the input into an expression tree. Look at how complex
// things are just to create an interpreter that can parse basic
// addition and subtraction input strings, e.g. "1 + 3 - 2".
public class Interpreter2
{
    private Context _context;

    public Interpreter2(Context context)
    {
        _context = context;
    }

    public int Interpret(string expression)
    {
```

```csharp
    IExpression expressionTree = BuildExpressionTree(expression);
    return expressionTree.Interpret(_context);
}


// Parse the input into an expression tree. This parser only
works with addition and subtraction.
private IExpression BuildExpressionTree(string input)
{
    var tokens = input.Split(' ');
    var output = new Queue<string>();
    var operators = new Stack<string>();

    // Shunting Yard Algorithm to convert infix to postfix
    foreach (var token in tokens)
    {
        if (int.TryParse(token, out _))
        {
            output.Enqueue(token);
        }
        else if (token == "+" || token == "-")
        {
            while (operators.Count > 0 && (operators.Peek() == "+" || operators.Peek() == "-"))
            {
                output.Enqueue(operators.Pop());
            }
            operators.Push(token);
        }
    }

    while (operators.Count > 0)
    {
        output.Enqueue(operators.Pop());
    }
```

```csharp
    var expressionStack = new Stack<IExpression>();

    while (output.Count > 0)
    {
      var token = output.Dequeue();

      if (int.TryParse(token, out int number))
      {
        expressionStack.Push(new NumberExpression(number));
      }
      else if (token == "+" || token == "-")
      {
        var right = expressionStack.Pop();
        var left = expressionStack.Pop();

        if (token == "+")
        {
          expressionStack.Push(new AdditionExpression(left, right));
        }
        else if (token == "-")
        {
          expressionStack.Push(new SubtractionExpression(left, right));
        }
      }
    }

    return expressionStack.Pop();
  }
}
```

Here's how a client would use this:

```
string input = "2 + 3 - 4 + 10";

Context context = new Context();
Interpreter2 interpreter = new Interpreter2(context);
int result = interpreter.Interpret(input);
System.Console.WriteLine("Result: " + result); // 11
```

What's going on here?

- **Client:** initiates the interpretation process by providing an input expression (1 + 2 * 3) to interpret, and creates the interpreter object. The context object is passed to the interpreter object.
- **Parsing and building the AST:**
    - The input expression is turned into an array of tokens (tokens are analogous to words in a sentence), and parsed via some algorithm to create an expression tree that represents the input.
    - Each operator and operand in the expression is represented by a corresponding expression object.
- **Expression evaluation:**
    - The interpreter traverses the expression tree and interprets each individual expression (node) as it goes.
    - For terminal expressions (the operands – such as 1, 2 and 3), their `Interpret()` methods directly return their numeric values.
    - For the non-terminal expressions (the operators, such as +, - and *), their `Interpret()` methods call their `left` and `right` subexpressions recursively and perform their respective operations (e.g. add, subtract or multiply).
- **Combining the interpreted results:**
    - The interpreter combines the results of the subexpressions according to the defined grammar rules, that should be represented by the expression tree.
    - In our example, following BODMAS, 2 * 3 should be evaluated first = 6.
    - Followed by the addition operation: 1 + 6 = 7. This final output is returned to the client.

GoF UML:

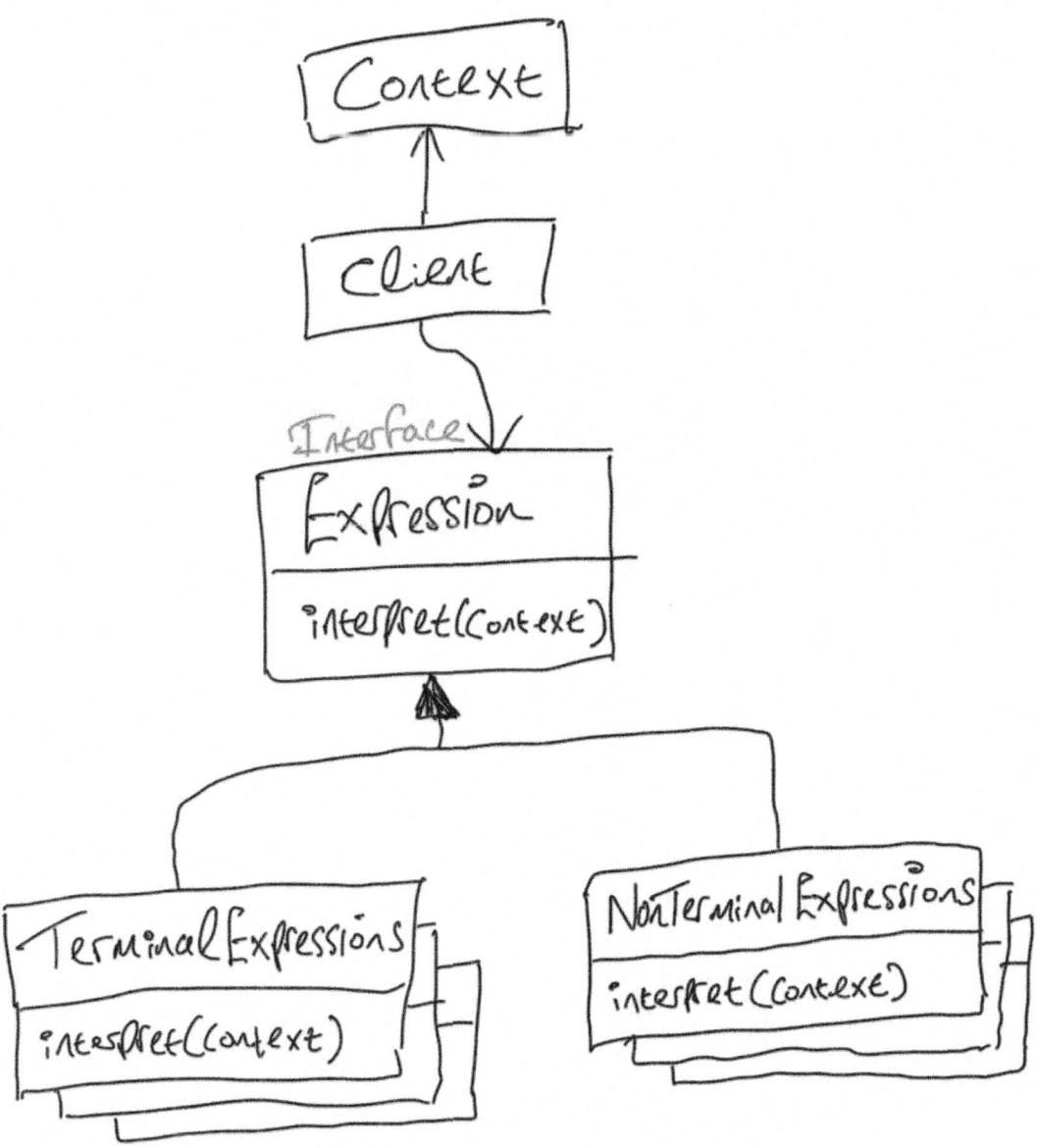

Some commonly-stated justifications for when to, and when not, to use the Interpreter pattern
- If you need to interpret and execute expressions or commands in a domain-specific language (DSL), the Interpreter pattern offers a flexible and extensible method for implementing the language's grammar and semantics.
- If your task only involves calculating simple operations that can be handled by a general-purpose programming language or a library, then using the Interpreter pattern adds a lot of unnecessary complexity.
- If the grammar of your language is complex, then the Interpreter pattern could lead to having a large number of classes and increased code

complexity. In this case, a dedicated parser generator or compiler could be a better option.

Why is the Interpreter pattern rarely used?
Steve Yegge, software developer and blogger, says "the [GoF] book contains 22 patterns and a practical joke" – the Interpreter pattern being the joke!

The problem with the Interpreter pattern is that you must turn your language into an Abstract Syntax Tree (AST). And as you saw earlier, creating a parser or algorithm for converting some input into an AST is very difficult to get right and time consuming. For anything other than the simplest of languages, creating a parser is very difficult!

How did the GoF book deal with this? They basically ignored the parsing problem and said that it was a separate problem to the Interpreter pattern. Here's what the GoF say:

"The Interpreter pattern doesn't explain how to create an abstract syntax tree. In other words, it doesn't address parsing. The abstract syntax tree can be created by a table-driven parser, by a hand-crafted (usually recursive descent) parser, or directly by the client."

But when we use the Interpreter pattern, we have to somehow generate an AST! We can't just ignore the complex problem of parsing!

This is why Yegge characterized the chapter as a practical joke. And why other programming techniques and patterns are almost always preferred to the Interpreter Pattern.

In your life as a software developer, most of you will rarely have to develop your own languages, so the other 22 design patterns will be of much greater use. However, there are, of course, some specific, good use cases for this pattern in the real world.

OK – you now know all of the GoF Behavioral design patterns. So, let's look at the Structural design patterns...

Structural design patterns

Structural design patterns focus on the composition of classes and objects to form larger structures and systems. These patterns primarily deal with how classes and objects can be combined to form larger, more complex structures while keeping these structures flexible and efficient. The key objective of structural design patterns is to provide solutions to design problems related to object composition and structure, allowing for better organization and management of code.

Structural design patterns help to achieve several important goals in software development:
- **Promote code reusability and modularity** by defining clear and standardized ways to compose and organize classes and objects. This makes the codebase more maintainable and scalable over time, as changes or additions to the system can be made more easily.
- **Enhance flexibility and extensibility** by allowing the system's structure to evolve without requiring major changes to the existing code. This is achieved by decoupling the components of the system and promoting loose coupling between different parts.
- **Improve performance and resource utilization** by optimizing the way objects interact and collaborate within the system, thereby enhancing overall system efficiency.

Overall, these patterns contribute to building robust, adaptable, and well-organized software systems that are easier to understand, maintain, and extend over time.

OK, let's learn some Structural design patterns!

Composite Pattern

The Composite pattern is a structural design pattern that enables the creation of tree-like structures to represent collections of objects, where both individual objects and groups of objects are treated in a unified manner.

To understand what this means, let's create a scenario, code up a simple, naive solution, then fix it with the Composite pattern.

Let's say that we get an Amazon delivery of a large package that contains multiple items:

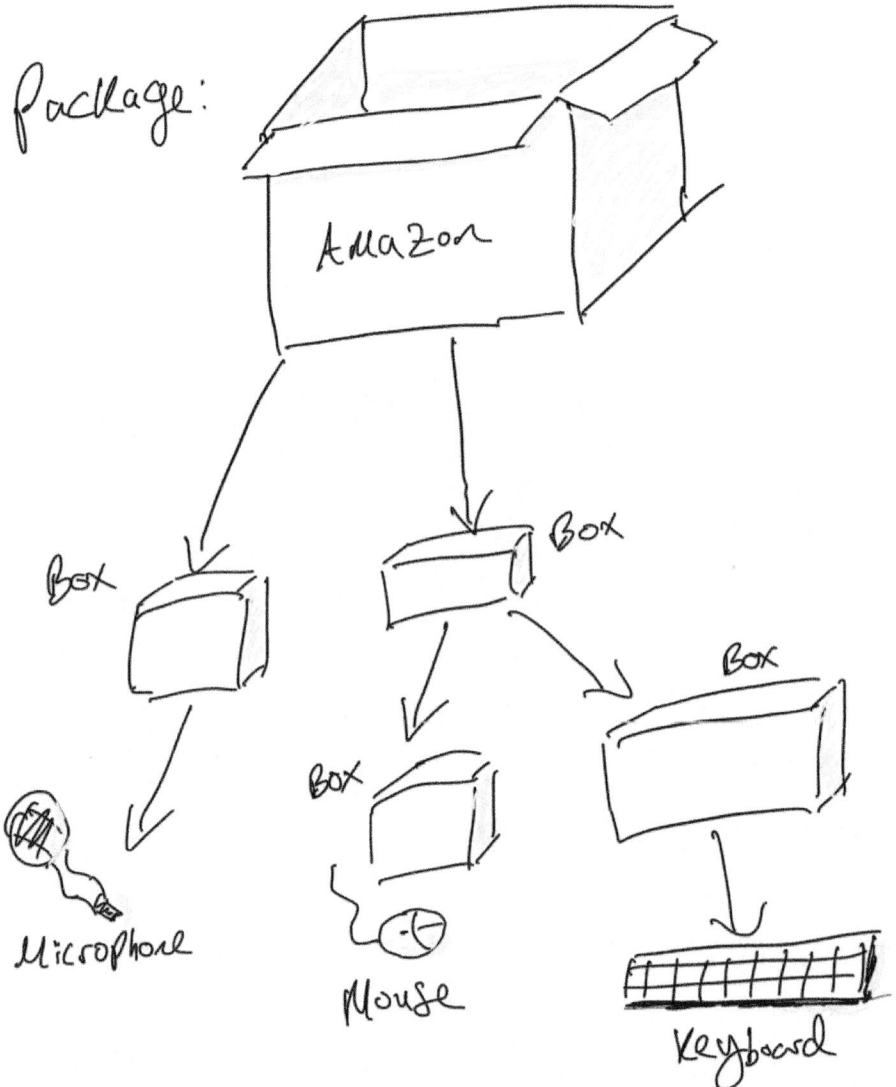

As you can see, boxes can contain groups of other boxes and items. The above diagram shows how a package of items can be represented as a tree structure.

Say that we needed to find the total price of the items within any package. The solution that naturally pops into the head is to create an array of boxes and items, then loop through them recursively to find the total price of the package. Here's a simple solution:

```
public class Keyboard
{
  public float Price { get; set; } = 40.00f;
}
```

```csharp
public class Microphone
{
    public float Price { get; set; } = 29.99f;
}

public class Mouse
{
    public float Price { get; set; } = 18.00f;
}

public class Box
{
    private List<object> items = new List<object>();

    public void Add(Object item)
    {
        items.Add(item);
    }

    // This method is UGLY!!! We need polymorphism!!
    public float CalculateTotalPrice()
    {
        float totalPrice = 0;
        foreach (var item in items)
        {
            if (item is Keyboard)
            {
                totalPrice += ((Keyboard)item).Price; // cast item to Keyboard object then we can get it's Price
            }
            else if (item is Mouse)
            {
                totalPrice += ((Mouse)item).Price;
            }
```

```
      else if (item is Microphone)
      {
         totalPrice += ((Microphone)item).Price;
      }
      else if (item is Box)
      {
         totalPrice += ((Box)item).CalculateTotalPrice(); // call
CalculateTotalPrice() recursively
      }
   }
   return totalPrice;
 }
}
```

Using this solution to create the package demonstrated in the previous tree diagram:

```
class Program
{
 static void Main(string[] args)
 {
   // the big package to deliver, containing box1 and box2
   var package = new Box();

   // box1 contains a microphone
   var box1 = new Box();
   box1.Add(new Microphone());

   // box2 contains box3 and box4
   var box2 = new Box();

   // box3 contains a mouse
   var box3 = new Box();
   box3.Add(new Mouse());

   // box4 contains a keyboard
```

```
    var box4 = new Box();
    box4.Add(new Keyboard());

    box2.Add(box3);
    box2.Add(box4);

    package.Add(box1);
    package.Add(box2);

    System.Console.WriteLine("Total price of package = " +
package.CalculateTotalPrice());
    // Total price of package = 87.99
  }
}
```

OK, the solution calculates the total price correctly, but it has some obvious issues:
- The `CalculateTotalPrice()` method contains lots of conditions. This is hard to read.
- Open/closed principle is violated: whenever we add a new item, we have to modify `Box`.

Whenever we have lots of conditionals that are checking the type of an object, and casting it to another object type, it's a good sign that we need to use polymorphism.

We can use polymorphism by creating an interface, called `Item` and extracting common methods, or logic, between the objects into that interface, like this:

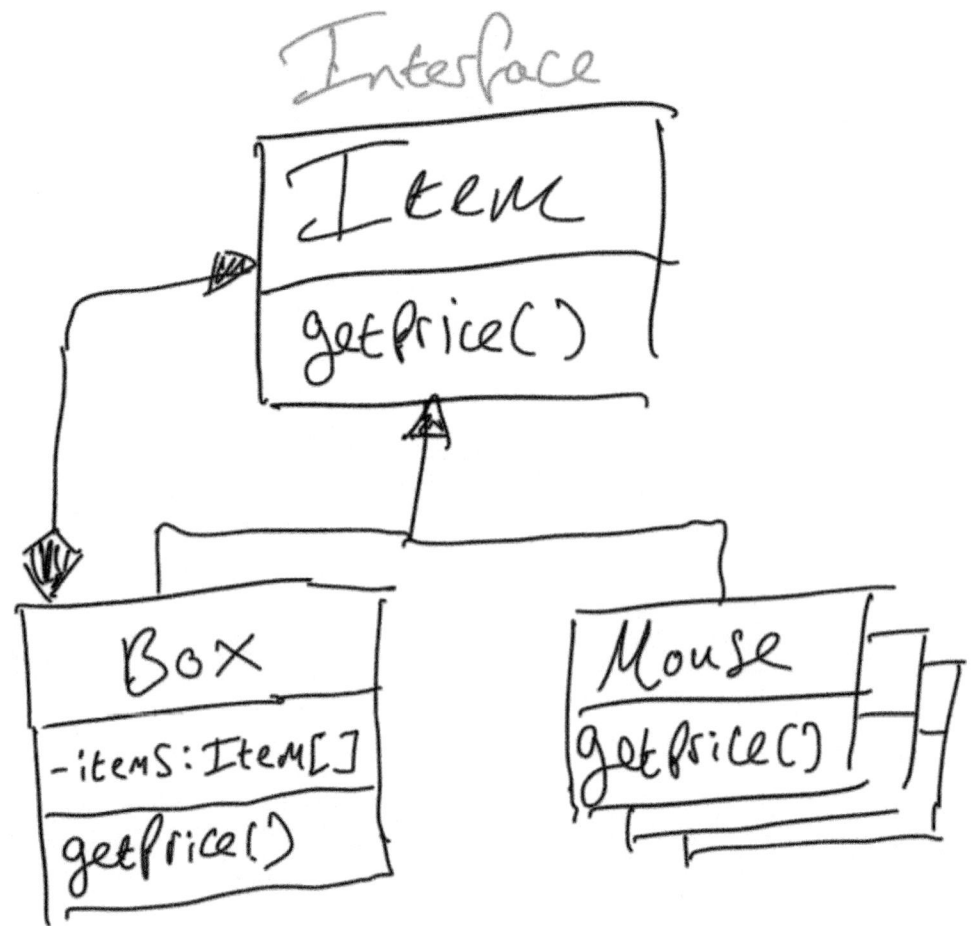

A box is essentially composed of a group of items (represented by the diamond arrow), but is also an item itself (represented by the arrow). A box is simply just a group of items.

Now, a box and its contents can be treated the same way – as items – thanks to polymorphism. Here's the code solution:

```
public interface Item
{
 public float GetPrice();
}

public class Keyboard : Item
{
 private float _price = 40.00f;
```

```csharp
    public float GetPrice()
    {
       return _price;
    }
}

public class Microphone : Item
{
  private float _price = 29.99f;

  public float GetPrice()
  {
     return _price;
  }
}

public class Mouse : Item
{
  private float _price = 18.00f;

  public float GetPrice()
  {
     return _price;
  }
}

public class Box : Item
{
  private List<Item> items = new List<Item>();

  public void Add(Item item)
  {
     items.Add(item);
  }
```

```
  public float GetPrice()
  {
    float total = 0f;
    foreach (var item in items)
    {
      total += item.GetPrice();
    }
    return total;
  }
}
```

Using this solution (not much change here):

```
class Program
{
 static void Main(string[] args)
 {
    // the big package to deliver, containing box1 and box2
    var package = new Box();

    // box1 contains a microphone
    var box1 = new Box();
    box1.Add(new Microphone());

    // box2 contains box3 and box4
    var box2 = new Box();

    // box3 contains a mouse
    var box3 = new Box();
    box3.Add(new Mouse());

    // box4 contains a keyboard
    var box4 = new Box();
    box4.Add(new Keyboard());
```

```
    box2.Add(box3);
    box2.Add(box4);

    package.Add(box1);
    package.Add(box2);

    System.Console.WriteLine("Total price of package = " +
package.GetPrice());
    // Total price of package = 87.99
  }
}
```

As you can see, there is little change in the way that a client would use this solution compared to before. The biggest change is in the method that calculates the price, `GetPrice()`. We can now treat all of the objects in the box as the same, as they all implement the `Item` interface, meaning we don't need conditionals to check the type of each item. This satisfies the open/closed principle, as our code is open for extension and closed for modification: we can create a new item class, extending our code, without needing to open any existing classes for modification.

Here is the GoF UML for the Composite pattern:

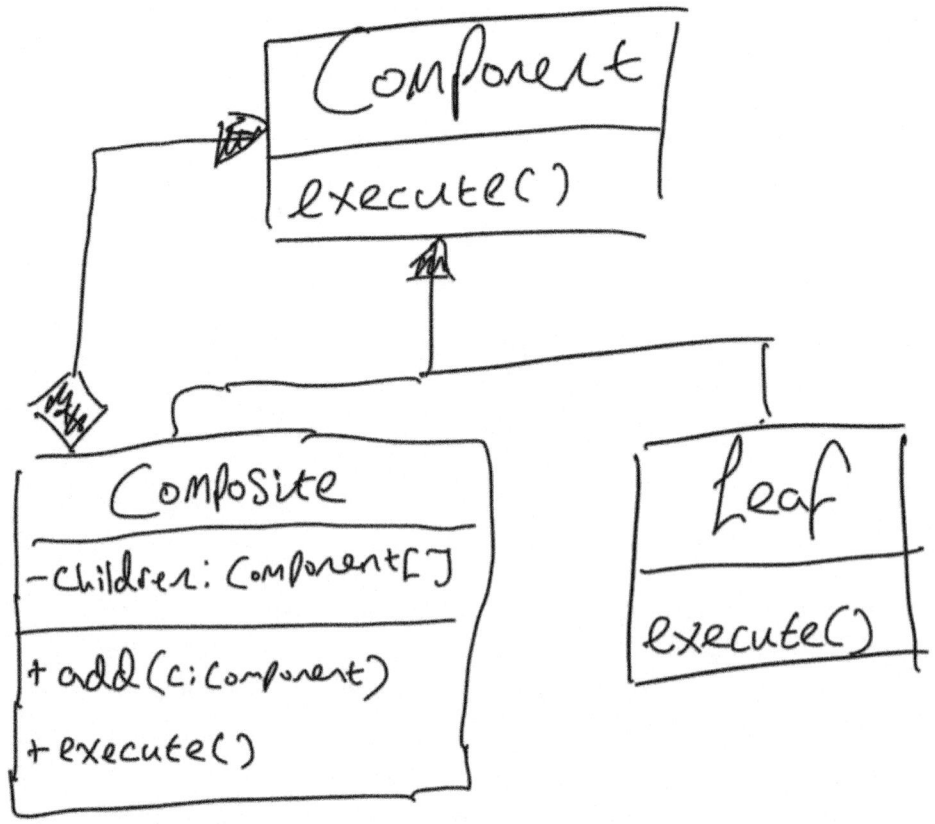

The Composite pattern is useful for representing tree structures, for example:

- Folders and files:

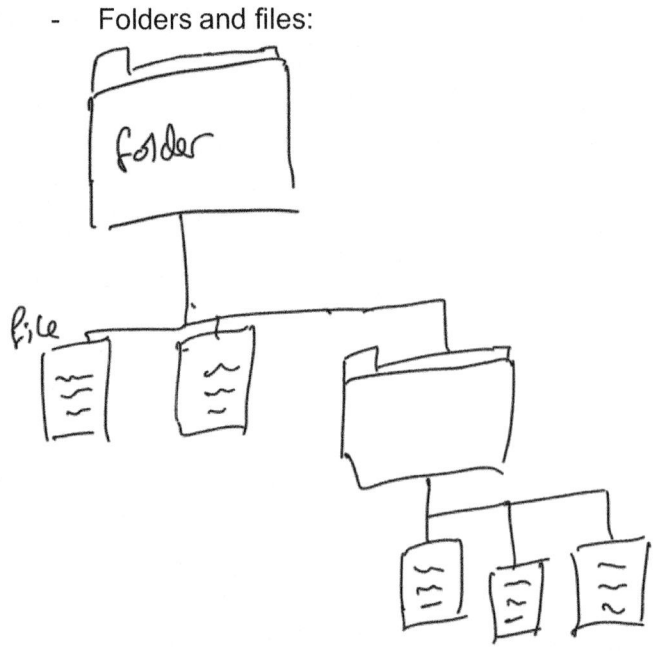

- A graphical editor, that allows you to group shapes together, and group groups of shapes together. When dragging a group, all shapes should move together in the same way:

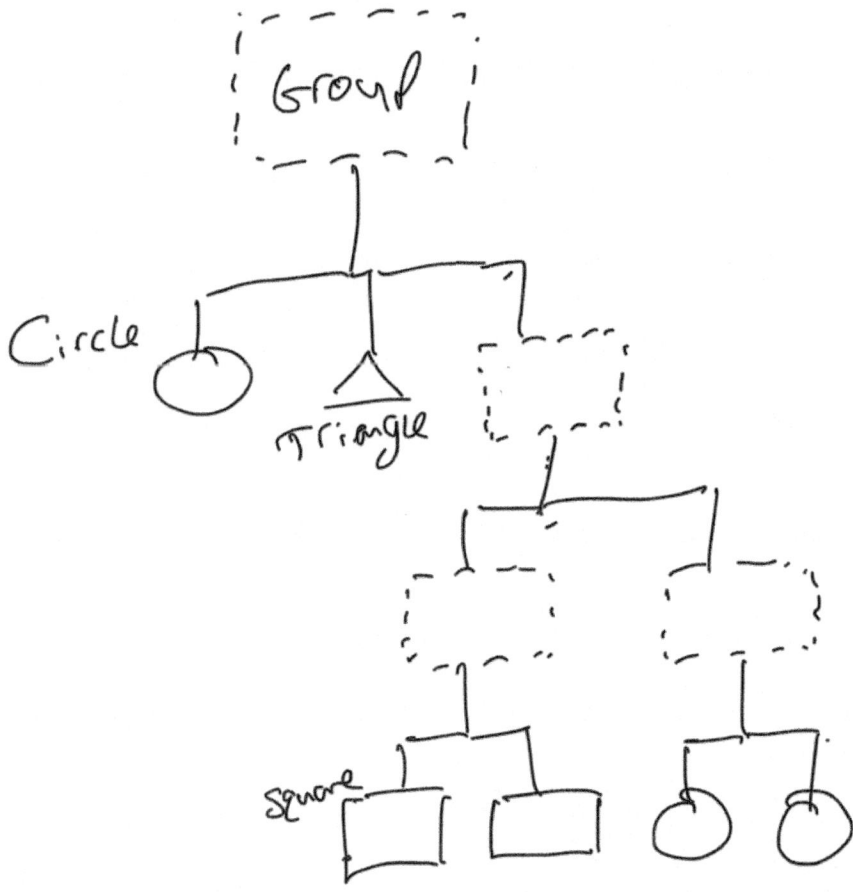

Adapter Pattern

The Adapter pattern is a structural design pattern that allows incompatible interfaces between classes to work together by providing a wrapper that translates one interface into another.

Let's create a scenario that will help you to understand this pattern, and its use-cases:

Say we have a video editing application that allows users to upload a video and change the color of the video. The application provides preset color options for the user to select, such as black and white, or midnight purple.

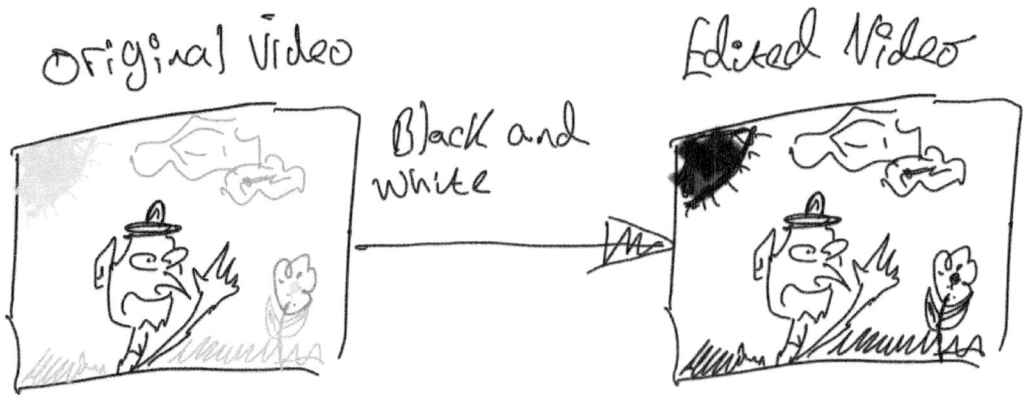

(if you're reading on a black and white device, just imagine the original video in color!)

The classes that change the color of the application are built by us, and implement a `Color` interface. Here's how the application looks:

```
public class Video
{
  // video fields and methods...
}

public interface Color
{
  void Apply(Video video);
}

public class BlackAndWhiteColor : Color
{
  public void Apply(Video video)
  {
     System.Console.WriteLine("Applying black and white color to video");
  }
}

public class MidnightColor : Color
```

```csharp
{
  public void Apply(Video video)
  {
    System.Console.WriteLine("Applying midnight-purple color to video"); ;
  }
}

public class VideoEditor
{
  private Video _video;

  public VideoEditor(Video video)
  {
    _video = video;
  }

  public void ApplyColor(Color color)
  {
    color.Apply(_video);
  }
}
```

Using this solution:

```csharp
var video = new Video();
var videoEditor = new VideoEditor(video);
videoEditor.ApplyColor(new BlackAndWhiteColor());
```

We then decide to install a 3rd-party library into our application that allows users to apply more types of colors to their videos.

The problem is that all concrete color classes are expected to implement our `Color` interface and have an `Apply()` method. But, the concrete color classes from the installed library do not, meaning that we can't pass them to our `videoEditor.ApplyColor()` method, like this:

```
// Rainbow is a color class from the 3rd-party library
videoEditor.ApplyColor(new Rainbow());
```

We cannot modify the 3rd-party library code to make the color classes implement our `Color` interface. So, how do we solve this…

We can solve this by converting the interface of the 3rd party color classes to a different form, using the Adapter pattern.

So far, we can't use `Rainbow` because it doesn't implement `Color`, and we can't make it implement `Color` because it's inside a 3rd party package:

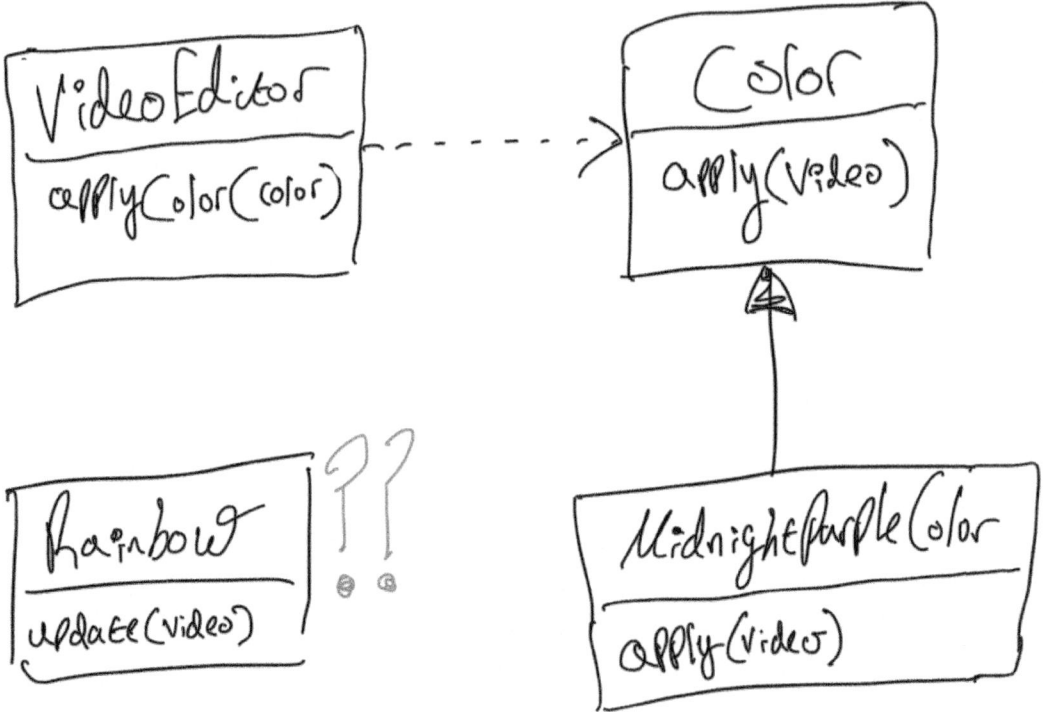

Solution:

We create a `RainbowColor` class that implements `Color` and is composed of the 3rd party `Rainbow` class. We can then call the `Apply()` method in `RainbowColor`, and, inside it, call whatever methods we need to call from `Rainbow` to apply the filter. We *adapt* the class to a different form:

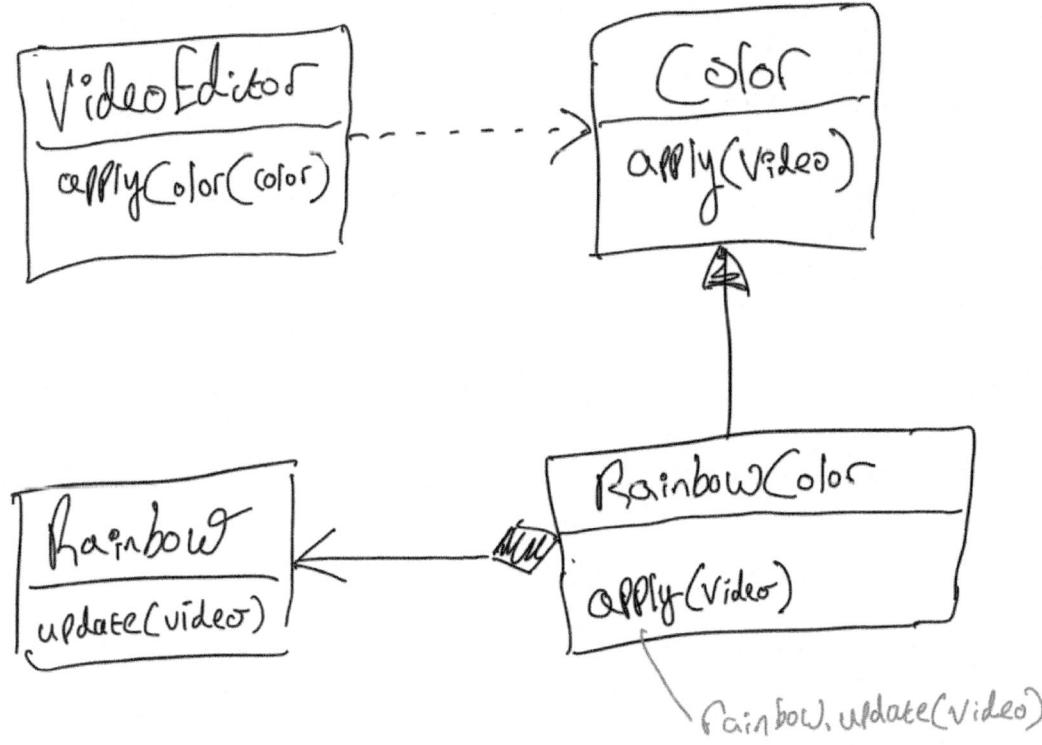

`RainbowColor` is the adapter: it's converting the interface of the `Rainbow` ("adaptee") class into a different form (`Color`).

GoF UML:

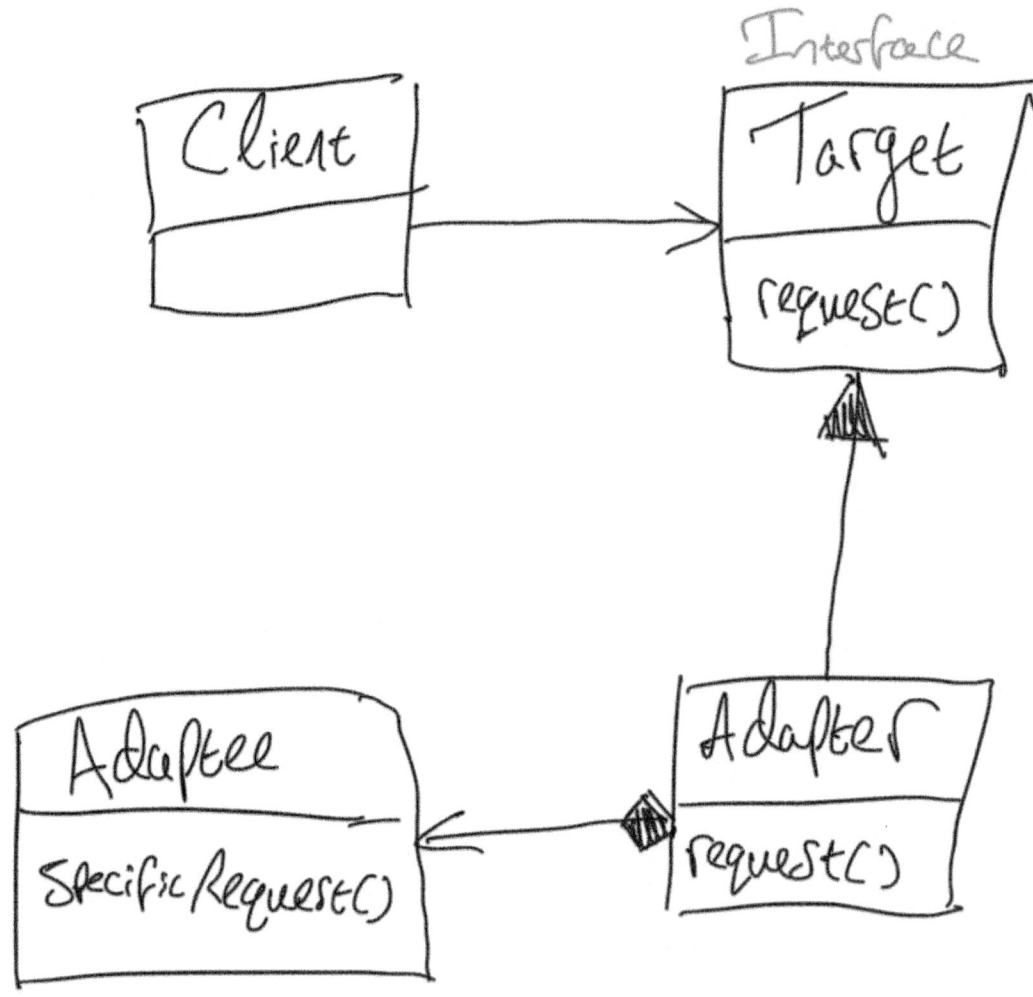

Let's now implement this in code:

Here's what the `Rainbow` class looks like from the 3rd-party library:

```
public class Rainbow
{
  public void Setup()
  {
     System.Console.WriteLine("Setting up rainbow filter");
  }

  public void Update(Video video)
  {
```

```csharp
    System.Console.WriteLine("Applying rainbow filter to video");
  }
}
```

Let's create an adapter class that adapts `Rainbow` to use our `Color` interface, so that it can be used by our `VideoEditor` class, without having to modify it:

```csharp
// Adapter class. Rainbow is the adaptee
public class RainbowColor : Color
{
  private Rainbow _rainbow; // "composition" -- RainbowColor is composed of, "has a", Rainbow. See RainbowAdapter for inheritance alternative.

  public RainbowColor(Rainbow rainbow)
  {
    _rainbow = rainbow;
  }

  public void Apply(Video video)
  {
    _rainbow.Setup();
    _rainbow.Update(video);
  }
}
```

We can now apply the rainbow color to our videos, just like the other colors:

```csharp
videoEditor.ApplyColor(new RainbowColor(new Rainbow()));
```

`RainbowColor` is a wrapper that translates one interface into another. Now, to use any other color from the library, we can create a new wrapper/adapter class to make it compatible with `VideoEditor` – satisfying the open/closed principle.

We created our adapter via composition, but it's also possible to use inheritance. Here's how the adapter looks using inheritance:

```
public class RainbowAdapter : Rainbow, Color
{
  public void Apply(Video video)
  {
    Setup();
    Update(video);
  }
}
```

This class does the same thing as `RainbowColor`, but uses inheritance, rather than composition. With inheritance, the `Rainbow` methods can be called directly.

Problem: this approach isn't as flexible as using composition, because, in C#, a class can only extend one class; so, if `Color` was an abstract class, we wouldn't be able to extend it. In this case, we're OK, because `Color` is an interface, but you can see that inheritance is less flexible than composition, and therefore composition should be preferred.

Bridge Pattern

The bridge pattern is a design pattern that separates a large class, or a set of related classes into two separate hierarchies so that they can be developed independently from each other.

Say that we have a remote for controlling a radio. There are multiple different brands of radio, and there are different types of remotes:

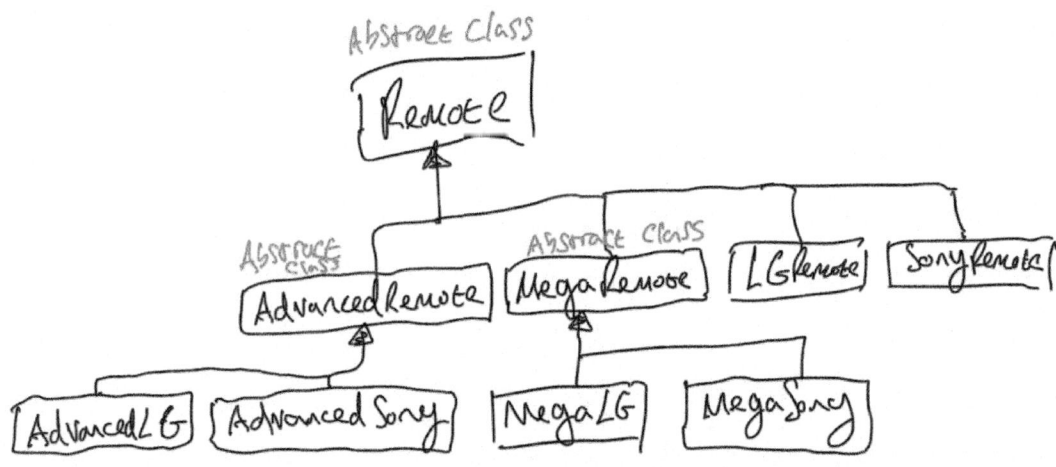

Every time that we add a new brand, e.g. Samsung, we'd have to create three new classes: SamsungRemote, AdvancedSamsungRemote and MegaSamsungRemote. And if we create a new type of remote, e.g. RadioAndTVRemote, then we'd have to create a new class for every brand, so RadioAndTVLG, RadioAndTVSony, RadioAndTVSamsung. This is not maintainable.

Here's this solution in code:

```
public abstract class RemoteControl
{
    public abstract void TurnOn();

    public abstract void TurnOff();

    public abstract void VolumeUp();

    public abstract void VolumeDown();
}

public abstract class AdvancedRemote : RemoteControl
{
    public abstract void SetChannel(int channel);
}

public abstract class RadioAndTVRemote : RemoteControl
```

```csharp
{
  public abstract void ControlTV();

  public abstract void ControlRadio();
}
```

For brevity, lets just implement this for LG devices:

```csharp
public class LGRemote : RemoteControl
{
  public override void TurnOff()
  {
    System.Console.WriteLine("Turning LG radio off");
  }

  public override void TurnOn()
  {
    System.Console.WriteLine("Turning LG radio on");
  }

  public override void VolumeDown()
  {
    System.Console.WriteLine("Turning LG radio volume down");
  }

  public override void VolumeUp()
  {
    System.Console.WriteLine("Turning LG radio volume up");
  }
}

public class AdvancedLGRemote : AdvancedRemote
{
  public override void SetChannel(int channel)
  {
```

```csharp
    System.Console.WriteLine("Setting LG channel to " + channel);
}

public override void TurnOff()
{
    System.Console.WriteLine("Turning LG radio off");
}

public override void TurnOn()
{
    System.Console.WriteLine("Turning LG radio on");
}

public override void VolumeDown()
{
    System.Console.WriteLine("Turning LG radio volume down");
}

public override void VolumeUp()
{
    System.Console.WriteLine("Turning LG radio volume up");
}
}

public class LGRadioAndTVLGRemote : RadioAndTVRemote
{
 public override void ControlRadio()
 {
    System.Console.WriteLine("Now controlling LG radio");
 }

 public override void ControlTV()
 {
    System.Console.WriteLine("Now controlling LG TV");
```

```csharp
    }

    public override void TurnOff()
    {
       System.Console.WriteLine("Turning LG device off");
    }

    public override void TurnOn()
    {
       System.Console.WriteLine("Turning LG device on");
    }

    public override void VolumeDown()
    {
       System.Console.WriteLine("Turning LG device volume down");
    }

    public override void VolumeUp()
    {
       System.Console.WriteLine("Turning LG device volume up");
    }
}
```

Using this solution:

```csharp
class Program
{
 static void Main(string[] args)
 {
    var lgRemote = new LGRemote();
    lgRemote.TurnOn(); // Turning LG radio on
    lgRemote.TurnOff(); // Turning LG radio off

    var lgRadioAndTVLGRemote = new LGRadioAndTVLGRemote();
    lgRadioAndTVLGRemote.ControlTV(); // Now controlling LG TV
```

```
    lgRadioAndTVLGRemote.TurnOn();   // Turning LG device on
    lgRadioAndTVLGRemote.VolumeUp(); // Turning LG device volume up
  }
}
```

This solution is very inflexible: add new remote type = need a new class for every brand of TV. Add a new brand = need a new class for every remote type.

The reason we ended up with this structure is because our hierarchy is growing in 2-dimensions: the abstract dimension (remote type) and an implementation dimension (the brand/device).

To simplify this hierarchy, we can break it down into two separate hierarchies:

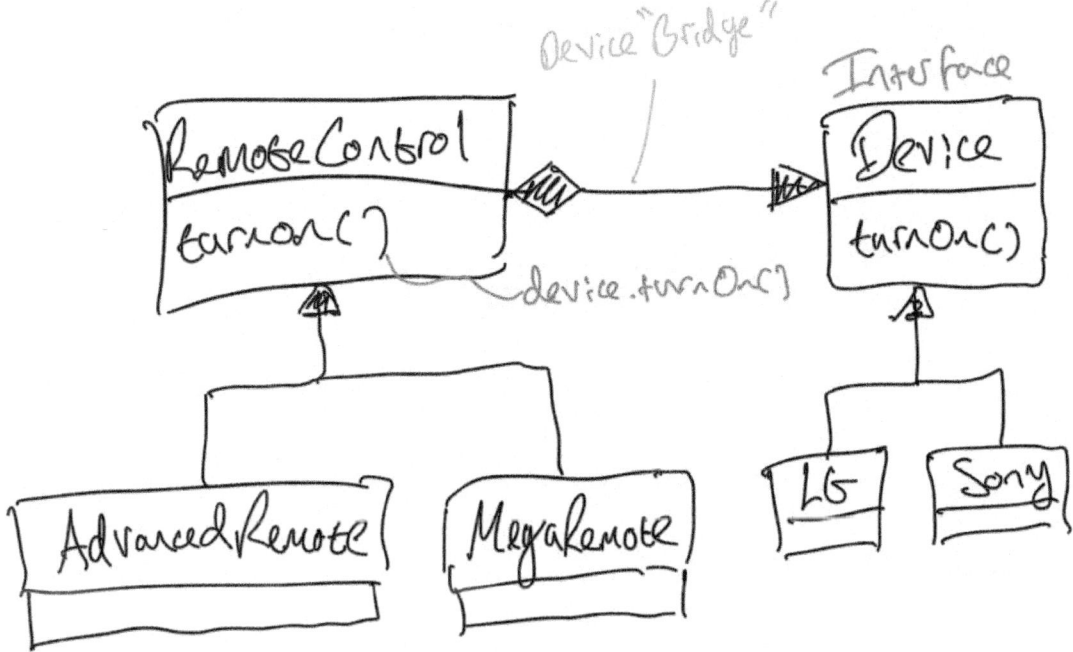

Whenever we have a hierarchy growing in two separate dimensions, we need to split them in half and connect them using a bridge.

The two hierarchies can now grow independently from each other.

GoF UML:

213

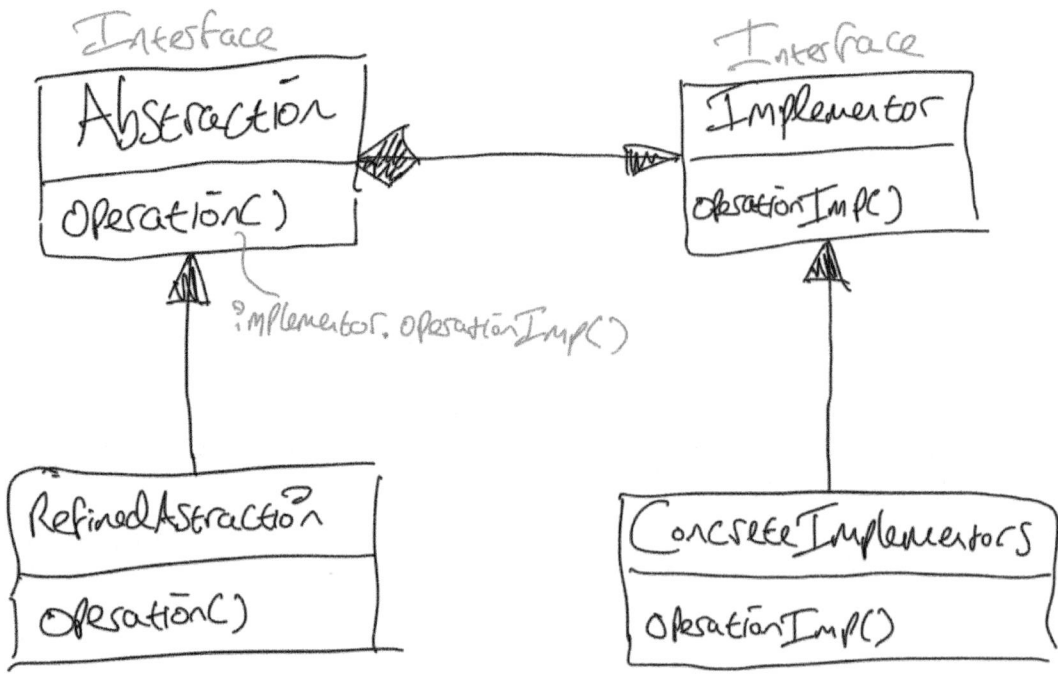

Let's implement this solution in code:

Using two separate hierarchies, composition, and a `Device` bridge to link the two hierarchies, clients now use remotes like so:

```
public interface Device
{
 public void TurnOn();

 public void TurnOff();

 public void SetChannel(int channel);
}

public class RemoteControl
{
 private Device _device;
```

```csharp
    public RemoteControl(Device device)
    {
       _device = device;
    }

    public void TurnOn()
    {
       _device.TurnOn();
    }

    public void TurnOff()
    {
       _device.TurnOff();
    }

    // other basic remote methods...
}

public class AdvancedRemote : RemoteControl
{
  public AdvancedRemote(Device device) : base(device)
   {
   }

   public void SetChannel(int channel)
   {
      System.Console.WriteLine("Setting channel to " + channel);
   }
}

public class LGRadio : Device
{
  public void TurnOff()
   {
```

```csharp
     System.Console.WriteLine("Turning LG radio off");
   }

  public void TurnOn()
  {
     System.Console.WriteLine("Turning LG radio on");
  }

  public void SetChannel(int channel)
  {
     System.Console.WriteLine("Setting LG radio channel to " + channel);
  }
}

public class SonyRadio : Device
{
  public void TurnOff()
  {
     System.Console.WriteLine("Turning Sony radio off");
  }

  public void TurnOn()
  {
     System.Console.WriteLine("Turning Sony radio on");
  }

  public void SetChannel(int channel)
  {
     System.Console.WriteLine("Setting Sony radio channel to " + channel);
  }
}
```

Here's how a client would use this solution:

```
class Program
{
  static void Main(string[] args)
  {
    var lgRemoteControl = new RemoteControl(new LGRadio());
    lgRemoteControl.TurnOn(); // Turning LG radio on
    lgRemoteControl.TurnOff(); // Turning LG radio off

    var advancedSonyControl = new AdvancedRemote(new SonyRadio());
    advancedSonyControl.TurnOn(); // Turning Sony radio on
    advancedSonyControl.TurnOff(); // Turning Sony radio off
  }
}
```

As remote control now delegates the work to the device via a bridge (composition), the device hierarchy and remote type hierarchy can grow independently from each other. Now, if we add a new brand of radio, we only need to create one new class. Our code is now more flexible and easier to maintain. Nice!

Proxy Pattern

The proxy pattern is a structural design pattern that provides a proxy, or agent, object to control access to another object, allowing for additional functionality such as caching, logging, lazy loading or access control, without changing the client's code.

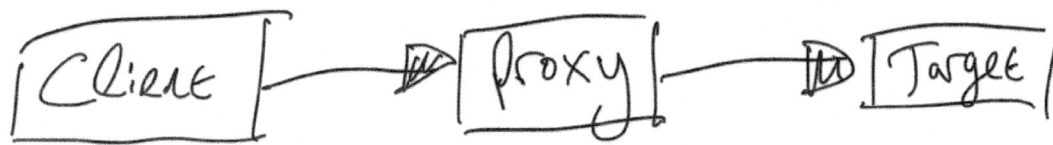

Let's say that we have an application that fetches a list of YouTube videos from YouTube's API, and displays them in a list. In our application we are using a 3rd-party YouTube package to handle fetching YouTube videos from the API, and then rendering the video on the screen with the video controls.

The problem is that every time a request is made to our application, our server has to re-download the videos from the YouTube API. This takes a long time, especially if lots of requests are made to our application at once.

Here's the interface for what a video object should look like from our third-party video library:

```
public interface Video
{
  void Render();

  string GetVideoId();
}
```

Here's what the class from the third-party library looks like for creating YouTube video objects:

```
public class YouTubeVideo : Video
{
  private string _videoId;

  public YouTubeVideo(string videoId)
  {
    _videoId = videoId;
    Download();
  }

  private void Download()
  {
    System.Console.WriteLine("Downloading video with id " + _videoId + " from YouTube API");
  }

  public void Render()
```

```csharp
    {
        System.Console.WriteLine("Rendering video " + _videoId);
    }

    public string GetVideoId()
    {
        return _videoId;
    }
}
```

As you can see, creating a new YouTube object causes the whole video to be downloaded (see the constructor).

Here's what *our* video list class looks like:

```csharp
public class VideoList
{
 private Dictionary<string, Video> _videoList = new Dictionary<string, Video>();

    public void Add(Video video)
    {
        _videoList.Add(video.GetVideoId(), video);
    }

    public void Watch(string videoId)
    {
        var video = _videoList[videoId];
        video.Render();
    }
}
```

And here's how this solution would be used:

```csharp
class Program
{
```

```
static void Main(string[] args)
{
    var videoList = new VideoList();
    String[] videoIds = { "1234", "abcde", "javasc123" };
    foreach (var videoId in videoIds)
    {
        videoList.Add(new YouTubeVideo(videoId));
    }
    // Logs from each loop:
    // 1. Downloading video with id 1234 from YouTube API
    // 2. Downloading video with id abcde from YouTube API
    // 3. Downloading video with id javasc123 from YouTube API

    videoList.Watch("abcde"); // Rendering video abcde
}
```

Just adding a video to our list class causes that whole video to be downloaded, even if the user doesn't want to watch that video. Above, the user only wants to watch video "abcde", so it would be much more efficient to download the video only after the user has selected a video from the video list. This is called "lazy loading" – delaying the loading of something for when it is required.

Problem is, the YouTubeVideo class is from a third-party library, so we are unable to modify it's code. The solution is to use a proxy object:

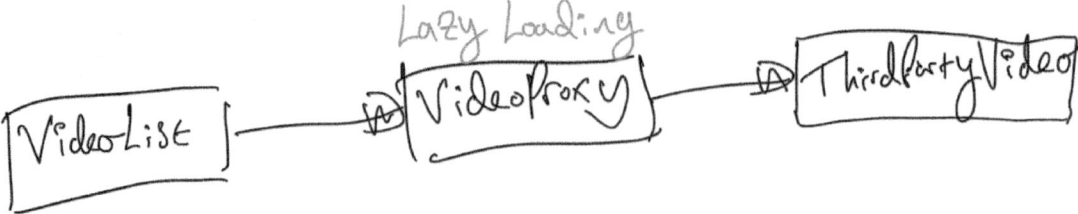

Our VideoList object will now talk to VideoProxy objects.

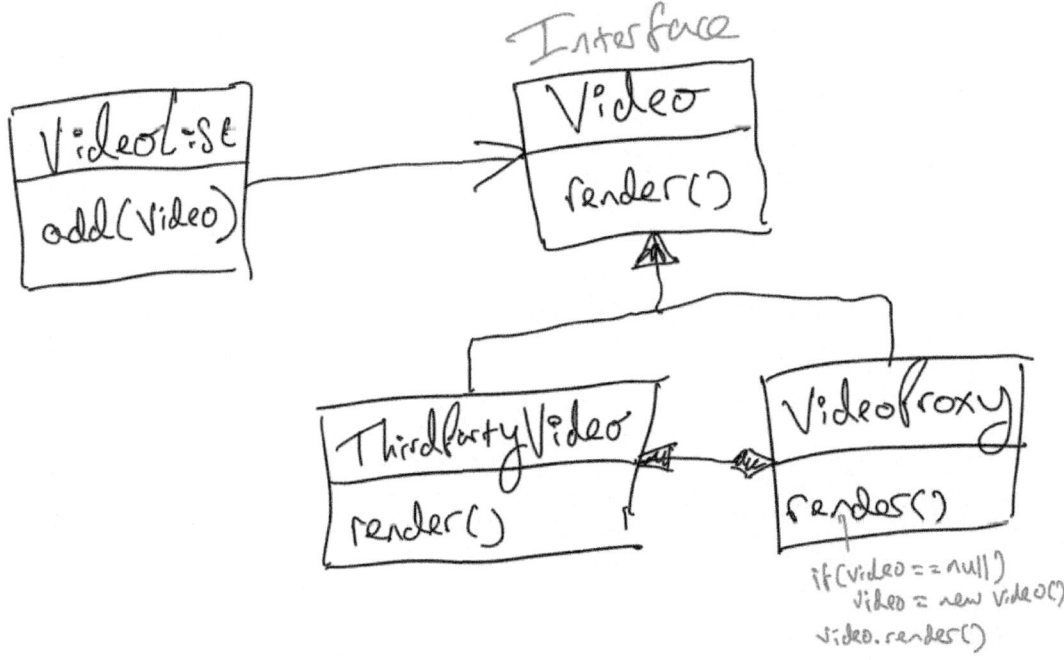

The above UML shows that our VideoProxy object will implement the third-party libraries Video interface, meaning that we can add these video proxy objects to our VideoList, and VideoList won't care whether it's a ThirdPartyVideo or a VideoProxy, as long as it is a Video.

GoF UML:

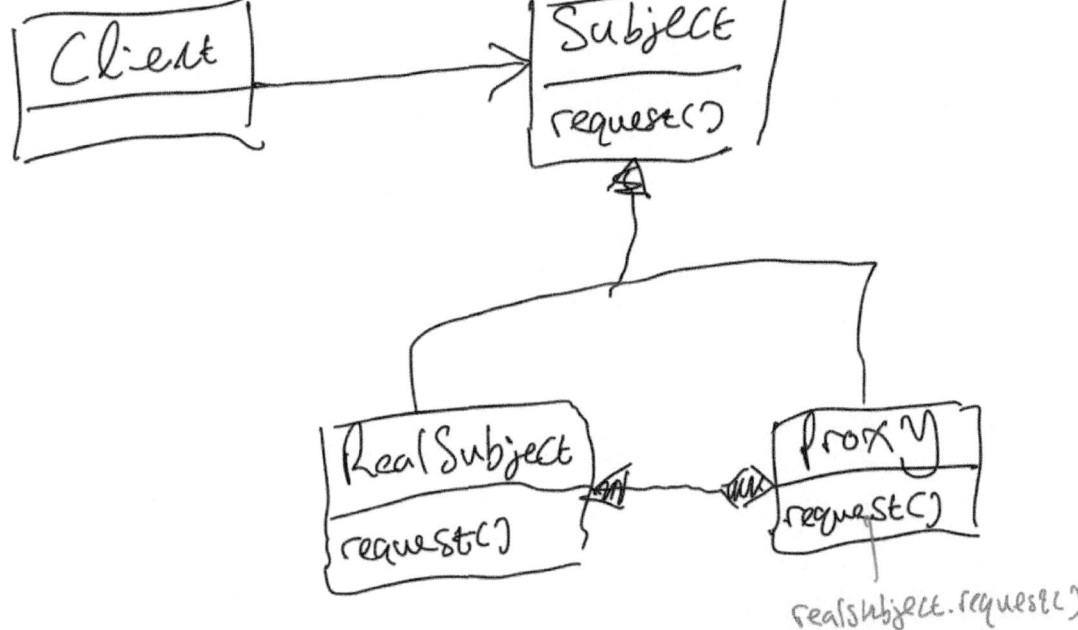

Let's now implement this Proxy pattern solution in code:

```
public class YouTubeVideoProxy : Video
{
 private string _videoId;
 private YouTubeVideo _youTubeVideo;

 public YouTubeVideoProxy(string videoId)
 {
    _videoId = videoId;
 }

 public void Render()
 {
    if (_youTubeVideo == null)
    {
       _youTubeVideo = new YouTubeVideo(_videoId);
    }

    _youTubeVideo.Render();
 }

 public string GetVideoId()
 {
    return _videoId;
 }
}
```

We now add these proxy objects in place of the real youtube video class:

```
class Program
{
 static void Main(string[] args)
```

```csharp
{
    var videoList = new VideoList();
    String[] videoIds = { "1234", "abcde", "javasc123" };
    foreach (var videoId in videoIds)
    {
        videoList.Add(new YouTubeVideoProxy(videoId)); // We now use our "placeholder", or "proxy" class
    }

    // Video is now only downloaded when user wants to watch it:
    videoList.Watch("abcde");
    // Logs:
    // Downloading video with id abcde from YouTube API
    // Rendering video abcde
}
}
```

Flyweight Pattern

The Flyweight pattern is a structural design pattern that aims to minimize memory usage by sharing common state between multiple objects, allowing efficient handling of large numbers of lightweight objects with shared characteristics.

Say that we have a farming game that includes different types of crops, such as potatoes, carrots and wheat. Each crop is represented by a crop object, that includes its x and y coordinates, the type of crop, and an icon:

In code:

```
public enum CropType
{
 Potato,
 Carrot,
 Wheat
}

public class Crop
{
 private int _x; // 4 bytes
 private int _y; // 4 bytes
 private CropType _cropType; // 4 bytes
 private byte[] _icon; // 40 KB -> if there are 1000 points to render, that's 40 MB of memory. Many mobile devices would struggle with that.

   public Crop(int x, int y, CropType cropType, byte[] icon)
```

```csharp
{
    _x = x;
    _y = y;
    _cropType = cropType;
    _icon = icon;
}

public void Render()
{
    System.Console.WriteLine($"Drawing {_cropType} at ({_x}, {_y})");
}
}

public class CropService
{
    public List<Crop> GetCrops()
    {
        List<Crop> cropList = new List<Crop>();

        // Simulate fetching from database
        var carrot = new Crop(1, 4, CropType.Carrot, null); // passing null for icon for convenience
        var carrot2 = new Crop(1, 5, CropType.Carrot, null);
        var carrot3 = new Crop(1, 6, CropType.Carrot, null);

        cropList.Add(carrot);
        cropList.Add(carrot2);
        cropList.Add(carrot3);
        return cropList;
    }
}
```

Using this:

```
class Program
{
  static void Main(string[] args)
  {
    var cropService = new CropService();
    foreach (var crop in cropService.GetCrops())
    {
      crop.Render();
    }

    // Logs:
    // Drawing Carrot at (1, 4)
    // Drawing Carrot at (1, 5)
    // Drawing Carrot at (1, 6)
  }
}
```

The problem with the above solution is that for every carrot created, we are storing a new object with all of the information about a carrot stored within that object. This means that if we create 1000 carrots, then we will be storing 1000 carrot icons in RAM – that is going to take up lots of memory, and many mobile devices will struggle to handle that.

What if we could share icons between crop objects of the same type...

If a carrot is created with the `Crop` class, then its `icon` and `cropType` fields will remain constant for the lifetime of the object; but its `x` and `y` coordinates will vary, as the crop can be harvested and moved around.

- State that remains the same throughout the object's life is called *internal state*.
- State that can change is called *extrinsic state*.

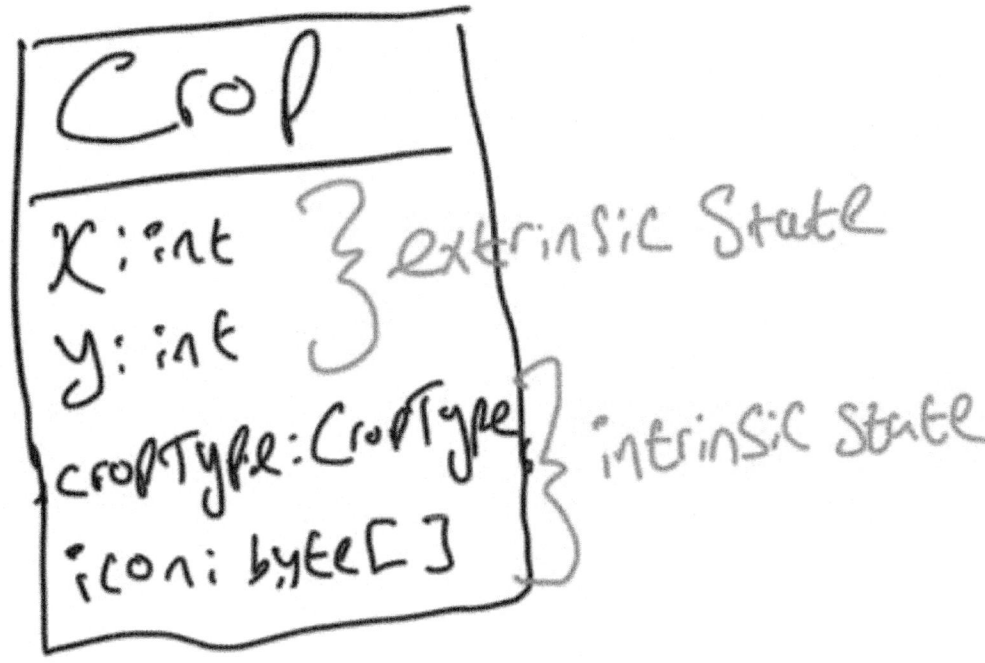

So, if we can extract the intrinsic state out of Crop, and place it into a new object, called CropIcon, then we would only need to create three CropIcon objects (for potato, carrot and wheat) in our application, even if there are 1000s of crops in the game.

We can then, for example, have just one carrot icon object stored in memory, then all crops of type carrot can reference, or reuse, that carrot icon object throughout the game:

An object that contains only intrinsic state is called a *Flyweight*.

But we shouldn't create `CropIcon` objects directly. We can create a factory class that creates an icon, depending on the icon type, and caches that icon in memory – ensuring that it's only created once, and stored in one place.

Here's the overall structure:

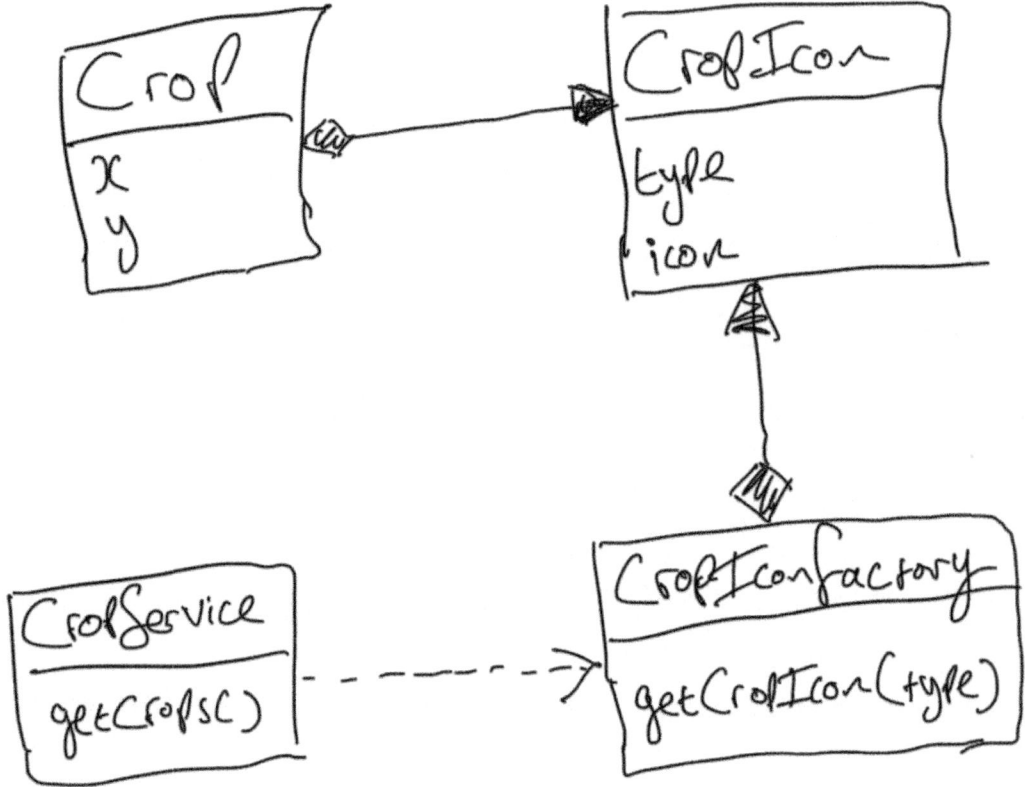

GoF:

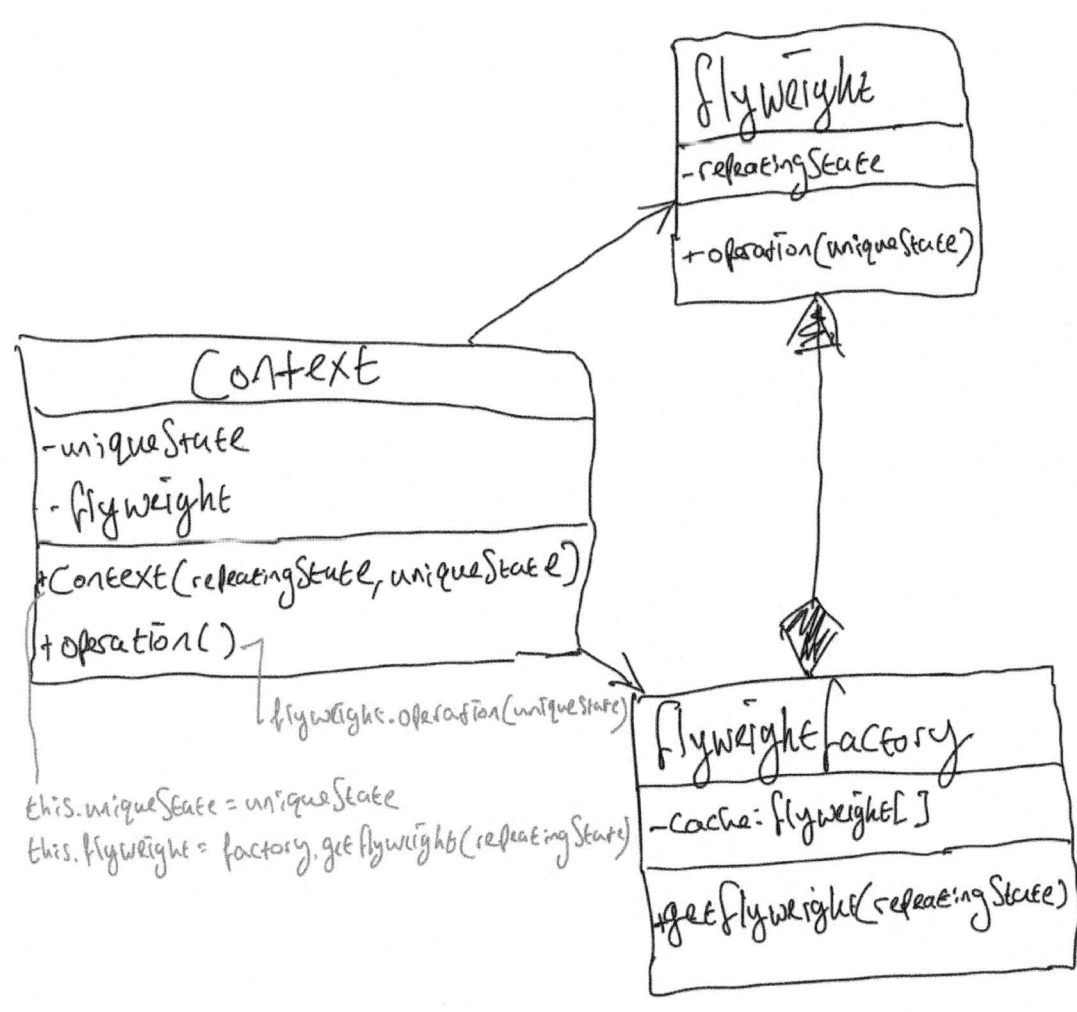

Lets now implement our farming game crops using the Flyweight pattern:

```
public enum CropType
{
  Potato,
  Carrot,
  Wheat
}

// Extrinsic, dynamic, state stored here. Intrinsic state,
// CropIcon -- the Flyweight class -- is referenced.
public class Crop
{
```

```csharp
   private int _x;
   private int _y;
   private CropIcon _cropIcon;

   public Crop(int x, int y, CropIcon cropIcon)
   {
      _x = x;
      _y = y;
      _cropIcon = cropIcon;
   }

   public void Render()
   {
      System.Console.WriteLine($"Drawing {_cropIcon.GetType()} at ({_x}, {_y})");
   }
}

// The Flyweight class stores intrinsic state -- the state that
// remains constant throughout the objects life
public class CropIcon
{
  // `readonly` ensures that once constructed, they cannot be
  // changed later on.
  private readonly CropType _type;
  private readonly byte[] _icon;

  public CropIcon(CropType type, byte[] icon)
  {
     _type = type;
     _icon = icon;
  }

  public CropType GetType()
```

```csharp
    {
        return _type;
    }
}

// This class ensures that each unique crop icon object is
// created only once, cached, and reused/shared between crop
// objects.
public class CropIconFactory
{
    // Icon cache
    private Dictionary<CropType, CropIcon> _icons = new Dictionary<CropType, CropIcon>();

    public CropIcon GetCropIcon(CropType cropType)
    {
        // check if icon already exists
        if (!_icons.ContainsKey(cropType))
        {
            // icon doesn't exist, so create one and add it to cache
            var icon = new CropIcon(cropType, null); // using null for convenience, but this could be, for example, a reference to file location
            _icons.Add(cropType, icon);
        }

        // here, we know the icon exists, so retrieve it from cache and return it
        return _icons[cropType];
    }
}

public class CropService
{
```

```
    private CropIconFactory _iconFactory;

    public CropService(CropIconFactory iconFactory)
    {
        _iconFactory = iconFactory;
    }

    public List<Crop> GetCrops()
    {
        List<Crop> crops = new List<Crop>();

        // all three carrots now reference the same CropIcon object, saving RAM
        var carrot = new Crop(1, 4, _iconFactory.GetCropIcon(CropType.Carrot));
        var carrot2 = new Crop(1, 5, _iconFactory.GetCropIcon(CropType.Carrot));
        var carrot3 = new Crop(1, 6, _iconFactory.GetCropIcon(CropType.Carrot));

        crops.Add(carrot);
        crops.Add(carrot2);
        crops.Add(carrot3);

        return crops;
    }
}
```

Using this solution is similar to before:

```
class Program
{
  static void Main(string[] args)
  {
```

```
// the only difference from before is that we now have to pass
a CropIconFactory object to CropService, to ensure icons are
cached, created only once, and reused between the same crops
    var cropService = new CropService(new CropIconFactory());
    foreach (var crop in cropService.GetCrops())
    {
        crop.Render();
    }

    // Logs:
    // Drawing Carrot at (1, 4)
    // Drawing Carrot at (1, 5)
    // Drawing Carrot at (1, 6)
  }
}
```

We created three carrot crop objects, but only one carrot crop icon object. This solution will save lots of RAM when rendering many crops at one time. Nice!

Facade Pattern

The Facade pattern is a structural design pattern that provides a simplified interface to a complex system, encapsulating the complexities of multiple subsystems into a single unified interface for clients.

Say that we have an eCommerce application that allows users to submit orders. Here are the steps involved:

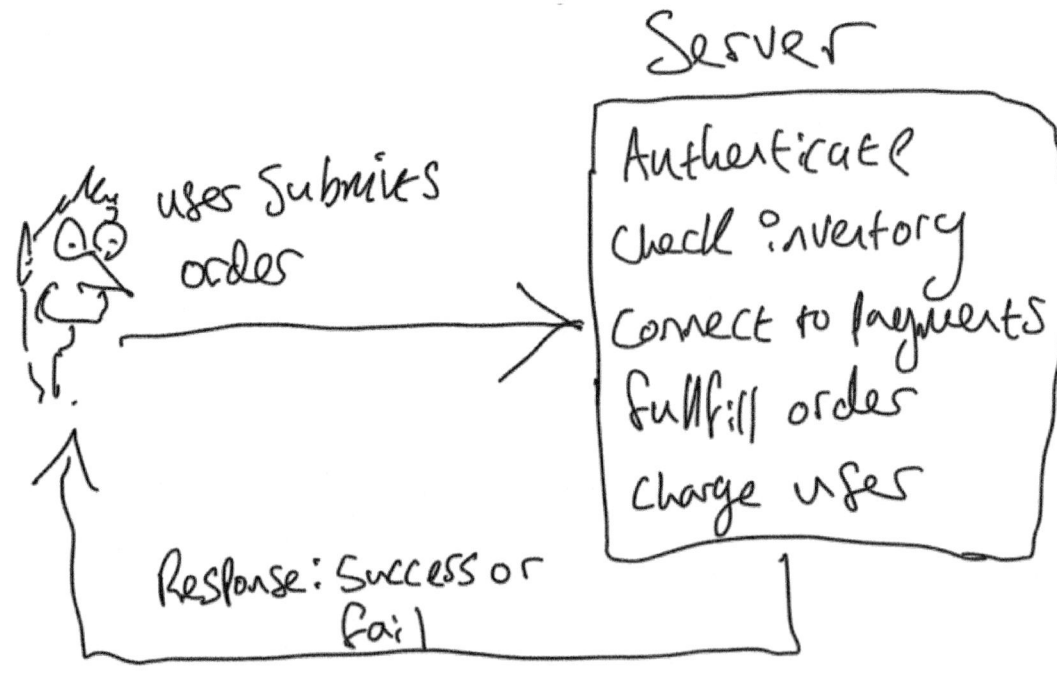

As you can see, there are five main steps involved in processing an order. Let's implement this roughly in code:

```
// Request object containing user-submitted data
public class OrderRequest
{
  public string Name { get; } = "danny";
  public string CardNumber { get; } = "1234";
  public float Amount { get; } = 20.99f;
  public string Address { get; } = "123 Springfield Way, Texas";
  // item ids user wants to order
  public string[] ItemIds { get; } = { "123", "423", "555", "989" };
}

public class Authenticate
{

}
```

```csharp
public class Inventory
{
 public bool CheckInventory(string itemId)
 {
   return true; // just return true to keep example simple
 }

 public void ReduceInventory(string itemId, int amount)
 {
   System.Console.WriteLine("Reducing inventory of " + itemId + " by " + amount);
 }
}

public class Payment
{
 private readonly string _name;
 private readonly string _cardNumber;
 private readonly float _amount;

 public Payment(string name, string cardNumber, float amount)
 {
   _name = name;
   _cardNumber = cardNumber;
   _amount = amount;
 }

 public void Pay()
 {
   System.Console.WriteLine("Charging card with name " + _name);
 }
}

public class OrderFulfillment
```

```csharp
{
  private Inventory _inventory;

  public OrderFulfillment(Inventory inventory)
  {
     _inventory = inventory;
  }

  public void Fulfill(string name, string address, string[] items)
  {
     System.Console.WriteLine("Inserting order into database");
     foreach (var item in items)
     {
        _inventory.ReduceInventory(item, 1);
     }
  }
}
```

Here's how a client would use this solution:

```csharp
class Program
{
  static void Main(string[] args)
  {
     // Order request contains info that user has submitted when requesting to make an order
     var orderReq = new OrderRequest();

     var auth = new Authenticate();

     var inventory = new Inventory();
     foreach (var id in orderReq.ItemIds)
     {
        inventory.CheckInventory(id);
     }
```

```
    var payment = new Payment(orderReq.Name, orderReq.CardNumber,
orderReq.Amount);
    payment.Pay();

    var orderFulfillment = new OrderFulfillment(inventory);
    orderFulfillment.Fulfill(orderReq.Name, orderReq.Address,
orderReq.ItemIds);

    // Logs:
    // Charging card with name danny
    // Inserting order into database
    // Reducing inventory of 123 by 1
    // Reducing inventory of 423 by 1
    // Reducing inventory of 555 by 1
    // Reducing inventory of 989 by 1
  }
}
```

As you can see, every client that needs to make an order has to go through all of these steps to make a single order. Every client becomes coupled to, or dependent on, four classes: `Authenticate`, `Inventory`, `Payment`, and `OrderFulfillment`.

If we had ten classes that needed to make an order, then we'd have ten classes dependent on these four classes – that's a lot of coupling. If one of these four classes changes, that's ten classes that may need updating. Not good.

Each client that needs to make an order will be dependent on four classes:

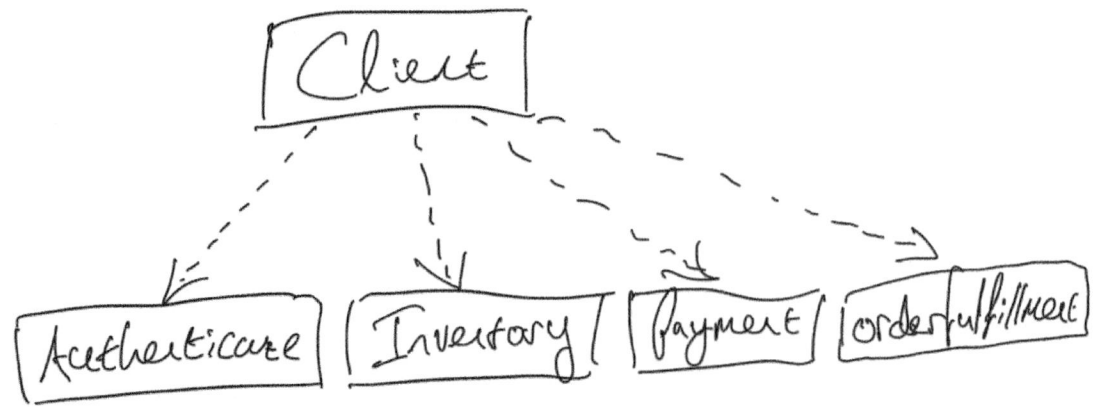

Facade pattern solution:
Clients making an order don't care about, or don't need to know about, the steps involved in making an order; they just want to make an order.

So, let's introduce a new class, OrderService, with a single method, order(), that abstracts all the logic, so all other classes that need to make an order only have to depend on this one class:

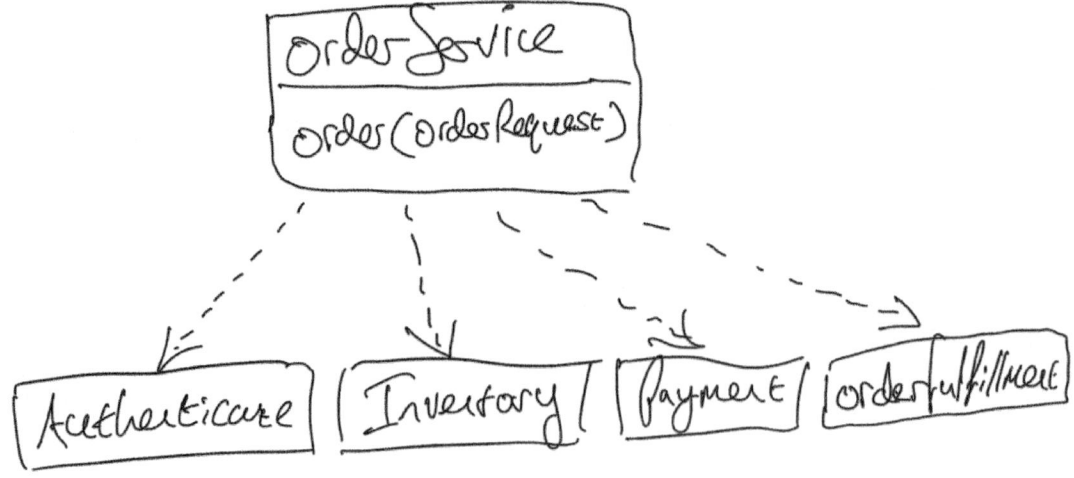

Now, all classes that need to be able to make an order only need to depend on the one OrderService class:

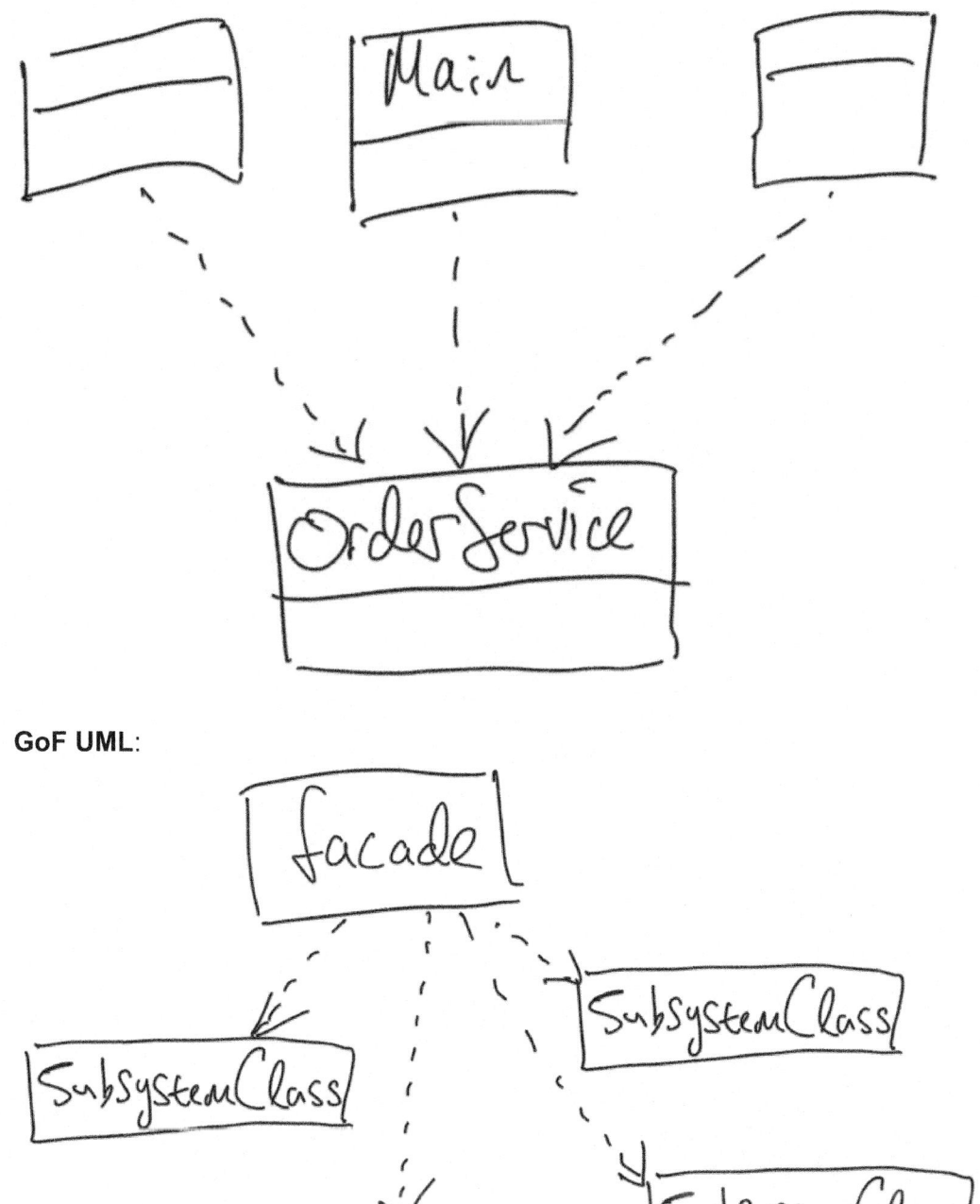

GoF UML:

Implementing `OrderService` in code:

```csharp
// "Facade" that encapsulates all the complexities and steps
// involved in making an order, so clients can make orders without
// having to know all of the details
public class OrderService
{
  public void Order(OrderRequest orderReq)
  {
    var auth = new Authenticate();

    var inventory = new Inventory();
    foreach (var id in orderReq.ItemIds)
    {
      inventory.CheckInventory(id);
    }

    var payment = new Payment(orderReq.Name, orderReq.CardNumber, orderReq.Amount);
    payment.Pay();

    var orderFulfillment = new OrderFulfillment(inventory);
    orderFulfillment.Fulfill(orderReq.Name, orderReq.Address, orderReq.ItemIds);
  }
}
```

Clients can now make orders without having to depend on many classes, and without having to know all of the complexities, as they have been abstracted away and encapsulated in the `OrderService` class:

```csharp
class Program
{
  static void Main(string[] args)
  {
    var orderReq = new OrderRequest();
    var orderService = new OrderService();
```

```
        orderService.Order(orderReq);

    // Logs:
    // Charging card with name danny
    // Inserting order into database
    // Reducing inventory of 123 by 1
    // Reducing inventory of 423 by 1
    // Reducing inventory of 555 by 1
    // Reducing inventory of 989 by 1
    }
}
```

Decorator Pattern

The Decorator pattern is a structural design pattern that allows behavior to be added to individual objects dynamically, enhancing functionality without altering the object's structure, and it's used to extend or modify the behavior of objects by wrapping them with additional functionality through composition.

Say that we have an application that allows users to store data in the cloud. The data can be sent to the cloud as it is, without any processing, and it can also be compressed and/or encrypted before it is saved to the cloud.

Here is the UML diagram:

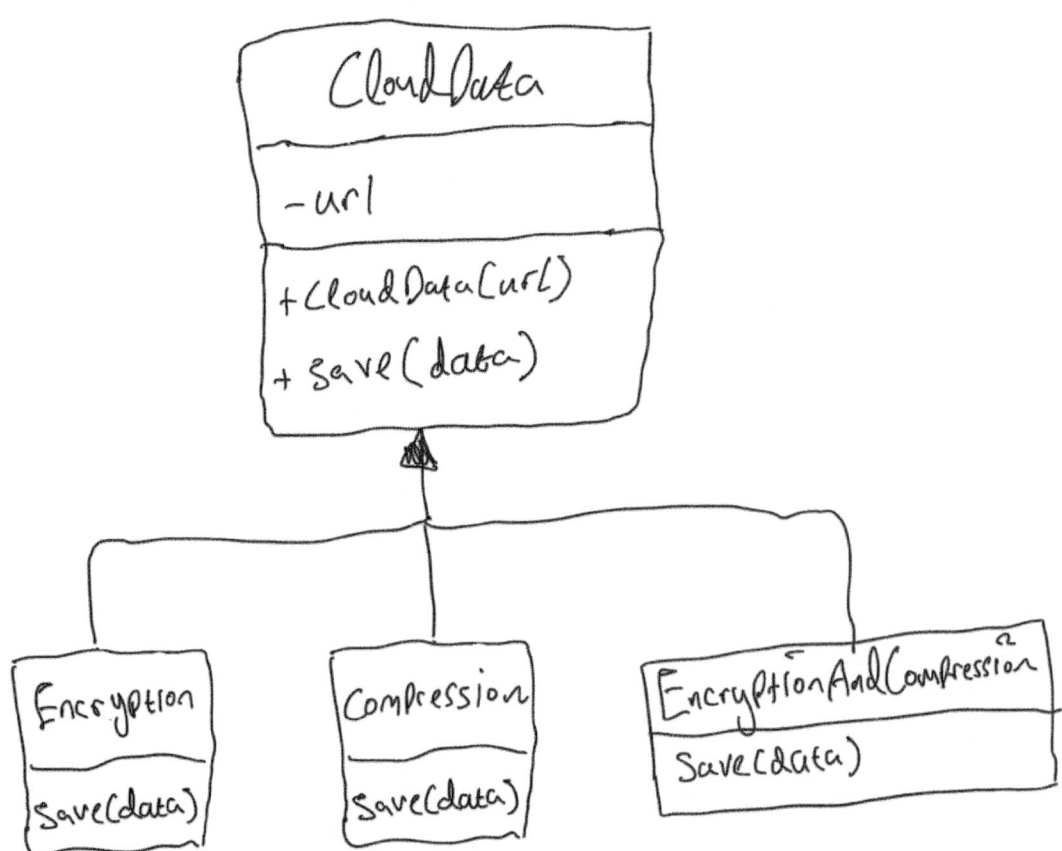

So far, everything looks OK. But then the boss says that we need to create a new validation class to validate and clean the data before it is sent to the cloud. Our code starts to look bloated as we need to make lots of new classes just to add an extra feature:

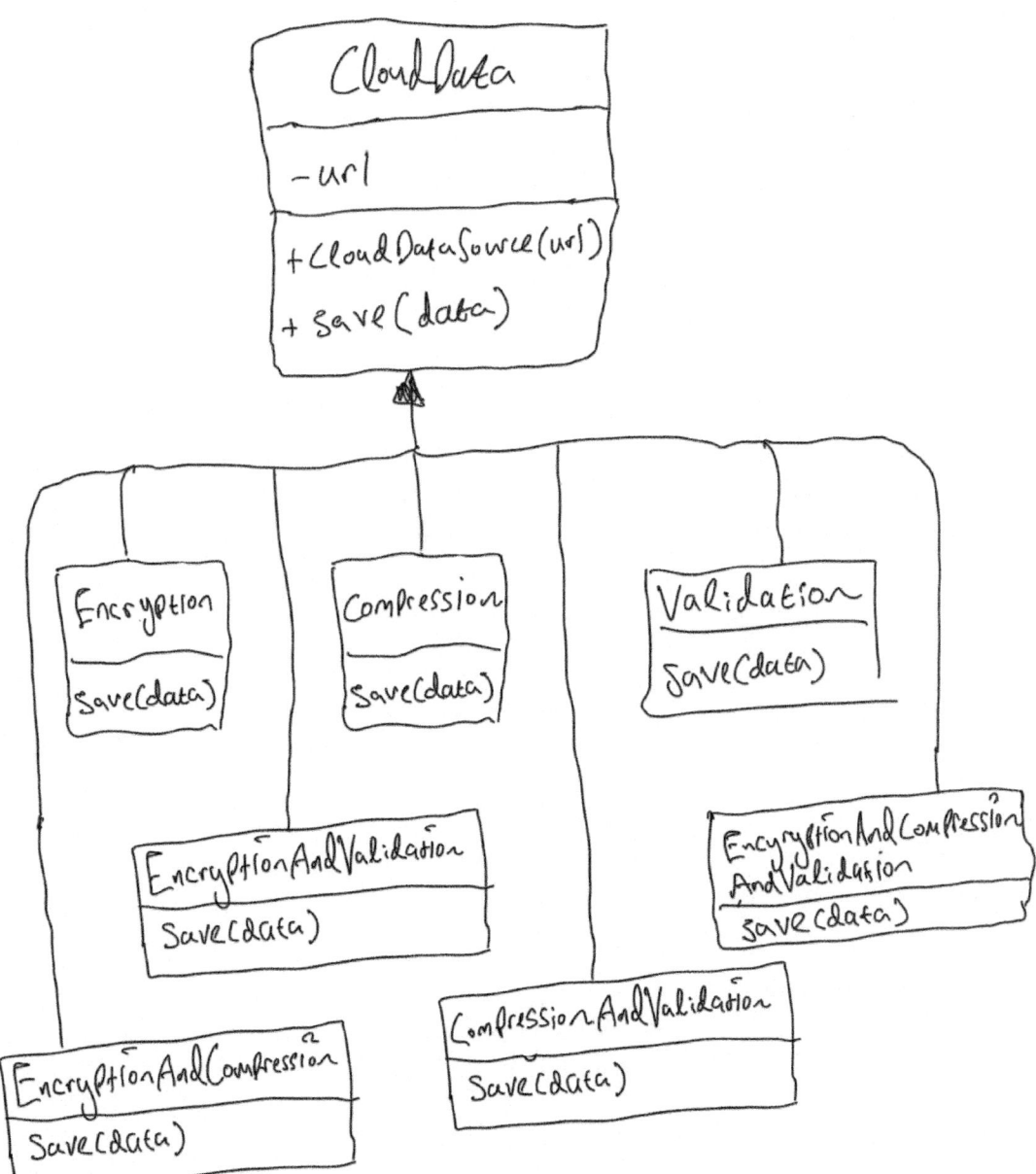

To add one new feature, we have to create four new classes. Our class library is growing exponentially – not good, not maintainable, not flexible!

Let's implement this solution in code:

```
public class CloudData
{
  protected string _url;
```

```csharp
  public CloudData(string url)
  {
    _url = url;
  }

  public virtual void Save(string data)
  {
    System.Console.WriteLine($"Saving data '{data}' to cloud at '{_url}'");
  }
}

public class CompressedData : CloudData
{
  public CompressedData(string url) : base(url)
  {
  }

  public override void Save(string data)
  {
    var compressed = Compress(data);
    base.Save(compressed);
  }

  public string Compress(string data)
  {
    return data.Substring(0, 9); // pretend to compress data
  }
}

public class EncryptedData : CloudData
{
  public EncryptedData(string url) : base(url)
```

```csharp
    {
    }

    public override void Save(string data)
    {
       var encrypted = Encrypt(data);
       base.Save(encrypted);
    }

    public string Encrypt(string data)
    {
       return "$dc&^*()';,,£@%%*(~)`"; // pretend to encrypt data
    }
}

public class CompressedAndEncryptedData : CloudData
{
  public CompressedAndEncryptedData(string url) : base(url)
    {
    }

    public override void Save(string data)
    {
       var compressed = new CompressedData(base._url).Compress(data);
       var encryptedAndComressed = new
EncryptedData(base._url).Encrypt(compressed);
       base.Save(encryptedAndComressed);
    }
}

class Program
{
  static void Main(string[] args)
  {
```

```
  // User input data:
  var url = "https://google.cloud.com";
  var data = "This is some data. Hello world. Facade Facade :)";
  var compress = true;
  var encrypt = true;

  // Now we have to select the correct cloud storage object
  var cloudData = new CloudData(url);

  if (compress && encrypt)
  {
    cloudData = new CompressedAndEncryptedData(url);
  }
  else if (compress)
  {
    cloudData = new CompressedData(url);
  }
  else if (encrypt)
  {
    cloudData = new EncryptedData(url);
  }

  // We have the correct data storage object, so now we can save
the data
  cloudData.Save(data);
 }
}
```

As we discussed, our total number of classes is going to increase exponentially with this solution. But another issue is that we have to perform lots of conditional checks in the client code; for example, if we add a `ValidatedData` class, then we'd have to add conditionals for `(encrypt && compress && validate)`, `(compress && validate)`, `(encrypt && validate)` and `(validate)` – four extra conditionals just to add one new feature! Not good at all! And this will continue to get worse and worse as we add more classes!! Terrible!!!

OK, so let's use a design pattern to solve this mess...

Solution: let's move away from inheritance and use composition instead

You may have noticed by this point that a lot of design patterns are based on moving away from inheritance and towards composition. With composition, one object has reference to another object, and delegates it some work. This allows you to use polymorphism and switch between objects at runtime, making your code flexible. Whereas with inheritance, the object itself is able to do that work, inheriting the behavior from its superclass. With inheritance we have to create lots of new classes; with composition, we can wrap, or decorate, existing objects to add new functionality.

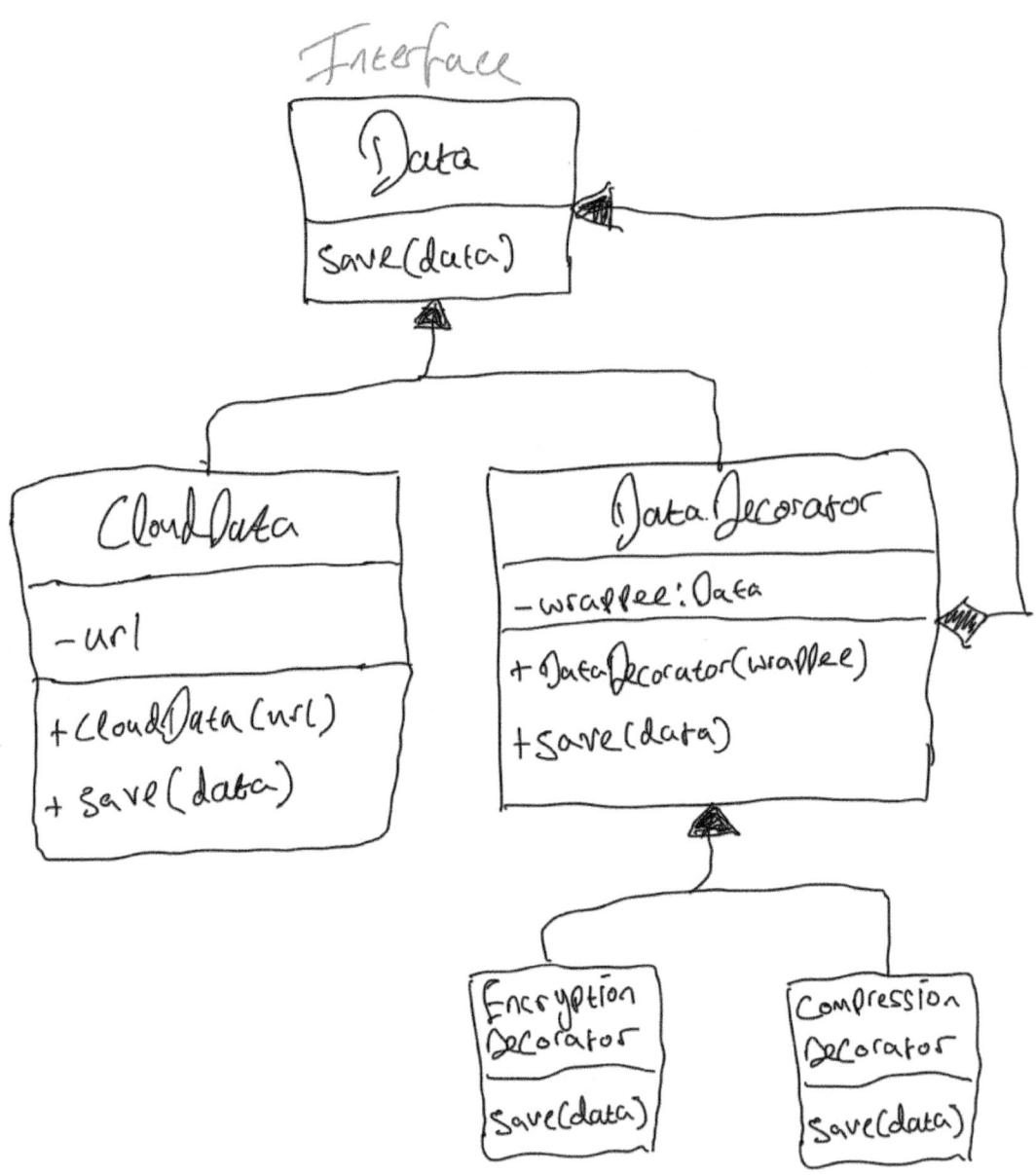

Above, we make the encryption and compression objects *decorators*, because they are decorating the `CloudData` object with some additional behavior. Because decorator classes have some common logic – e.g. referencing a `CloudData` object – we have created a `DataDecorator` class where this logic can be inherited to prevent code repetition.

Our decorator classes are *composed* of (or are *decorating/wrapping*) a `CloudData` object (or any object that implements the `Data` interface).

GoF UML:

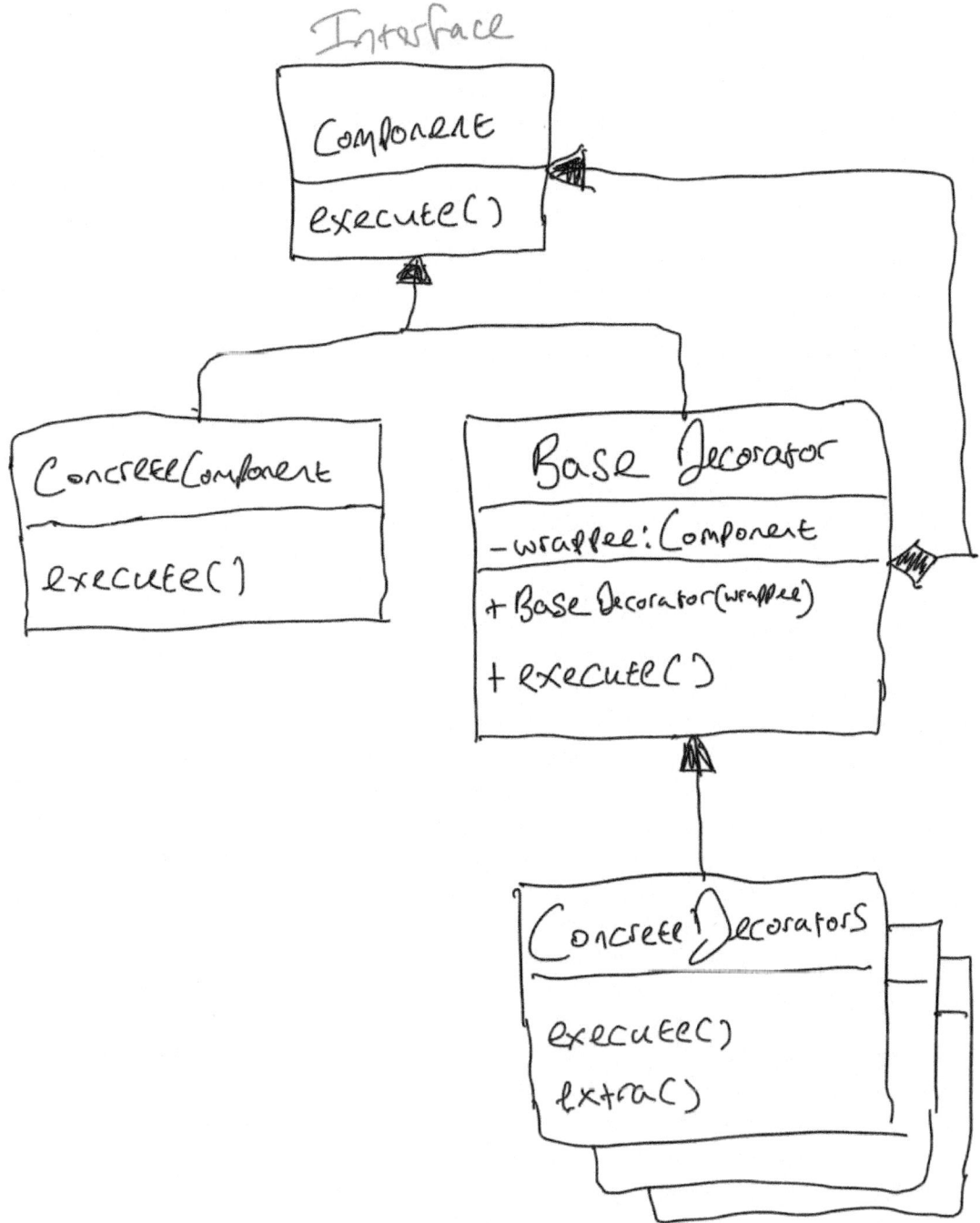

If this is not making much sense, then don't worry – things will become clearer as you code-out this solution:

```csharp
public interface Data
{
    void Save(string data);
}

public class CloudData : Data
{
    private string _url;

    public CloudData(string url)
    {
        _url = url;
    }

    public void Save(string data)
    {
        System.Console.WriteLine($"Saving data '{data}' to cloud at '{_url}'");
    }
}

public abstract class DataDecorator : Data
{
    protected Data _data;

    public DataDecorator(Data data)
    {
        _data = data;
    }

    public abstract void Save(string data);
}

public class CompressionDecorator : DataDecorator
{
```

```csharp
    public CompressionDecorator(Data data) : base(data)
    {
    }


    public override void Save(string data)
    {
       System.Console.WriteLine("Compressing data");
       var compressed = Compress(data);
       base._data.Save(compressed);
    }


    private string Compress(string data)
    {
       return data.Substring(0, 9); // pretend to compress data
    }
}

public class EncryptionDecorator : DataDecorator
{
 public EncryptionDecorator(Data data) : base(data)
    {
    }


    public override void Save(string data)
    {
       System.Console.WriteLine("Encryping data");
       var encrypted = Encrypt(data);
       base._data.Save(encrypted);
    }

    // This can now be private, encapsulating this code
    private string Encrypt(string data)
    {
       return "$dc&^*()';,,£@%%*(~)`"; // pretend to encrypt data
```

```
    }
}
```

By using the Decorator pattern, the client now only needs one conditional per data type. This is because we can now decorate/wrap the `CloudData` object by using composition:

```
class Program
{
  static void Main(string[] args)
  {
    // User input data:
    var url = "https://google.cloud.com";
    var data = "This is some data. Hello world. Facade Facade :)";
    var compress = true;
    var encrypt = true;

    Data cloudData = new CloudData(url);

    if (encrypt)
    {
      cloudData = new EncryptionDecorator(cloudData);
    }
    if (compress)
    {
      cloudData = new CompressionDecorator(cloudData);
    }

    cloudData.Save(data);

    // Logs:
    // Compressing data
    // Encryping data
    // Saving data '$dc&^*()';,,£@%%*(~)`' to cloud at 'https://google.cloud.com'
```

}
}

Nice!

Creational design patterns

Last, but not least: Creational design patterns. Massive congratulations on getting this far – and your reward: Creational design patterns are probably the easiest group of design patterns to learn and understand. So, if you feel like giving up – don't; the hardest work has been done!

Let's go!

Creational design patterns are a category of design patterns that focus on object creation, dealing with the best way to create objects while hiding the creation logic and making the system independent of how its objects are created, composed, and represented.

Benefits of Creational Design Patterns:
1. **Encapsulation of Object Creation**: Creational patterns encapsulate object creation logic, hiding it from clients. This promotes loose coupling and allows the system to be more flexible to changes in how objects are instantiated.
2. **Enhanced Flexibility and Extensibility**: Creational patterns promote flexibility by providing ways to create objects dynamically based on varying requirements or conditions. This makes the system more adaptable to changes and new features.
3. **Improved Code Reusability**: By encapsulating object creation logic in reusable patterns, such as factories or builders, developers can leverage existing patterns to create similar objects in different parts of the application, promoting code reuse.
4. **Promotion of Separation of Concerns**: Creational patterns help separate the responsibility of object creation from the rest of the system's logic. This separation of concerns improves code maintainability and readability.
5. **Support for Dependency Injection**: Creational patterns often play a crucial role in supporting Dependency Injection (DI) by providing mechanisms to manage the creation and injection of dependencies, promoting modularity and testability.

6. **Centralized Control over Object Creation**: Creational patterns centralize control over how objects are created, allowing developers to apply consistent instantiation strategies across the application.
7. **Enforcement of Design Principles**: Creational patterns encourage adherence to important design principles such as abstraction, encapsulation, and separation of concerns, contributing to a more robust and scalable architecture.

In summary, creational design patterns offer numerous benefits that contribute to the overall quality, flexibility, and maintainability of software systems by providing effective solutions to object creation challenges and promoting best practices in software design. Each pattern addresses specific aspects of object creation, catering to different scenarios and requirements in software development.

Now, let's learn all of the GoF Creational design patterns…

Prototype Pattern

The Prototype pattern is a creational design pattern that allows objects to be copied or cloned, providing a mechanism to create new instances by copying existing objects without explicitly invoking their constructors, and it is used to efficiently produce new instances with identical properties to existing objects.

Say that we have a GUI that allows the user to create new shapes on the screen, such as circles and rectangles. When the user right-clicks on a shape, an actions menu opens up. The user can then select "duplicate" to clone the shape:

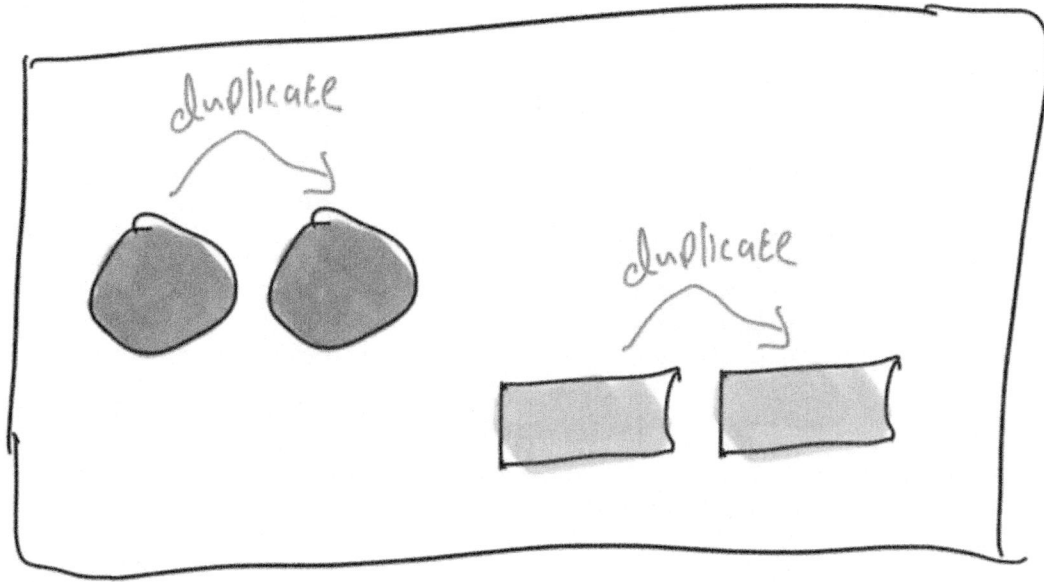

Let's come up with a solution:

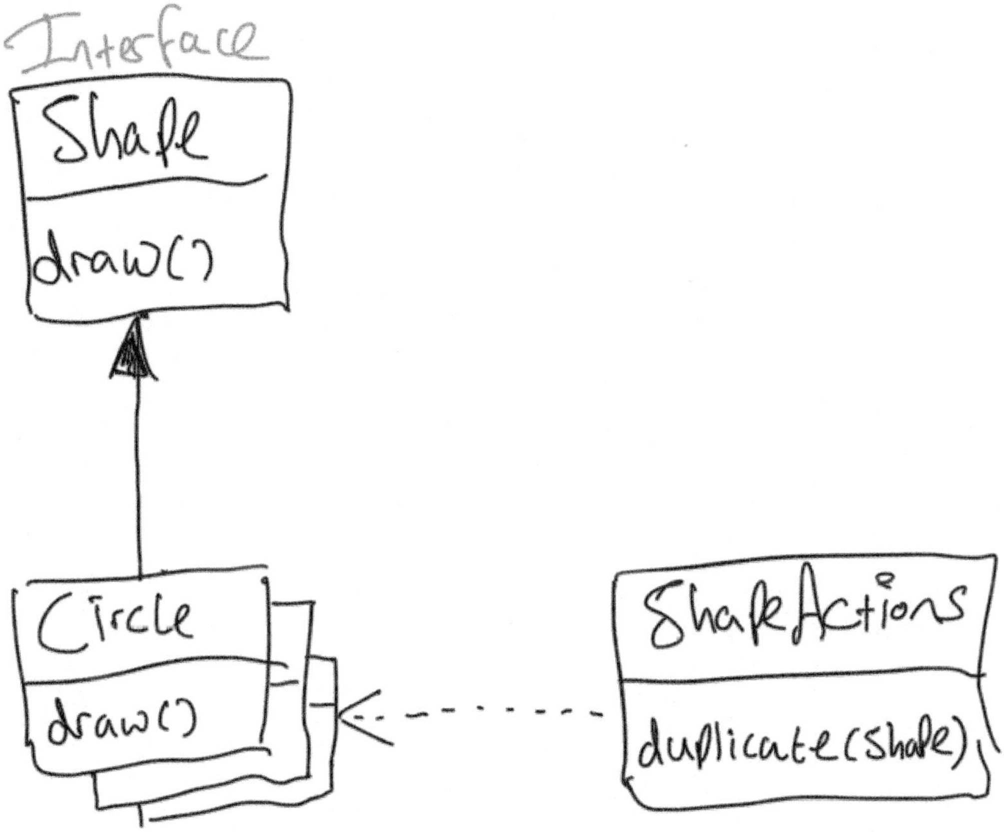

We have concrete shape classes that implement the Shape interface. The ShapeActions class contains the logic for duplicating each shape, and is dependent on all of the shapes that can be duplicated.

Can you see the issue with this solution? What SOLID principle are we violating?

Let's code this solution out to make the issues clear:

```
public interface Shape
{
  void Draw();


  // other shape methods...
}

public class Circle : Shape
{
  public int Radius { get; set; } = 5; // give a default radius of 5 for newly-created circles

  public void Draw()
  {
     System.Console.WriteLine("Drawing circle");
  }
}

public class Rectangle : Shape
{
  public int Width { get; set; } = 10;
  public int Height { get; set; } = 5;

  public void Draw()
  {
     System.Console.WriteLine("Drawing rectangle");
  }
}
```

```csharp
public class ShapeActions
{
    public void Duplicate(Shape shape)
    {
        if (shape is Circle)
        {
            var copiedShape = (Circle)shape; // the copied shape
            var newShape = new Circle(); // the clone
            newShape.Radius = copiedShape.Radius;
            newShape.Draw();
        }
        else if (shape is Rectangle)
        {
            var copiedShape = (Rectangle)shape;
            var newShape = new Rectangle();
            newShape.Width = copiedShape.Width;
            newShape.Height = copiedShape.Height;
            newShape.Draw();
        }
        else
        {
            throw new ArgumentException("Invalid shape provided");
        }
    }
}
```

Here's how a client could use this solution:

```csharp
class Program
{
    static void Main(string[] args)
    {
        // User adds a new circle to GUI
        var circle = new Circle();
```

```
        circle.Draw();
        // User clicks and drags on circle to resize
        circle.Radius = 12;

        // User adds a new rectangle to GUI
        var rectangle = new Rectangle();
        rectangle.Draw();
        // User clicks and drags rectangle to resize
        rectangle.Width = 20;
        rectangle.Height = 12;

        // User right-clicks the shapes and clicks "duplicate"
        var shapeActions = new ShapeActions();
        shapeActions.Duplicate(circle);
        shapeActions.Duplicate(rectangle);

        // Logs:
        // Drawing circle
        // Drawing rectangle
        // Drawing circle
        // Drawing rectangle
    }
}
```

Look at how ugly the `Duplicate()` method is in the `ShapeActions` class!

Here are some obvious issues that I spot:

- We are violating the open-closed principle, as we need to modify the `ShapeActions` class every time we add (extend our code base) a new shape.
- `ShapeActions` is coupled to the concrete shape classes – so far, `Circle` and `Rectangle`. So `ShapeActions` has to know about, or depend on, all kinds of shapes and their specific fields and methods.

- At the time of writing code, ShapeActions has to know about all of the shapes that we support. What if we wanted to make this app extensible, so that other people can build plugins for it -- so they can define other types of shapes that can be added to a GUI? That can't be achieved with the current implementation, because at the time of writing code or at compile time, ShapeActions has to know about all of the kinds of shapes. Not a flexible solution. It currently depends on concrete implementations of shapes.

Solution:

The logic for duplicating a shape can be moved to each concrete shape class, rather than having it all in ShapeActions.Duplicate(). We can then decouple ShapeActions from all of the concrete shapes, and have it talk to the Shape interface. Flexible, maintainable, nice!

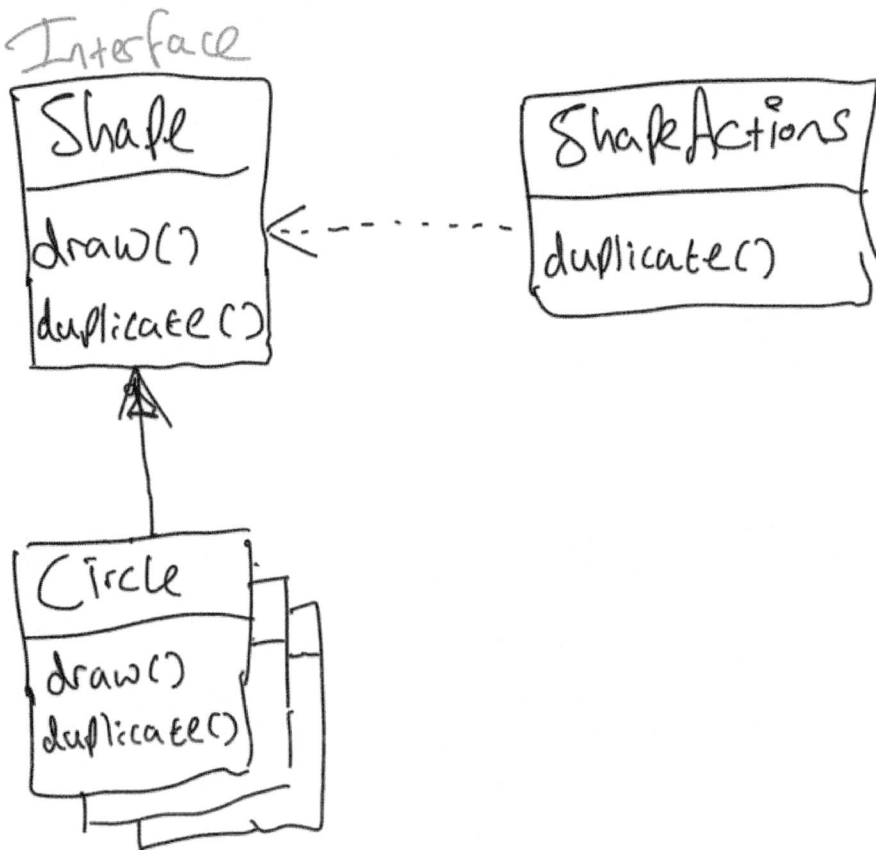

Note how ShapeActions has been lifted up to talk to the single Shape interface, rather than talking to the many concrete classes.

GoF:

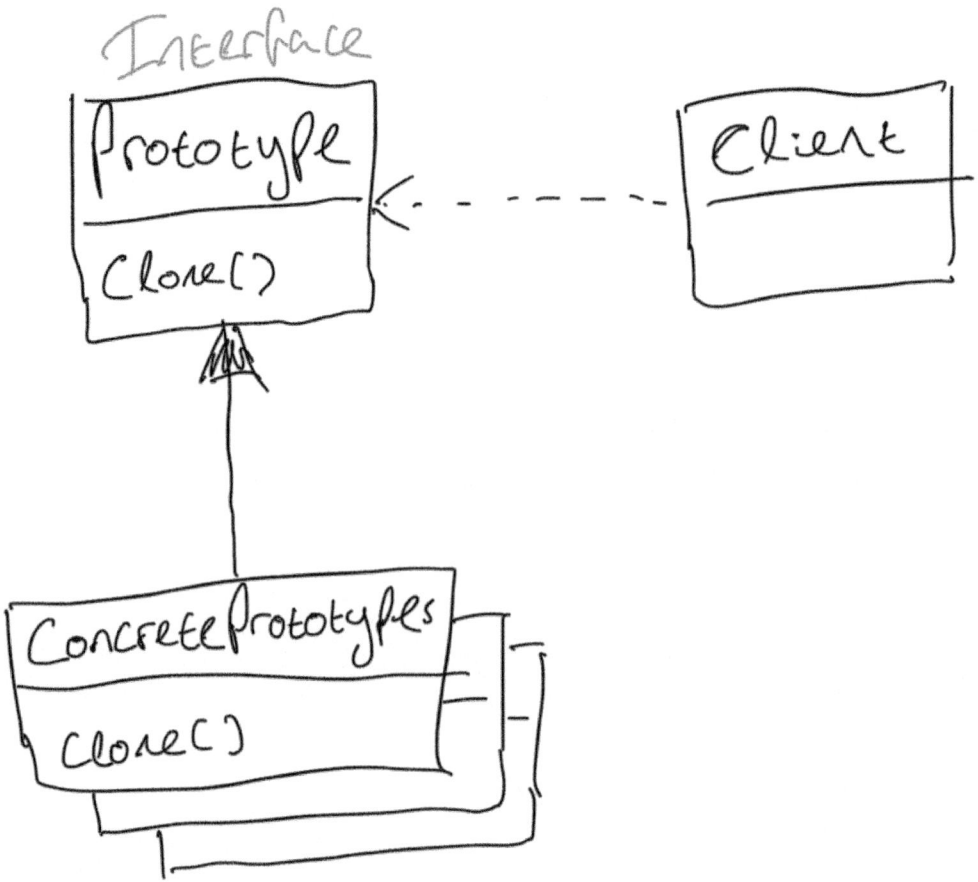

Time to implement this in code:

```
public interface Shape
{
  void Draw();
  Shape Duplicate();
}

public class Circle : Shape
{
  public int Radius { get; set; } = 5; // give a default radius of
  5 for newly-created circles

  public void Draw()
```

```csharp
    {
        System.Console.WriteLine("Drawing circle");
    }

    public Shape Duplicate()
    {
        var newCircle = new Circle();
        newCircle.Radius = Radius;
        return newCircle;
    }
}

public class Rectangle : Shape
{
    public int Width { get; set; } = 10;
    public int Height { get; set; } = 5;

    public void Draw()
    {
        System.Console.WriteLine("Drawing rectangle");
    }

    public Shape Duplicate()
    {
        var newRectangle = new Rectangle();
        newRectangle.Width = Width;
        newRectangle.Height = Height;
        return newRectangle;
    }
}

public class ShapeActions
{
    public Shape Duplicate(Shape shape)
```

```csharp
    {
        System.Console.WriteLine("Duplicating shape");
        return shape.Duplicate();
    }
}
```

Client:

```csharp
class Program
{
    static void Main(string[] args)
    {
        // User adds a new circle to GUI
        var circle = new Circle();
        circle.Draw();
        // User clicks and drags on circle to resize
        circle.Radius = 12;

        // User adds a new rectangle to GUI
        var rectangle = new Rectangle();
        rectangle.Draw();
        // User clicks and drags rectangle to resize
        rectangle.Width = 20;
        rectangle.Height = 12;

        // User right-clicks the shapes and clicks "duplicate"
        var shapeActions = new ShapeActions();
        var circleClone = shapeActions.Duplicate(circle);
        circleClone.Draw();
        var rectangleClone = shapeActions.Duplicate(rectangle);
        rectangleClone.Draw();

        // Logs:
        // Drawing circle
        // Drawing rectangle
```

```
    // Duplicating shape
    // Drawing circle
    // Duplicating shape
    // Drawing rectangle
  }
}
```

We can now add new shapes without having to modify existing code – nice!

Singleton Pattern

The Singleton pattern is a creational design pattern that ensures a class has only one instance and provides a global point of access to that instance. The single instance is commonly used for managing shared resources, configuration settings, or logging functionality within an application.

A common use case of the Singleton pattern is to use a single global instance of a database object throughout an application. This means that all clients that need to connect to a database will retrieve the same database object, and not be creating new, separate ones. The database object is only created once, the first time it is needed, and then all other clients that need to connect and query the database will use this same object.

Here's a user making a request to fetch some products:

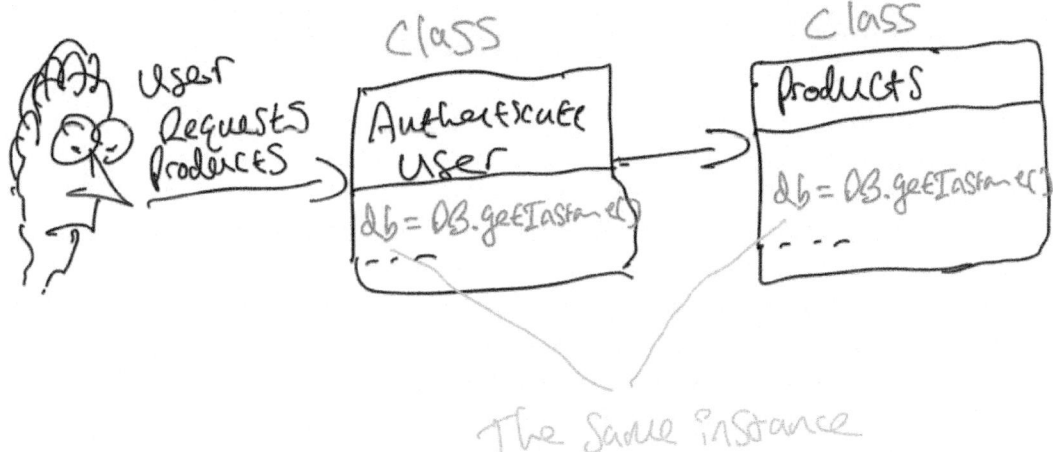

There are two classes – `UserAuthentication` and `Products`. Both require fetching things from the same database. Notice that we are not using the `new`

keyword to get the database object; we are using a method called `getInstance()` that returns the exact same database object throughout the application, ensuring that we always use a single database connection.

You may be wondering why we can't just create a new database object every time we need to connect to the database. Here are some good reasons to use a single global database object in all clients:

1. **Resource Efficiency**: Database connections and resources are typically limited and can be expensive to establish. By using a single instance of a database object, you minimize the overhead of creating and managing multiple connections, optimizing resource utilization.
2. **Consistency and State Management**: Having a single database instance ensures consistent state management and transaction handling across different parts of the application. Changes made to the database state are visible universally within the application, avoiding inconsistencies that could arise from multiple database instances.
3. **Simplified Configuration and Management**: With a singleton database instance, configuration settings such as connection parameters, credentials, and initialization logic are centralized and managed in one place. This simplifies application setup and maintenance.
4. **Performance Optimization**: By reusing a single database instance, you can optimize database query performance and reduce latency associated with establishing new connections or reinitializing database resources.

The singleton pattern is also great for storing app configuration settings, logging configuration, session information, authentication tokens – and making this information available globally via a single instance, ensuring that it is the same throughout the app.

Say that we need to keep an `AppSettings` object, that stores global variables such as the name of the app, the database configuration (e.g. the database we are using, username, password) and logger settings (e.g. the filepath of our log file, the format – e.g. text vs JSON). We need to create only a single instance of this object throughout our app to ensure that it only needs to be configured once in one place, and to ensure consistency throughout the app.

First, a bad solution:

```
public class AppSettings
```

```csharp
{
    private Dictionary<string, object> _settings = new Dictionary<string, object>();

    public object Get(string key)
    {
        if (!_settings.ContainsKey(key))
            return null;

        return _settings[key];
    }

    public void Set(string key, object value)
    {
        _settings[key] = value;
    }
}

class Program
{
    static void Main(string[] args)
    {
        // Configure the app settings
        var settings = new AppSettings();
        settings.Set("app_name", "Design Pattern Mastery");
        settings.Set("app_creator", "Danny");
        System.Console.WriteLine(settings.Get("app_name")); // Design Pattern Mastery

        // Accessing settings somewhere else in the app (i.e. in another class)...
        var test = new Test();
        test.Run();
```

```
    }
}

public class Test
{
    public void Run()
    {
        var settingsElsewhere = new AppSettings();
        System.Console.WriteLine(settingsElsewhere.Get("app_name"));
// null -- we need to use Singleton pattern to ensure a single
instance of AppSettings is maintained throughout our app
    }
}
```

Above, every time we need to use the `AppSettings` object, we are using the `new` keyword, and so creating a new, unconfigured object

SOLUTION: Singleton pattern

To ensure we have only a single instance of this class, first we have to make the constructor private (notice -ve UML symbol) -- so we can't use the `new` operation with this class.

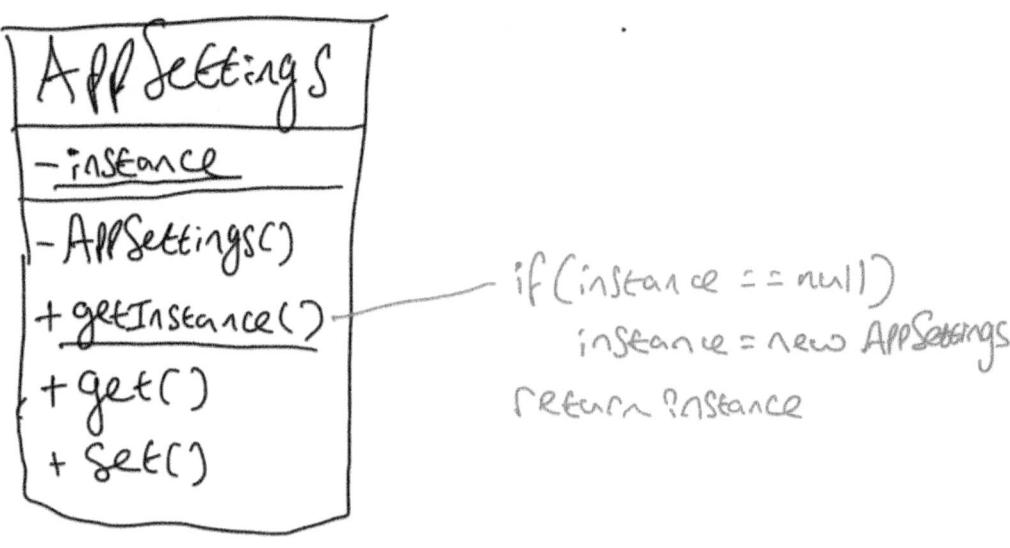

We also add a private static (symbolized by underlining) `instance` field that holds an instance of the `AppSettings` class – i.e. the class is responsible for maintaining a single instance of itself.

`getInstance()` is a static method for getting that single instance. Static because static fields are only visible to static methods.

GoF:

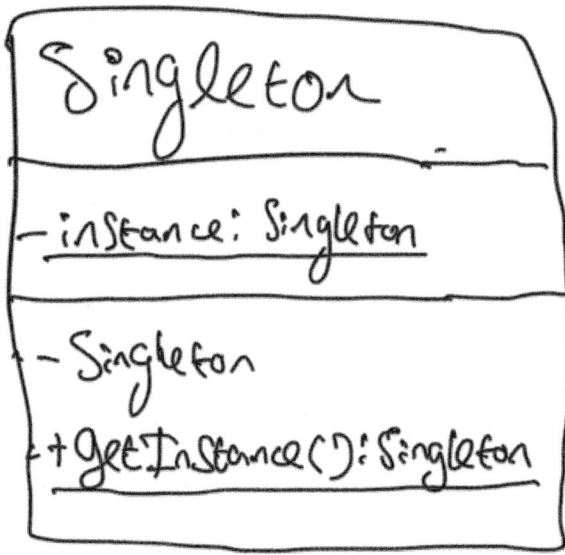

So, to implement the Singleton pattern, you have to:
1. Make the constructor private, so that the `new` keyword can't be used to create multiple instances of the class
2. Create a private static `instance` field to keep reference to the single instance
3. Create a public static `getInstance()` for creating that single instance the first time the method is called in the application, then returning that same instance every time the method is called.

Implementing this in code:

```
public class AppSettings
{
    private static AppSettings _instance;
```

```csharp
  private Dictionary<string, object> _settings = new
Dictionary<string, object>();

  // make constructor private
  private AppSettings() { }

  // method for creating a single instance of this class
  public static AppSettings GetInstance()
  {
    if (_instance == null)
    {
      _instance = new AppSettings();
    }
    return _instance;
  }

  public object Get(string key)
  {

    if (!_settings.ContainsKey(key))
      return null;

    return _settings[key];
  }

  public void Set(string key, object value)
  {
    _settings[key] = value;
  }
}

class Program
{
  static void Main(string[] args)
```

```csharp
{
    var settings = AppSettings.GetInstance();
    settings.Set("app_name", "Design Pattern Mastery");
    settings.Set("app_creator", "Danny");
    System.Console.WriteLine(settings.Get("app_name")); // Design Pattern Mastery

    // Accessing settings somewhere else in the app (i.e. in another class)...
    var test = new Test();
    test.Run();
  }
}

public class Test
{
 public void Run()
 {
    var settings = AppSettings.GetInstance();
    System.Console.WriteLine(settings.Get("app_creator")); // Danny
  }
}
```

Perfect!

Now, if we try to create a new instance of `AppSettings` directly, VSCode gives us an error, as the constructor is private:

Factory Method Pattern

The Factory Method pattern is a creational design pattern that defines an interface for creating objects, but allows subclasses to alter the type of objects that will be created, providing a way to delegate the instantiation logic to subclasses, enabling flexibility in object creation without changing the client code.

Say that we are developing a new Model-View-Controller backend framework, to rival the popular PHP framework, Laravel.

We create a base `Controller` class to handle requests made to our application:

```
public class Controller
{
  public void Render(string fileName, Dictionary<string, object> data)
  {
    var viewEngine = new BladeViewEngine(); // PROBLEM: Controller is tightly coupled to this particular view engine -- not flexible
    var html = viewEngine.Render(fileName, data);
    System.Console.WriteLine(html);
  }
}
```

Then, developers can extend the base controller class to create their own controllers to handle requests to their application – such as a controller that deals with order-related requests:

```
public class OrdersController : Controller
{
  public void ListOrders()
  {
    // Simulate fetching user's previous orders from db
    var orders = new Dictionary<string, object>{
            {"Red socks", "$12.98"},
            {"Black socks", "$12.98"},
            {"Pink T-shirt", "29.00"}
```

```
      };

   Render("orders.php", orders);
 }

 public void GetOrder(int id)
 {
    // Simulate getting single order by id from db
    var order = new Dictionary<string, object>{
         {"Red Socks", "$12.98"}
      };

   Render("order.php", order);
 }
}
```

Here's how we implement the view engine:

```
public interface ViewEngine
{
 string Render(string fileName, Dictionary<string, object> data);
}

public class BladeViewEngine : ViewEngine
{
 public string Render(string fileName, Dictionary<string, object> data)
  {
    return "View rendered from " + fileName + " by Blade";
  }
}
```

Our backend framework code, where our base `Controller` class is stored, will be downloaded by developers as a third-party framework, so developers won't be able to modify the code directly. This means that if the developer wants to use a different view engine (also known as "template engines"), the above solution is poor, as our `Controller` class is tightly coupled to the `BladeViewEngine`, and cannot be changed by developers.

So, we try a different approach. What if we allowed developers to pass a view engine as an argument to the `Controller.Render()` method, like so:

```
public class Controller
{
  public void Render(string fileName, Dictionary<string, object> data, ViewEngine viewEngine)
   {
     var html = viewEngine.Render(fileName, data);
     System.Console.WriteLine(html);
   }
}
```

Then developers can select a view engine every time they call `Controller.Render()`:

```
public class OrdersController : Controller
{
  public void ListOrders()
   {
     // Simulate fetching users previous orders from db
     var orders = new Dictionary<string, object>{
             {"Red socks", "$12.98"},
             {"Black socks", "$12.98"},
             {"Pink T-shirt", "29.00"}
         };

     // Problem: we have to pass the view engine every time we call Render.
     Render("orders.php", orders, new TwigViewEngine());
   }
```

```
public void GetOrder(int id)
{
    // Simulate getting single order by id from db
    var order = new Dictionary<string, object>{
            {"Red Socks", "$12.98"}
        };

    Render("order.php", order, new TwigViewEngine());
}
}
```

But, usually, developers will be using one view engine for all of the templates in their application, so it doesn't make much sense to make them keep passing a view engine every time render is called.

Solution: create a factory method

We can add a `createViewEngine()` factory method in the `Controller` class. By default, we return the Blade view engine. But if the developer wants to switch to a different view engine, such as Twig, then they can use our alternative controller class, `TwigController`, that overrides the `createViewEngine()` factory method:

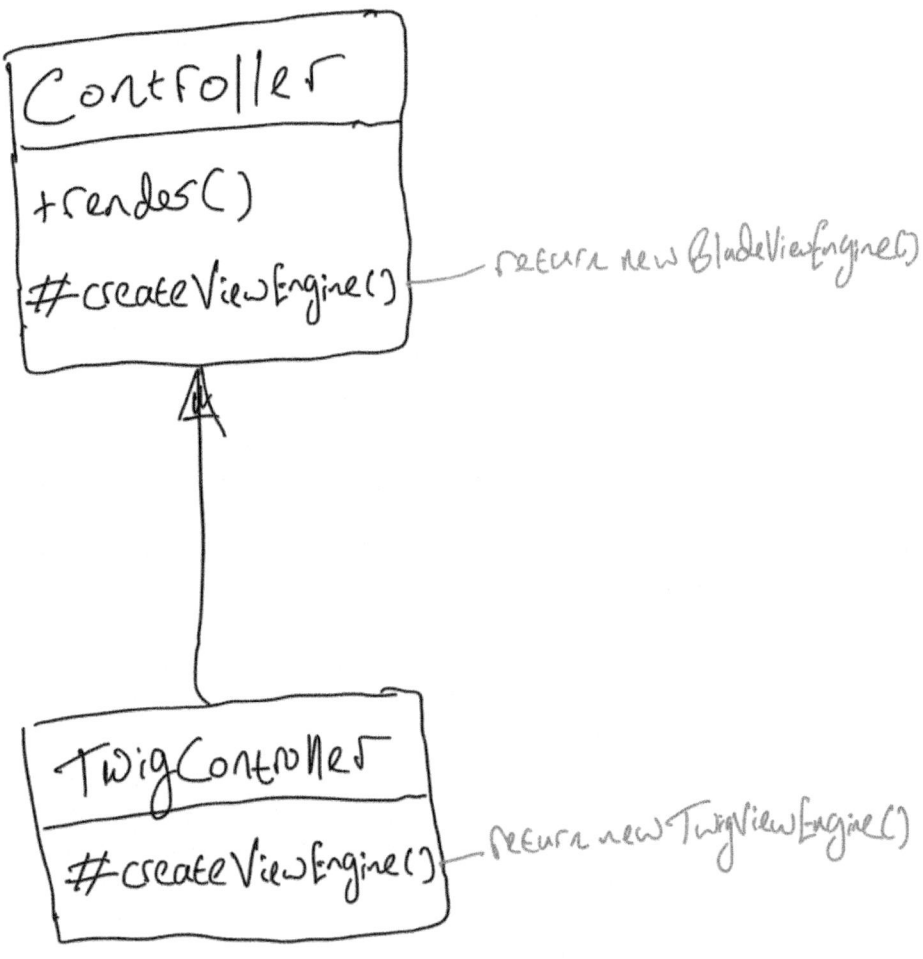

Here's the solution:

```
public abstract class Controller
{
  public void Render(string fileName, Dictionary<string, object> data)
  {
     var viewEngine = CreateViewEngine();
     var html = viewEngine.Render(fileName, data);
     System.Console.WriteLine(html);
  }

  // By default, the view engine for our framework will be Blade
```

```
    protected virtual ViewEngine CreateViewEngine()
    {
        return new BladeViewEngine();
    }

    // Note that we could also implement our factory method as an
    // abstract method, and so providing no default view engine, and
    // force the developer to select one.
    // protected abstract ViewEngine CreateViewEngine();
}

public class TwigController : Controller
{
    protected override ViewEngine CreateViewEngine()
    {
        return new TwigViewEngine();
    }
}
```

If the developer wants to switch to the Twig view engine, they can extend our `TwigController` class:

```
public class OrdersController : TwigController
```

`createViewEngine()` is acting as a factory method -- it returns a new object.

We have deferred the creation of an object (the view engine) to a subclass (`TwigController` is a subclass of `Controller`).

Another option would be to make `createViewEngine()` an abstract method, and force subclasses to implement it.

GoF:

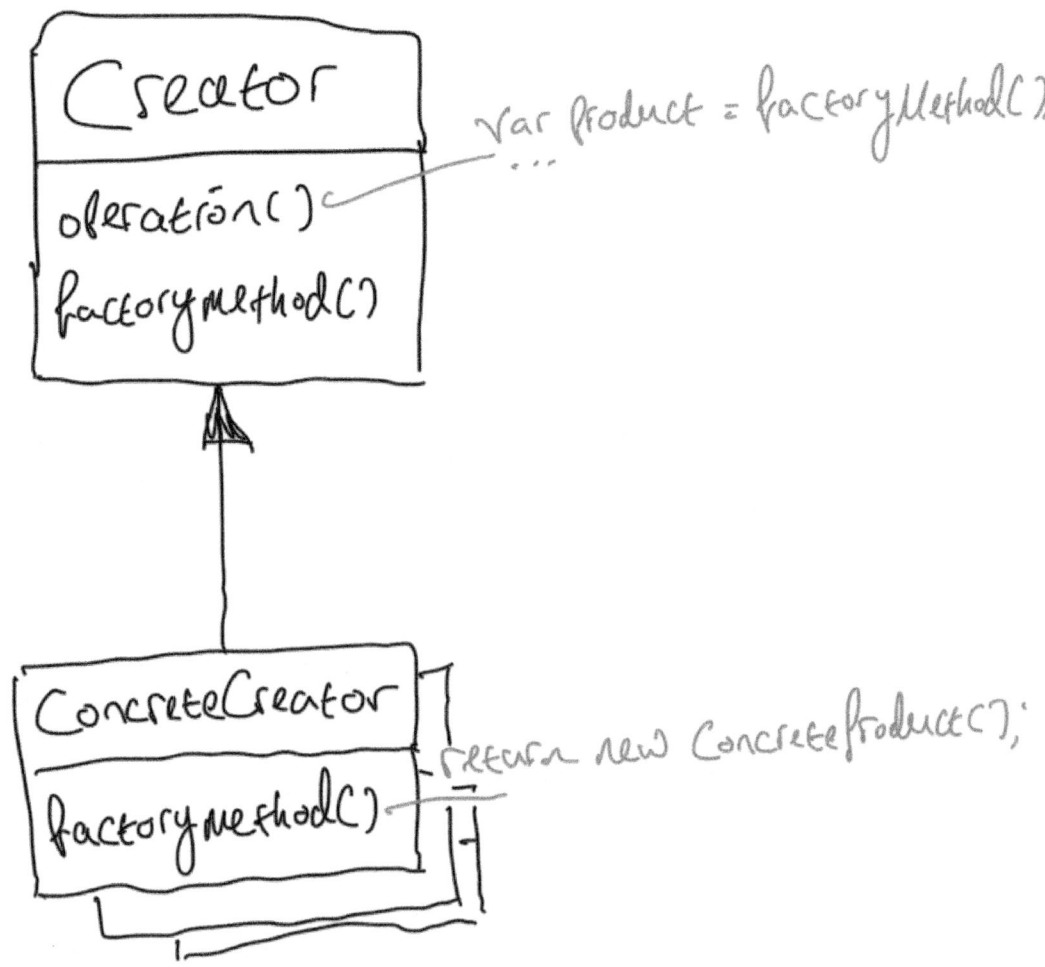

The objects returned from factory methods are referred to as "products".

The Factory Method Pattern is often misunderstood. It relies on inheritance and polymorphism to add flexibility to the design. Inheritance allows methods to be overridden in subclasses, and polymorphism allows different objects to be returned from the overridden methods.

Many people implement the Factory Method Pattern incorrectly, e.g. using a static method, such as:

```
var engine = ViewEngineFactory.createViewEngine();
```

But static methods cannot be overridden, so there is no flexibility with this approach, and it isn't correct. We cannot change the implementation of the `createViewEngine()` method.

Using the Factory method pattern, we can defer the creation of an object to subclasses, and this is possible through inheritance.

Abstract Factory Pattern

The Abstract Factory pattern is a creational design pattern that provides an interface for creating families of related objects without specifying their concrete classes, promoting encapsulation and allowing for the creation of object families that can vary independently.

Say that you have an app for Windows and Mac. The UI components – such as buttons, checkboxes, and textboxes – are different for each operating system, but each type of UI component will have the same behaviors – e.g. a checkbox, whether on Windows or Mac, will have an `onSelect()` method.

So, our app needs a way of knowing what the current operating system is, and then select the appropriate family of UI components for that operating system.

First, let's implement a more obvious solution:

```
public enum OperatingSystemType
{
  Windows,
  Mac
  // In future, we may need to support Linux, Web, Android...
}

public interface IUIComponent
{
  void Render();
}

public interface ICheckbox : IUIComponent
{
  // checkbox methods, e.g. OnSelect()...
}
```

```csharp
public interface IButton : IUIComponent
{
  // button methods, e.g. OnClick()...
}
```

Now for the concrete Windows components:

```csharp
// /Windows/WindowsButton.cs
public class WindowsButton : IButton
{
 public void Render()
 {
    System.Console.WriteLine("Windows: render button");
 }
}

// Windows/WindowsCheckbox.cs
public class WindowsCheckbox : ICheckbox
{
 public void Render()
 {
    System.Console.WriteLine("Windows: render checkbox");
 }
}
```

The concrete Mac components:

```csharp
// Mac/MacButton.cs
public class MacButton : IButton
{
 public void Render()
 {
    System.Console.WriteLine("Mac: render button");
 }
}
```

```csharp
// /Mac/MacCheckbox.cs
public class MacCheckbox : ICheckbox
{
  public void Render()
  {
    System.Console.WriteLine("Mac: render checkbox");
  }
}
```

Now for the app that we are building. Let's say we have a user settings form:

```csharp
// /App/UserSettingsForm.cs
public class UserSettingsForm
{
  public void Render(OperatingSystemType os)
  {
    // PROBLEM: open-closed principle violated: if add new OS, we have to modify this class
    if (os == OperatingSystemType.Windows)
    {
      // PROBLEM: too easy to make mistake -- e.g. easy to accidentally render a Mac button here.
      new WindowsButton().Render();
      // PROBLEM: UserSettingsForm is tightly coupled to many concrete implementations of widgets.
      new WindowsCheckbox().Render();
    }
    else if (os == OperatingSystemType.Mac)
    {
      new MacButton().Render();
      new MacCheckbox().Render();
    }
  }
}
```

We can then render the correct form for the operating system like so:

```
class Program
{
  static void Main(string[] args)
  {
    var os = OperatingSystemType.Mac;

    var userSettingsForm = new UserSettingsForm();
    userSettingsForm.Render(os);

    // Logs:
    // Mac: render button
    // Mac: render checkbox
  }
}
```

The problems with this simple solution can be seen in `UserSettingsForm`. For every UI that we develop, we will need conditionals to check what the current OS is, and render the correct concrete UI components for that particular UI. This is a maintenance nightmare, as every time we add or remove a type of OS, we have to modify a load of classes – violating the open/closed principle.

Another issue is that because we have to conditionally render concrete UI components, it is easy to make mistakes, such as accidentally rendering a Windows checkbox on Mac.

Solution: create an Abstract factory class to create families of UI components, such as the family of Windows UI components.

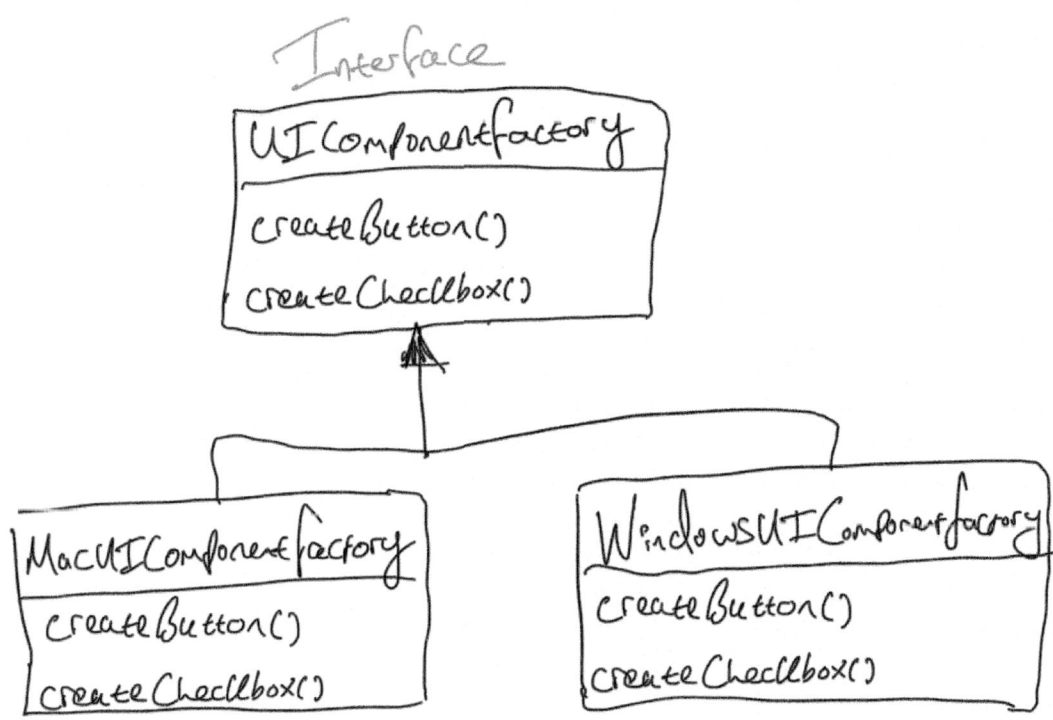

GoF:

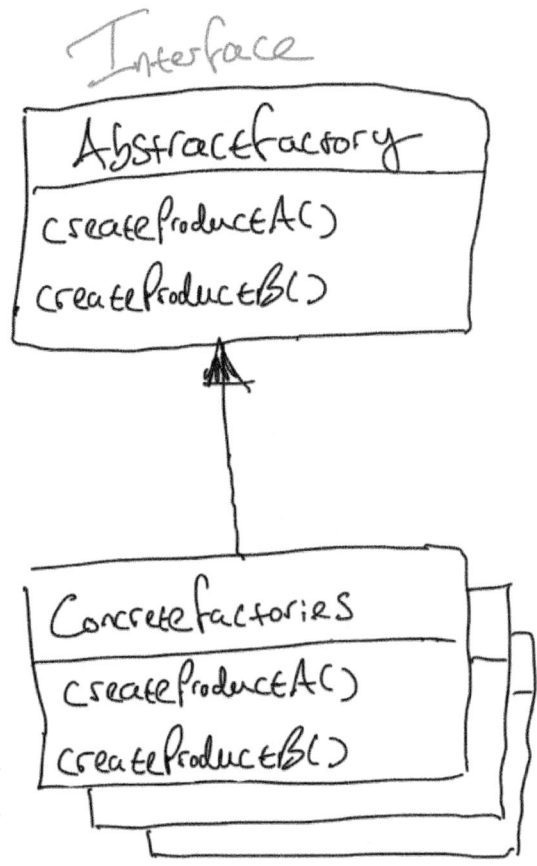

Let's implement this in code. Continuing from our previous code, we create the abstract factory interface:

```
public interface IUIComponentFactory
{
    IButton CreateButton();
    ICheckbox CreateCheckbox();
}
```

The concrete factories:

```
// /Mac/MacUIComponentFactory.cs
public class MacUIComponentFactory : IUIComponentFactory
{
```

```csharp
    public IButton CreateButton()
    {
        return new MacButton();
    }

    public ICheckbox CreateCheckbox()
    {
        return new MacCheckbox();
    }
}

// /Windows/WindowsUIComponentFactory.cs
public class WindowsUIComponentFactory : IUIComponentFactory
{
    public IButton CreateButton()
    {
        return new WindowsButton();
    }

    public ICheckbox CreateCheckbox()
    {
        return new WindowsCheckbox();
    }
}
```

Now, in our form, we are using polymorphism by talking to a factory interface to create related UI components – with no knowledge of the specific operating system being necessary:

```csharp
public class UserSettingsForm
{
    // Polymorphism used here, so that this client requires no
    // knowledge of specific uiComponentFactory.
    public void Render(IUIComponentFactory uiComponentFactory)
    {
```

```csharp
        uiComponentFactory.CreateButton().Render();
        uiComponentFactory.CreateCheckbox().Render();
    }
}
```

Here's how this solution would be used. This would usually be done just once, upon app initialisation. Then, throughout the app, the `uiComponentFactory` can be used to ensure that the correct family of UI components are used for current operating system:

```csharp
class Program
{
    static void Main(string[] args)
    {
        // App initialisation -- we only have to do these operating
        // system checks upon starting the app, so that we can begin using
        // the correct UI library for this operating system throughout the
        // app.
        var os = OperatingSystemType.Mac;
        IUIComponentFactory uiComponentFactory;

        if (os == OperatingSystemType.Windows)
        {
            uiComponentFactory = new WindowsUIComponentFactory();
        }
        else if (os == OperatingSystemType.Mac)
        {
            uiComponentFactory = new MacUIComponentFactory();
        }
        else
        {
            throw new Exception("Unsupported operating system");
        }

        new UserSettingsForm().Render(uiComponentFactory);
```

```
        // Logs:
        // Mac: render button
        // Mac: render checkbox
    }
}
```

Builder Pattern

The builder pattern is a creational design pattern used to construct complex objects step by step, providing clarity and flexibility in the creation process.

Let's say that we have a class, Car, that creates car objects. We also have a Manual class that is used to create car manuals:

```
public class Car
{
    public CarType _type;
    public int _seats;
    public Engine _engine;
    public bool _isConvertible;
    public Dashboard _dashboard;
    public Wheels _wheels;
    public GPSNavigator _gpsNavigator;

    // Fields specific to this class:
    public double Fuel { get; set; }

    public Car(
        CarType type,
        int seats,
        bool isConvertible,
        Engine engine,
        Dashboard dashboard,
```

```
        Wheels wheels,
        GPSNavigator gpsNavigator
    )
    {
        _type = type;
        _seats = seats;
        _isConvertible = isConvertible;
        _engine = engine;
        _dashboard = dashboard;
        _wheels = wheels;
        _gpsNavigator = gpsNavigator;
    }
}

public class Manual
{
    public CarType _type;
    public int _seats;
    public bool _isConvertible;
    public Engine _engine;
    public Dashboard _dashboard;
    public Wheels _wheels;
    public GPSNavigator _gpsNavigator;

    public Manual(
        CarType type,
        int seats,
        bool isConvertible,
        Engine engine,
        Dashboard dashboard,
        Wheels wheels,
        GPSNavigator gpsNavigator
    )
    {
```

```
        _type = type;
        _seats = seats;
        _isConvertible = isConvertible;
        _engine = engine;
        _dashboard = dashboard;
        _wheels = wheels;
        _gpsNavigator = gpsNavigator;
    }

    public string Print()
    {
        var text = "";

        text += "Car type: " + _type + "\n";
        text += "Seats: " + _seats + "\n";
        text += "Wheels: diameter in inches = " +
_wheels.GetDiameterInInches() + "\n";
        text += "Engine: info on engine... \n";
        text += "GPS Navigator: ";
        if (_gpsNavigator != null)
        {
            text += "Info on gps... \n";
        }
        else
        {
            text += "N/A \n";
        }

        return text;
    }
}
```

Here's how a client would use this solution:

```
class Program
```

```csharp
{
  static void Main(string[] args)
  {
    var sportsCar = new Car(CarType.Sports, 2, false, new
Engine(), new Dashboard(hasRevCounter: true), new
Wheels(diameterInInches: 20), new GPSNavigator());
    sportsCar.Fuel = 100;

    var suvCar = new Car(CarType.SUV, 5, false, new Engine(), new
Dashboard(hasRevCounter: true), new Wheels(diameterInInches: 19),
new GPSNavigator());
    suvCar.Fuel = 40;com

    var sportsCarManual = new Manual(CarType.Sports, 2, false, new
Engine(), new Dashboard(hasRevCounter: true), new
Wheels(diameterInInches: 20), new GPSNavigator());
    System.Console.WriteLine(sportsCarManual.Print());
    // Car type: Sports
    // Seats: 2
    // Wheels: diameter in inches = 20
    // Engine: info on engine...
    // GPS Navigator: Info on gps...

    var suvManual = new Manual(CarType.SUV, 5, false, new
Engine(), new Dashboard(hasRevCounter: true), new
Wheels(diameterInInches: 19), new GPSNavigator());
    System.Console.WriteLine(suvManual.Print());
    // Car type: SUV
    // Seats: 5
    // Wheels: diameter in inches = 19
    // Engine: info on engine...
    // GPS Navigator: Info on gps...
  }
}
```

As you can see, there are a large number of configuration variables that we have to pass to the constructor when creating a car or car-manual object. It's pretty ugly. Also, a large number of the configuration options are not needed most of the time – e.g. most cars are not convertibles.

One way of not having to specify all of the configuration options when creating a new object would be to create subclasses for each type of car or manual, e.g.:

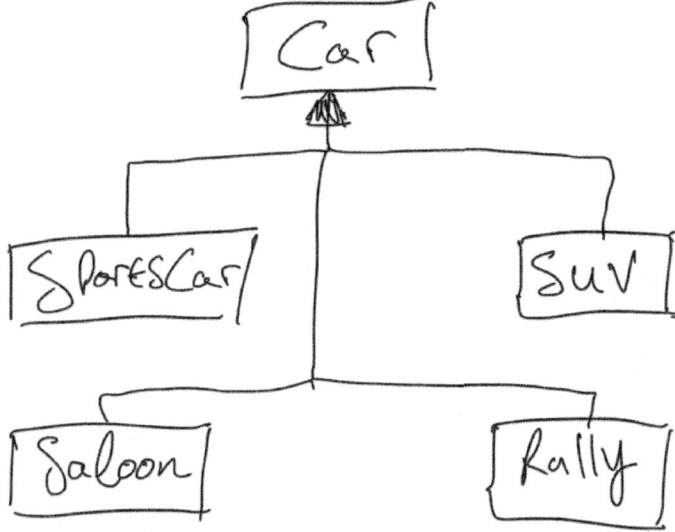

Then to create the manuals for these cars:

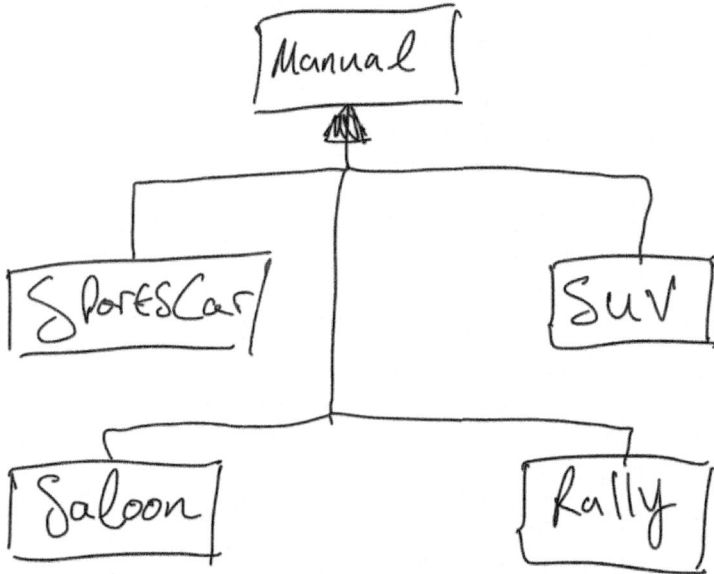

Problem is, our library of subclasses is likely to grow very large as more configuration variables are added to `Car`.

Also, if we, for example, change the wheel size on `SportsCar`, then we'd also have to change the `SportsCarManual` class.

The above solutions are ugly and difficult to maintain. Let's use the Builder pattern to solve this:

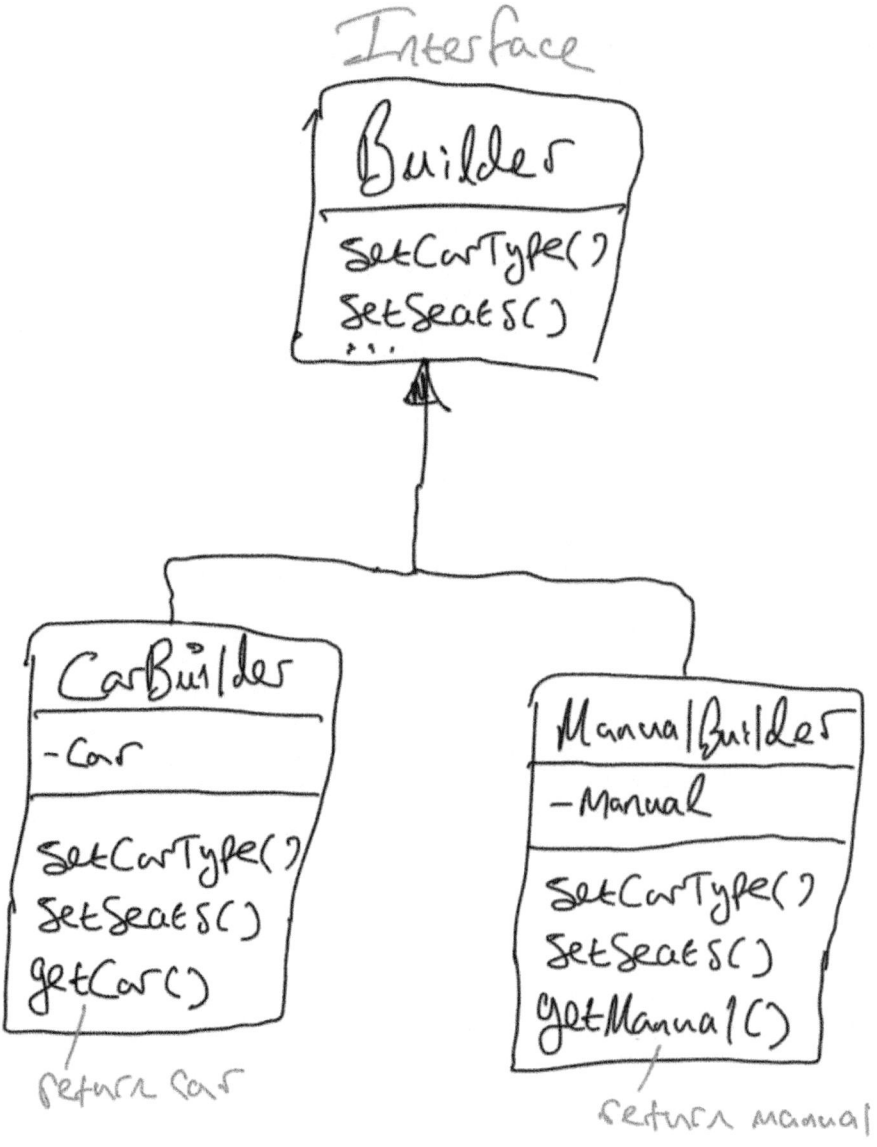

A car and its manual are two different objects that don't share a common interface; however, they can be constructed using the same steps, as each specific component in a car needs to be documented in its manual. By abstracting the object creation logic into builder classes, we can create cars and manuals by only specifying the steps required to build that specific car or manual:

```csharp
public class Car
{
  public CarType Type { get; set; }
  public int Seats { get; set; }
  public bool isConvertible { get; set; }
  public Engine Engine { get; set; }
  public Dashboard Dashboard { get; set; }
  public Wheels Wheels { get; set; }
  public GPSNavigator GpsNavigator { get; set; }

  // Fields specific to this class:
  public double Fuel { get; set; }
}

public class Manual
{
  public CarType Type { get; set; }
  public int Seats { get; set; }
  public bool isConvertible { get; set; }
  public Engine Engine { get; set; }
  public Dashboard Dashboard { get; set; }
  public Wheels Wheels { get; set; }
  public GPSNavigator GpsNavigator { get; set; }

  public string Print()
  {
     var text = "";

     text += "Car type: " + Type + "\n";
     text += "Seats: " + Seats + "\n";
```

```
   text += "Wheels: diameter in inches = " +
Wheels.GetDiameterInInches() + "\n";
   text += "Engine: info on engine... \n";
   text += "GPS Navigator: ";
   if (GpsNavigator != null)
   {
     text += "Info on gps... \n";
   }
   else
   {
     text += "N/A \n";
   }

   return text;
  }
}
```

The builder interface, that contains all possible steps for building a car or manual:

```
public interface IBuilder
{
 void Reset();
 IBuilder SetCarType(CarType type);
 IBuilder SetSeats(int seats);
 IBuilder IsConvertible(bool isConvertible);
 IBuilder SetEngine(Engine engine);
 IBuilder SetWheels(Wheels wheels);
 IBuilder SetDashboard(Dashboard dashboard);
 IBuilder SetGPSNavigator(GPSNavigator gpsNavigator);
}
```

The concrete builders:

```
public class CarBuilder : IBuilder
{
```

```csharp
private Car _car;

public CarBuilder()
{
    Reset();
}

public void Reset()
{
    _car = new Car();
}

public IBuilder SetCarType(CarType type)
{
    _car.Type = type;
    return this;
}

public IBuilder SetDashboard(Dashboard dashboard)
{
    _car.Dashboard = dashboard;
    return this;
}

public IBuilder SetEngine(Engine engine)
{
    _car.Engine = engine;
    return this;
}

public IBuilder SetGPSNavigator(GPSNavigator gpsNavigator)
{
    _car.GpsNavigator = gpsNavigator;
    return this;
```

```csharp
    }

    public IBuilder SetSeats(int seats)
    {
       _car.Seats = seats;
       return this;
    }

    public IBuilder IsConvertible(bool isConvertible)
    {
       _car.isConvertible = isConvertible;
       return this;
    }

    public IBuilder SetWheels(Wheels wheels)
    {
       _car.Wheels = wheels;
       return this;
    }

    public Car GetCar()
    {
       var car = _car;
       Reset();
       return car;
    }
 }

 public class CarManualBuilder : IBuilder
 {
  private Manual _manual;

    public CarManualBuilder()
    {
```

```csharp
    Reset();
}

public void Reset()
{
    _manual = new Manual();
}

public IBuilder SetCarType(CarType type)
{
    _manual.Type = type;
    return this;
}

public IBuilder SetDashboard(Dashboard dashboard)
{
    _manual.Dashboard = dashboard;
    return this;
}

public IBuilder SetEngine(Engine engine)
{
    _manual.Engine = engine;
    return this;
}

public IBuilder SetGPSNavigator(GPSNavigator gpsNavigator)
{
    _manual.GpsNavigator = gpsNavigator;
    return this;
}

public IBuilder SetSeats(int seats)
{
```

```csharp
      _manual.Seats = seats;
      return this;
   }

   public IBuilder IsConvertible(bool isConvertible)
   {
      _manual.isConvertible = isConvertible;
      return this;
   }

   public IBuilder SetWheels(Wheels wheels)
   {
      _manual.Wheels = wheels;
      return this;
   }

   public Manual GetManual()
   {
      var manual = _manual;
      Reset();
      return manual;
   }
}
```

The client:

```csharp
class Program
{
 static void Main(string[] args)
 {
    var carBuilder = new CarBuilder();

carBuilder.SetCarType(CarType.Sports).SetSeats(2).SetEngine(new
Engine()).SetDashboard(new Dashboard(hasRevCounter:
true)).SetWheels(new Wheels(diameterInInches: 20));
```

```
        var sportsCar = carBuilder.GetCar();
        sportsCar.Fuel = 100;

        var manualBuilder = new CarManualBuilder();

manualBuilder.SetCarType(CarType.Sports).SetSeats(2).SetEngine(ne
w Engine()).SetDashboard(new Dashboard(hasRevCounter:
true)).SetWheels(new Wheels(diameterInInches: 20));
        var sportsCarManual = manualBuilder.GetManual();
        System.Console.WriteLine(sportsCarManual.Print());
        // Car type: Sports
        // Seats: 2
        // Wheels: diameter in inches = 20
        // Engine: info on engine...
        // GPS Navigator: N/A
    }
}
```

This is a nicer solution, as we now only need to specify the car or manual properties that we need, e.g. we don't need to specify if the car is convertible, like we did before.

Also, notice how we can conveniently "chain" methods onto each other because we are returning the current object from each method call. You could also return `void` from each method, and then call each method line-by-line, but having the option to chain is convenient.

Problem is, we still have to specify a large number of fields when creating cars and manuals. Also, because `CarBuilder` and `CarManualBuilder` both implement the same `IBuilder` interface, we can now use polymorphism to create cars and manuals, as producing a manual for a specific type of car, e.g. sports car, requires the exact same steps – e.g. if a car has a gps, then it needs to be documented in the manual.

We can implement this using a "Director" class:

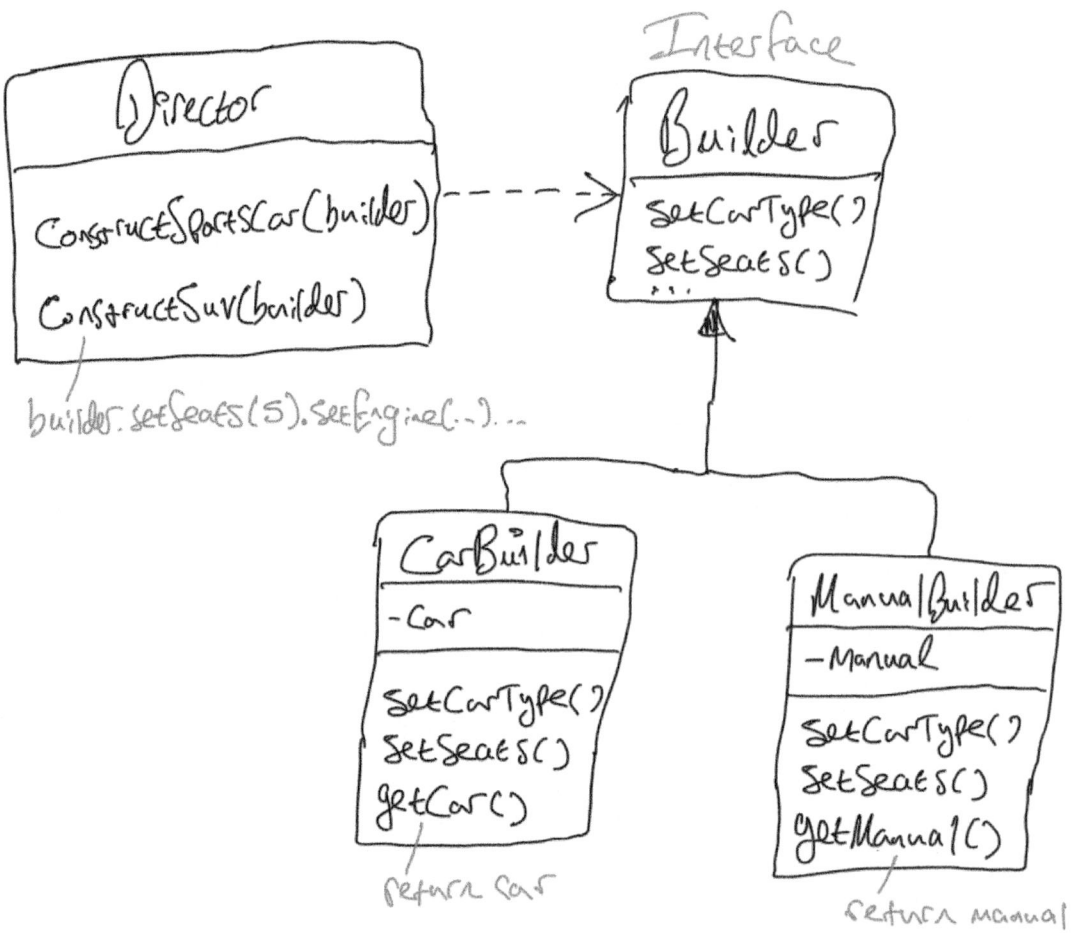

The director class is optional in the builder pattern, as the build steps can be specified in the client; but it's often useful for containing common construction routines so that they can be reused throughout the app.

GoF:

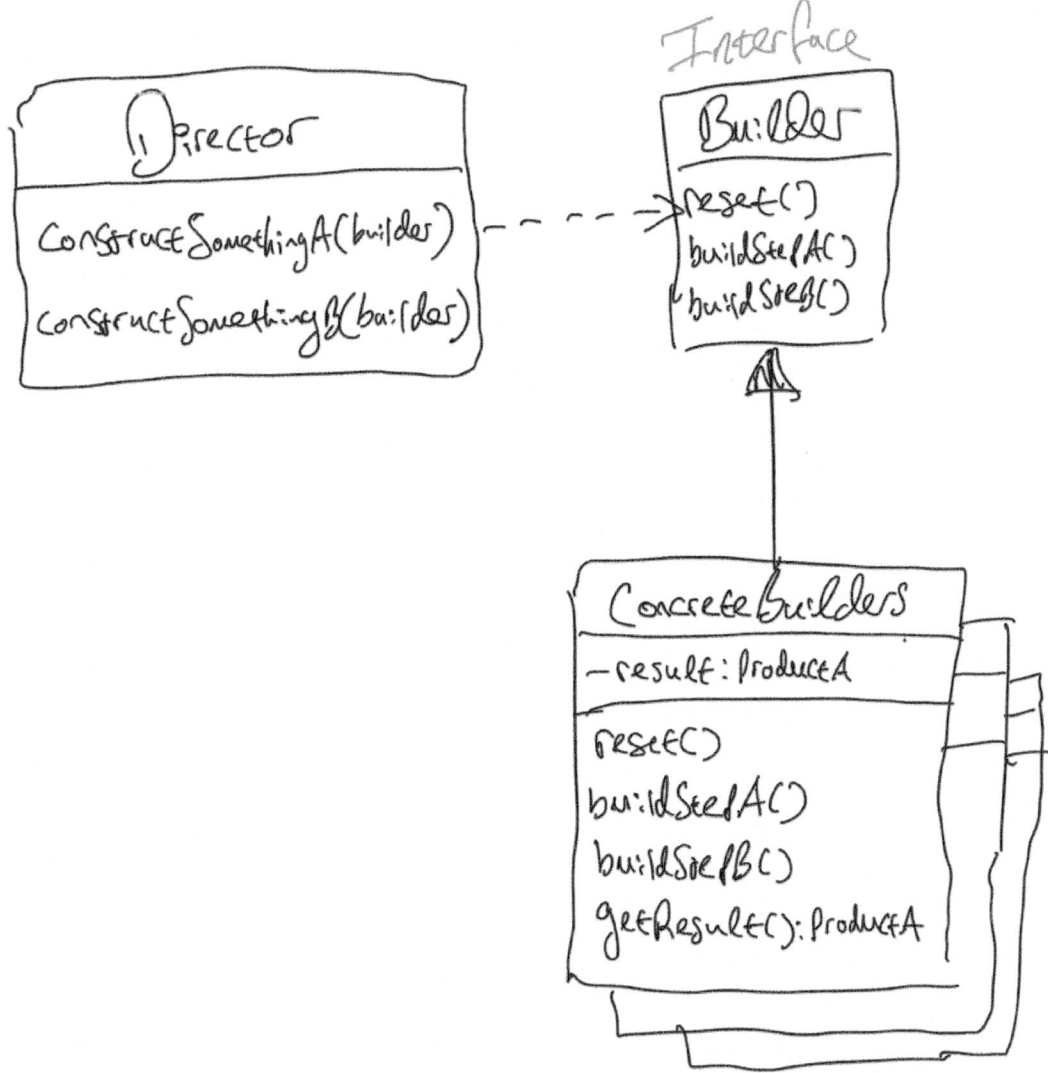

Note that, above, we are passing a builder to each method in the director class. But it's also fine to store a reference to a builder, and use methods for changing the builder at runtime, like so:

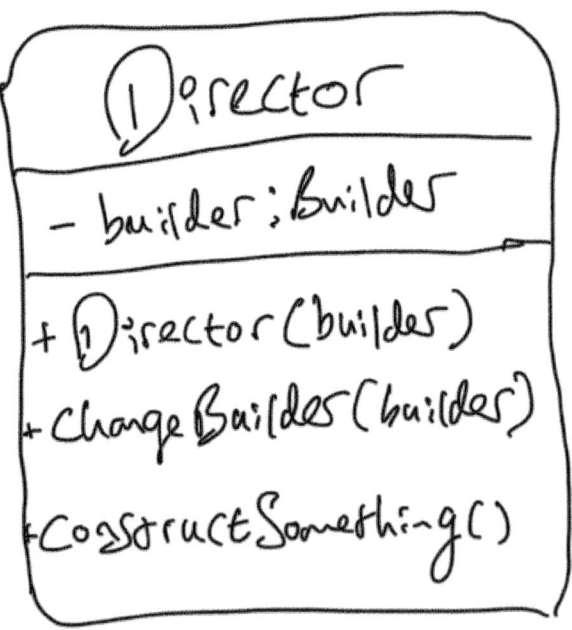

Here's the director class in code:

```
public class Director
{
 public void ConstructSportsCar(IBuilder builder)
 {
    builder.SetCarType(CarType.Sports);
    builder.SetDashboard(new Dashboard(hasRevCounter: true));
    builder.SetEngine(new Engine());
    builder.SetSeats(2);
    builder.SetWheels(new Wheels(diameterInInches: 20));
 }

 public void ConstructSUV(IBuilder builder)
 {
    builder.SetCarType(CarType.SUV);
    builder.SetDashboard(new Dashboard(hasRevCounter: true));
    builder.SetEngine(new Engine());
    builder.SetGPSNavigator(new GPSNavigator());
```

```
      builder.SetSeats(5);
      builder.SetWheels(new Wheels(diameterInInches: 19));
  }
}
```

Note that we don't return the product (e.g. car or manual) from the director; each product is returned from its respective concrete builder. This is because `Car` and `Manual` objects don't share a common interface.

Here's how the client can use the director:

```
class Program
{
  static void Main(string[] args)
  {
    var carBuilder = new CarBuilder();
    var director = new Director();

    director.ConstructSportsCar(carBuilder);
    var sportsCar = carBuilder.GetCar();
    sportsCar.Fuel = 100;

    director.ConstructSUV(carBuilder);
    var suvCar = carBuilder.GetCar();
    suvCar.Fuel = 40;

    var manualBuilder = new CarManualBuilder();
    director.ConstructSportsCar(manualBuilder);
    var sportsCarManual = manualBuilder.GetManual();
    System.Console.WriteLine(sportsCarManual.Print());
    // Car type: Sports
    // Seats: 2
    // Wheels: diameter in inches = 20
    // Engine: info on engine...
    // GPS Navigator: N/A
```

```
        director.ConstructSUV(manualBuilder);
        var suvManual = manualBuilder.GetManual();
        System.Console.WriteLine(suvManual.Print());
        // Car type: SUV
        // Seats: 5
        // Wheels: diameter in inches = 19
        // Engine: info on engine...
        // GPS Navigator: Info on gps...
    }
}
```

We have used the Builder pattern to reuse the same object construction code (build steps) to build different kinds of products – cars and their corresponding manuals.

Other creational patterns focus on producing objects that share a common interface. The Builder pattern differs in that it can construct objects of different types, providing that they share a common set of build steps.

Conclusion

Congratulations! You now have all of the tools to create readable, maintainable, flexible, top-quality software. This will:

- Save you lots of time and headaches throughout your life as a programmer
- Allow you to work and collaborate more effectively in a team
- Land more interesting, better-paying jobs on larger projects

I hope that you found this book useful. Thanks for reading!

If you found this book useful, it would be great if you could leave me a review!

For More From Me

My YouTube channel:
https://www.youtube.com/channel/UC0URylW_U4i26wN231yRqvA

Twitter: https://x.com/DoableDanny

Gumroad: https://doabledanny.gumroad.com/

Freecodecamp: https://www.freecodecamp.org/news/author/danny-adams/

Dev.to: https://dev.to/doabledanny

Thank you!

Printed in Great Britain
by Amazon